SEGMENTED TURNING

A COMPLETE GUIDE

SEGMENTED TURNING

A COMPLETE GUIDE

RON HAMPTON

GUILD OF MASTER CRAFTSMAN PUBLICATIONS

First published 2003 by
Guild of Master Craftsman Publications Ltd
Castle Place, 166 High Street,
Lewes, East Sussex BN7 1XU

ISBN 1 86108 337 8

Publisher: Paul Richardson
Art Director: Ian Smith
Managing Editor: Gerrie Purcell
Commissioning Editor: April McCroskie
Production Manager: Stuart Poole
Editor: Stephen Haynes
Designer: Lorna Cowan
Photographer: Ron Hampton, except where otherwise stated
Illustrator: Simon Rodway

Set in Times and Humanist

Colour origination by Icon Reproduction
Printed and bound by Stamford Press, Singapore

CONTENTS

FOREWORD BY KEVIN NEELLEY

It seems to me that more woodturners are becoming interested in adding segmented turning to their skill repertory. I can attest to this by the great volume of emails I have recently received, and by the numbers of new members at the segmented woodturning groups on Yahoo and MSN. I'm sure Ron Hampton has also seen the increase in segmented-related emails on his website, www.woodturningplus.com. I have been frequently asked if there are any books on segmented woodturning. Up until now my answer has not been very hopeful.

I am very glad that Ron Hampton has done the research and put together this wonderfully concise book. I wish there had been a book like this when I was just starting out; it would have saved me several years of trial and error. Novices will appreciate Ron's easy-to-follow approach, and even the pros might find some interesting and new construction methods described here. There are several great techniques detailed in this book that are probably not known by many except the most gnarled old segmented woodturner. I believe that anyone who has completed all nine projects in this book should be able to design and construct just about any segmented project on their own.

Ron has put years of his own experience into this book. Each of the nine projects shows a different aspect of segmented construction, and Ron has not left out any detail that could help the reader understand the process. It might take years for a woodturner to achieve proficiency in all these different aspects without the help of this book.

As I have already said, I believe that the printing of this book coincides with an upsurge in segmented woodturning interest. The major woodturning symposia have had fine segmented turning demonstrators for a number of years. Galleries and collectors are beginning to show a keen interest in this new art form. I hope that each reader of this book will go on to create their own segmented turned art.

Kevin Neelley
Lenexa, Kansas

Leaf-patterned vase by Kevin Neelley
(photo by courtesy of Kevin Neelley)

FOREWORD BY ED ZBIK

Segmented turning is by far the most difficult form of woodturning. All turners must be concerned with consistent wall thickness, a fine finish and a graceful form that complements the wood grain. But the segmented turner has the additional task of *creating* the appearance of the wood itself. This involves both substantial skills in the art of design, and techniques accurate to thousandths of an inch. All of these aspects are clearly and thoroughly covered in this book.

Segmented turning requires careful planning, both in drawing and in the determination of cutting angles. Formulas for angle calculation are provided, as well as detailed tables for both ring and stave construction. Examples of calculations are provided, including sample cutting lists. Accurate, tight joints are the hallmark of good segmented turning, and the text reviews several ways of achieving these, some using only the simplest of tools.

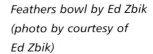

Feathers bowl by Ed Zbik
(photo by courtesy of
Ed Zbik)

Having covered the fundamentals, Ron clarifies and expands on the construction techniques via nine complete projects, providing detailed instructions, drawings and photos for all phases of construction. A wide variety of techniques are presented, including segmented rings, stave construction, intarsia, and pewter inlay.

The last section of the book presents an extensive gallery of contemporary segmented turnings to provide design inspiration for the reader's newly acquired skills.

The difficulty of segmented turning is exacerbated by the lack of books on the subject, and the lack of books is in turn exacerbated by the limited readership. Hopefully this book will help break the cycle and expand the ranks of segmented woodturners.

Ed Zbik
San Diego, California

Dedication

To Barbara, Jennifer Beth, and Sarah: the three most important people in my life. Thank you! You can never know how much your love and support mean to me.

Acknowledgements

I would like to thank J. P. (Jim) Davis of Midland, Texas for allowing me to reproduce the tables on pages 134–47. Also I want to thank my office staff: Barbara Hampton, Lynne Peavy, and Sarah Whitten-Morris. They have put up with me these last 18 months when the only thing I talked about was segmented turning and 'the book'.

Measurements

Although care has been taken to ensure that the metric measurements are true and accurate, they are only conversions from imperial; they have been rounded up or down to the nearest whole millimetre, or to the nearest convenient equivalent in cases where the imperial measurements themselves are only approximate. When following the projects, use either the metric or the imperial measurements; do not mix units.

INTRODUCTION

Woodturners are artists who work with wood. We strive to bring forth the hidden beauty that lies just below the surface. We are always looking for new and better ways to manipulate wood for our artistic ends – to allow the beauty of wood to show through our art. Wood is a wonderful material to work with: its warmth, its wonderful rich colours, and its textures stir a deep sense of appreciation in almost all art lovers.

Woodturning is experiencing tremendous growth in popularity around the world. Many people are finding that they now have the time and money to enjoy new hobbies; others would like to try a new career direction. Woodturning is a wonderfully satisfying hobby and can be a terrific source of additional income. For the hobbyist, woodturning can be richly rewarding as a means of artistic expression and as a means of relaxation. For the professional, it offers a pleasant lifestyle and a desirable form of employment.

Segmented turning – in which the workpiece is built up from many separate pieces of wood before turning – offers many artistic advantages. You can use different-coloured woods to make beautiful and unique patterns or images in your turnings. Very often, contrasting woods can make a beautiful artistic statement that you would be hard pressed to achieve with one-piece turnings. Figuring out new ways to make attractive patterns becomes an enjoyable challenge. Inlaying veneer into turned work allows you to carry your art to a higher level.

A significant advantage over 'wet'-wood turning is that segmented turners are always using dry, stable wood. This avoids the problem of the bowl warping or cracking after it has dried for a while. Any piece of dried wood can be used by the creative segmented turner: your scraps from a large project could end up in numerous small turnings.

Hopi bowl by Ed Zbik (photo by courtesy of Ed Zbik)

Segmented turning does require significantly more time: while one-piece turnings can be completed in one or two days' work, segmented pieces will often take a month to a year to complete. However, the artistic possibilities of segmented turning far outweigh this disadvantage. This book will focus on projects that can usually be completed in one to two weeks. By concentrating on such pieces, the student will learn a lot about the techniques without becoming hopelessly bogged down in a year-long project.

Calculating angles can be a challenge for the beginner. When I made my first segmented ring in 1993, I spent three days making adjustments at the tablesaw before I obtained a ring with no gaps. By that time I had lost my enthusiasm for making a 'museum-quality' vase. In this book I have worked to make the maths easy – if you *want* to understand it. If you do not want to read these sections, that is OK: I have provided tables that will allow you to make any bowl you want without ever doing an equation.

Cutting flawless angles does not need to be a major obstacle. Using either a home-made cutting board or a high-quality mitre gauge, making perfect rings can become an effortless process. Once cutting accurate mitre angles has become easy, you are then free to plan more advanced and beautiful vessels. Therefore the first part of the book will concentrate on how to make perfect rings easily. Then we will progress to more advanced techniques as your skill improves.

Segmented turning is fun and artistically rewarding. Take your time learning the techniques described in this book. You will be rewarded by improved woodworking skills and a new world of artistic possibilities. Have fun, and continue to learn.

Holly and walnut vase by Colin Delory

PART I
PLANNING AND PREPARATION

1
HEALTH AND SAFETY

Safety first

Segmented turning can be a lot of fun and it can be done safely. However, it is necessary to pay attention and follow some safety rules. Any and all tools can be dangerous!

Power saw safety

All power saws can be very dangerous. To use them safely it is necessary to:

- operate the saw correctly in accordance with the manufacturer's instructions
- use appropriate safety equipment
- stay alert and sober
- keep your hands and fingers away from the blade.

Power saw accidents occur to beginners and experienced woodworkers alike. Beginners have accidents because they do not know the rules for safe saw use. Experienced workers have accidents because they ignore the rules, work too fast, or lose their concentration.

You must be mentally alert and paying attention at all times. If you are compromised by fatigue, alcohol, or medication you must quit and go to the house. Any one of these factors will affect your judgement and reflexes. Remember that the saw blade does not care if you are tired or in a hurry.

Paying attention

In segmented turning you will be making the same saw cut over and over. Repetitive cutting is one of the most dangerous aspects of segmented work. Most people will make the first cut safely by paying attention and following the safety procedures. The difficulty for segmented turners lies in paying attention on the tenth or five-hundredth cut. **You must be just as careful on the last cut as on the first (Fig 1.1).**

Basic tablesaw rules

1 Pay attention

Think how you need to do the job so that you do it safely. Try to think of any situation that could cause you an accident. **Repetitive cuts in segmented turning are dangerous because your mind can wander and you could stick your hand into a moving saw blade.**

Fig 1.1 Don't let your attention wander in repetitive cutting; the last cut is as dangerous as the first

Fig 1.2 Face masks and respirators offer varying levels of protection against dust; the respirator helmet shown at left protects eyes as well as lungs

Fig 1.3 Never use the saw without wearing either earplugs or muffs

Fig 1.4 Loose clothing or hair can be caught in an instant, with devastating results. This loose sleeve could easily be caught by the saw

Fig 1.5 Do not stand directly behind the wood that is being cut; otherwise you might be hurt in the event of a kickback

Fig 1.1

Fig 1.2

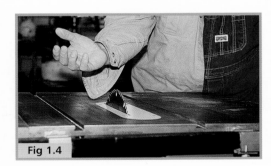

Fig 1.3

Fig 1.4

Fig 1.5

2 Clean the work area

Make sure the work area of the saw is clean and uncluttered.

3 Eye protection

Always wear a safety shield or plastic protective glasses when operating a saw. It is very easy to damage your eyes.

4 Lung protection

Always wear some sort of dust filtration. All sawdust is a lung irritant; some types cause cancer. Avoid breathing sawdust at all times. My preference is to wear a face shield that has automatic air filtration in the mask; this deals with points 3 and 4 together (Fig 1.2).

5 Hearing protection

Loud noise can lead to permanent hearing loss. Use some type of ear protection (either plugs or muffs) every time you turn the saw on (Fig 1.3).

6 Loose clothing

Anything long and loose will eventually get caught in moving machinery. Do not wear any long or loose clothing near machinery (Fig 1.4); long hair must be tied back.

7 Use a splitter

To help prevent kickback, some type of splitter may be advisable to prevent the rip-fence side of the wood from being deflected toward the saw blade; but in practice these devices do not always work well.

8 Body position

Stand to one side of the wood that is being cut (Fig1.5), so that if there is a kickback the wood will not be kicked into your stomach. Kickbacks occur when the stock becomes wedged between the blade and a stationary object such as the rip fence or safety guard. The blade catches the stock and throws it backwards with great speed.

9 Blade sharpness

Keep a sharp blade on your saw. A dull blade will require you to use more force, and more force means less control.

10 Blade height

Adjust your saw blade so that it projects no more than ¼in (6mm) above the wood stock. The less the blade is exposed, the safer it is. However, even a small amount of exposure from a saw blade can still do a tremendous amount of damage to your fingers or hand. **You must always pay attention!**

11 Safety zone

Always keep your fingers 3–5in (75–125mm) away from the saw blade at any time when the blade has any movement.

12 Safety devices

Whenever possible, use appropriate safety devices to hold and push your work. Featherboards hold the work against the rip fence and help to prevent kickback. Push sticks help you push the stock into the saw while keeping your fingers a safe distance away from the blade (Fig 1.6).

13 Accidental starts

Unplug the saw before changing a blade or making any adjustments to the blade (Fig 1.7). **Never put your hand down inside the machine while it is still plugged in.**

14 Safety guard

In principle, it is a good idea to use a safety guard whenever possible. It offers you protection from kickback by incorporating a splitter, and makes it harder for you to stick your hand into the saw blade. However, the safety guards that I know of are usually not practical for segmented work. Do use all the safety devices you can.

15 Inserts

Zero-clearance inserts are an important safety device for the tablesaw. They must fit snugly around the saw blade to prevent thin pieces of wood from becoming lodged between the blade and the insert.

16 Socializing

I like friends to visit my shop, but no socializing is done while working. Turn the saw off, sit down and share a cup of coffee or tea with your friend.

Fig 1.6 Keep your fingers well away from the danger zone while the blade is moving. Featherboards and push sticks are invaluable

Fig 1.7 Always unplug your saw before making any adjustments

Fig 1.8 Essential equipment for lathe safety includes face shield or respirator helmet, ear protection, and a shop apron

LATHE SAFETY

1 Speed kills!

This is just as true of machinery as it is of cars. If by mischance the workpiece breaks loose or comes apart, it can become a lethal flying object. The lathe speed must be slow enough to avoid unnecessary vibration. Also, high speed can cause pieces to come apart through excessive centrifugal force. **You must always wear a face shield when using the lathe, because you never know when your turning might come apart.**

2 Sober and alert

When working in the shop, you must always be sober and alert. If you are too tired, or in too much of a hurry, to do something the correct way, then it is time for you to quit and go to the house.

3 Safety equipment

Always wear the proper safety equipment (Fig 1.8). **This means that you always put a face shield on before turning on the lathe – always!** Whenever you are making any dust, you must have a respirator or air filter on. If you are too tired to wear the filter and face shield, then you are too tired to work.

4 Apron

Use a proper workshop apron, with no loose sleeves or strings which might get caught in the lathe. A heavy apron will give you a considerable degree of protection if the turning comes apart. Mine is home-made from fire-resistant imitation leather.

Fig 1.6

Fig 1.7

Fig 1.8

5 Plastic face shield

Always use a full face shield when turning; plastic glasses are not enough. It is fairly common to hear of turners being hit in the face with a heavy section of wood. If the turner is wearing a face shield it is just a sad story of losing a beautiful piece of work when it was almost finished. If not, then it is a story about a trip to the hospital.

6 Clothing

Do not wear any loose jewellery (watches, chains, rings), hair, or clothing in the vicinity of moving equipment. Lathes are especially dangerous because you are working close to a rotating shaft. Always be alert to the fact that anything loose might be caught, with disastrous results.

7 Have nothing in the line of fire

Position your toolrest between you and the turning. If your turning comes apart, the rest gives you some protection. With the toolrest in place between you and the turning, any flying object will almost always travel in a straight line away from the lathe, or straight up. Make sure that your friends or dog are not in the line of fire.

8 No unattended machines

If you leave the machine, turn it off. Never walk away from a running lathe, and never walk across the path of a running lathe.

9 Vibrations

Make sure that your turning is in balance and not causing the lathe to vibrate. Whenever possible, hold the turning at both ends by moving up your tailstock.

10 Sharp tools

Use sharp tools and a light touch when cutting. Dull tools require more force to cut the wood. This excess force makes the tool harder to control, and may cause your turning to come apart. Also, dull tools will not give a smooth finish cut.

PAY ATTENTION, wear your safety equipment, and control your speed. Turning is fun and safe when done properly. If you are a beginner turner, it is a good idea to get some instruction from an expert. There are also many good videos that can help get you started safely in turning.

2
DRAWING
MADE EASY

Most turners will benefit from having a detailed drawing to go by. The drawing will be a blueprint that will guide you through the entire segmented procedure. It will simplify the whole process, because it will show you what size rings to make and how many are needed. You will be able to construct your rings with the proper amount of overlap to achieve the bowl or vase shape that you intended.

Drawings are fun and simple to do once you have learnt the proper techniques. As for the amount of work involved, I can do a nice drawing from scratch in about five minutes. I can then ink in the colours and special designs in about another ten minutes. I will take about another 20 minutes to draw in the diameter and the width of the segments. Next I make a table on the left side of the drawing to show the diameters of the individual rings, and a table on the right side to show the segment widths. Drawings of this kind can be seen on pages 21 and 71, for example. All of this takes about one hour of total time. Since I usually do my drawings in intervals between work, making a drawing does not require any workshop time. You could just as easily do the drawing while you sit watching television.

Just four or five basic shapes will allow you to create most of the bowls that you want. Remember that all drawings can be increased or decreased in size as much as necessary with the aid of a photocopier that has enlarging and shrinking capabilities.

DRAWING BY HAND

For a drawing like that shown in Fig 2.1 you need a few basic supplies:

- paper
- a sharp, fine-leaded pencil
- a straightedge
- a fine felt-tip pen
- coloured pencils or coloured ink pens
- a big eraser.

Use a thin pencil for your drawings. Start off by folding a piece of lined paper down the middle. Draw a line down the crease of the paper; this will allow you to line up your paper with one below it if you want to trace from a previous drawing. Use a straightedge to draw a base line for half the shape. Next draw a pleasant curve for the bottom of the bowl (Fig 2.2). If you are not satisfied, use your eraser and redraw.

Fig 2.1 Four or five basic drawings will allow you to make just about any shape that you like. One drawing can be made into a vase that either flares out (shaded green) or narrows down (red) at the mouth

Fig 2.2 The lower part of the shape drawn freehand

Fig 2.3 The complete half-outline drawn and corrected

Fig 2.4 The half-drawing traced through the folded paper

Fig 2.5 The completed outline

Fig 2.6 Changing the width of the outline by increasing or decreasing the length of the base

Draw in the top curve next. This will often be an S-curve, but it could also be a simple curve so that the overall shape is an ogee. Use your eraser and redraw until you have a nice shape for half of your bowl (Fig 2.3).

Now fold the paper along the crease line and place the unused side of the paper facing up. Place the paper on a light box, or any piece of plastic or glass that has a light shining through from the back; this will make the pencil line show through. Trace over the line so that the half-drawing now appears on the back of the paper (Fig 2.4).

Open the page up and lay it face up on the light box. Trace the lines that show through from the back. This completes both sides of the drawing (Fig 2.5).

Varying the shape

The width of the bowl can be easily changed, simply by making the lines of the top and bottom of the bowl longer or shorter. This allows you to create many different forms with a limited amount of drawing. In Fig 2.6 the only difference between the upper shape and the original shape at the bottom is the length of the legs A and B.

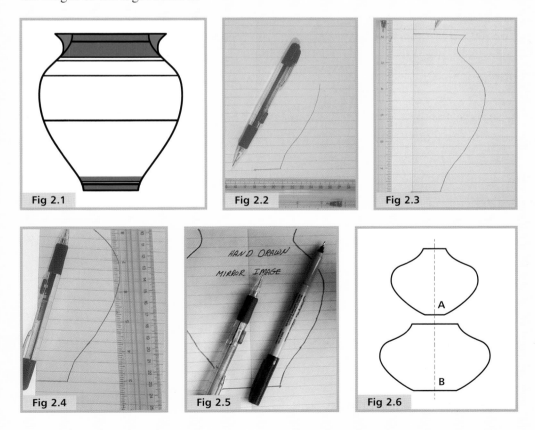

Fig 2.1

Fig 2.2

Fig 2.3

Fig 2.4

Fig 2.5

Fig 2.6

You might also want to put two or three tops on the same bowl; in this way you have three different design possibilities from the same drawing (Fig 2.7).

Practice drawings

To gain practice, it is a good idea to draw several small bowls on the same sheet of paper and refine the shapes that you like. Use the same method as before, but draw three different shapes on the same sheet (Fig 2.8). With just a little practice you will be drawing the shapes that you like.

Colouring in the drawing

Once you have completed a drawing to your satisfaction, make numerous copies and put them in a safe place for future use.

Ink in your drawing to help decide the wood colours and patterns that you want to use. I like the top and bottom of a bowl to be of the same wood. Then ink in the body and the feature ring (Fig 2.9).

DRAWING WITH A COMPUTER

Drawing with a CAD (computer-aided drawing) program can be fun. I bought a modestly priced one which does not have all the capabilities of the more expensive programs.

First use the 'straight line' button to draw half the bottom of the bowl. Then use 'fitted curve' to draw the right side of the bowl. Use the pointer to draw a rectangle around the drawing, then select the 'rubber stamp' or 'duplicate' option; this will make a duplicate of the right side of the drawing. You now have two right sides and no left side. Now select the duplicate and 'mirror-image' that part of the drawing. Move the mirror image to align with the right side, and the outline is complete. Note that you can make your vase as wide or as narrow as you want to at this stage. Name your drawing and save it into the computer. You can print out as many copies as you want; you can also enlarge and reduce as you choose to.

Computer programs for segmented turning

There are several new computer programs specially designed for the segmented turner. These will help you make a drawing easily, and do all the calculations at the same time. You decide how many segments are in each

Fig 2.7 A single drawing showing three alternative shapes for the top

Fig 2.8 A practice sheet with three drawings, all made by the folding method

Fig 2.9 Experiment on paper with different colours and patterns; I like my bowls to have a considerable amount of visual symmetry

ring, and what type or colour of wood you want to use. You can easily change the colour of any ring. The programs allow you to build the turning one ring at a time. As you add each ring, the program draws the bowl instantly. Some of the programs have 2D modelling, and some have 3D modelling for viewing the drawing. With 3D modelling you can rotate and translate the bowl to see it from any angle.

These programs make all of the calculations for you. It is very easy to add or delete rings wherever you want. You can print out the entire project and carry it with you to the workshop. The print-out will include a drawing of the vessel, a full description of each ring, and an itemized list of the wood used. This bill of goods will show you how much wood you need to purchase for your project.

Some programs allow you to put gaps between the segments to create open-segment turnings (see page 126 for an example of this type of work). There is usually a 'preferences' list where you can choose parameters such as width of saw kerf, minimum waste, accuracy of measurement, and metric or imperial measurements.

I will not go into details of individual programs, because computer software is constantly being updated and any information I could give here would soon be out of date. However, programs which I have found particularly useful include Lloyd Johnson's Woodturner Pro, Bill Kandler's Segmented Project Planner and Jerry Bennett's Woodturner Studio. Some of these come with ready-made projects which you can use or adapt, and some have associated websites from which designs can be downloaded.

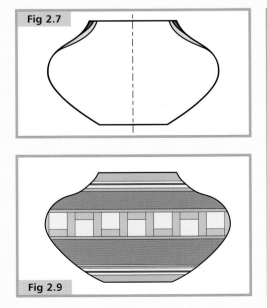

Fig 2.7

Fig 2.9

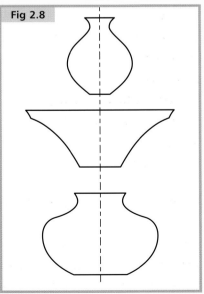

Fig 2.8

*Southwestern vase by Allen Quandee
(photo by courtesy of Allen Quandee)*

3
PLANNING
THE SEGMENTS

SEGMENTS AND ANGLES

Segmented turning is very much concerned with calculating the angles needed for the ring segments and determining how to make the correct sizes of ring. This chapter will go through the mathematics involved in calculating any angle you need for segmented turning. If you are not really interested in maths, don't worry. You do not need to be able to do any of these calculations, because you can look up any answer that you need in the tables on pages 134–47.

Note that in all calculations metric measurements may be substituted for imperial if you prefer, with no effect on the calculations.

DESCRIPTION OF A SEGMENT

Segmented turning involves cutting and gluing segments into rings that are later assembled to make bowls. A segment is a four-sided wedge shape (a trapezoid in American terminology, a trapezium in British usage). It is described by: width, height (or thickness), length, and the angle ϑ (theta) that is cut at each end (Fig 3.1). The width is determined by the width of the stock you use. The height (thickness) is determined by how thick your stock is. You must determine the length to make the correct size of circle. The angle ϑ (which I will usually call the 'mitre angle') is determined by how many segments you choose to have in your ring (Fig 3.2).

CALCULATING THE SEGMENT ANGLE

All rings are circles and therefore contain 360 degrees. Each segment has an identical mitre angle (ϑ) at each end. A ring may be made from any number of segments, typically from 4 to 40. It is important to know the correct angle ϑ for the number of segments in any given ring. Since each segment has the angle ϑ cut at each end, the amount of taper the segment has is 2ϑ; that is, twice as much as the angle that you cut.

The formula is:

Angle ϑ (mitre angle) = $360° \div 2n$

or, to simplify:

$\vartheta = 180° \div n$
where n stands for the number of segments in the ring.

Fig 3.1 The features of a segment

Fig 3.2 The mitre angle ϑ depends on the number of segments to be used

In plain English this reads: the mitre angle equals 180° divided by the number of segments. This is a good equation to understand and remember.

Example: What is the mitre angle ϑ to be cut for a 12-segment bowl?

$180° \div 12 = 15°$, so in this case $\vartheta = 15°$.

Table 1 shows the mitre angle for some commonly used rings.

TABLE 1

No. of segments	Mitre angle ϑ (°)	No. of segments	Mitre angle ϑ (°)
4	45	16	11.25
5	36	17	10.588
6	30	18	10
7	25.714	19	9.474
8	22.5	20	9
9	20	21	8.571
10	18	22	8.182
11	16.364	23	7.826
12	15	24	7.5
13	13.846	25	7.2
14	12.857	26	6.923
15	12	28	6.428

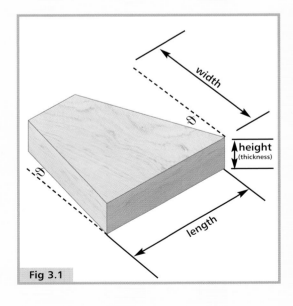

Fig 3.1

Fig 3.2

SEGMENT LENGTH AND RING DIAMETER

Knowing the tangent of the mitre angle (tan ϑ) is useful in determining the diameter of the ring and the length of the corresponding segments. (By 'length' I mean the length of material which has to be cut; the finished size after turning will be somewhat smaller.) An inexpensive hand calculator with basic mathematical functions makes this calculation very easily. Note that, although I have given measurements to three decimal places for completeness, accuracy to 0.1in (or to the nearest millimetre) is all that is needed when cutting the pieces.

Example: Making a 12-segment ring that is 9in in diameter.

Mitre angle $\vartheta = 180° \div 12 = 15°$
Tan $\vartheta = 0.2679$
Segment length = tan ϑ x diameter = 0.2679 x 9in = 2.411in

If you prefer metric units, simply substitute 230mm for 9in. In this case:

Segment length = 0.2679 x 230mm = 61.617mm

Table 2 shows tangents for rings of up to 40 segments.

TABLE 2

No. of segments	Mitre angle ϑ (°)	Tan ϑ	No. of segments	Mitre angle ϑ (°)	Tan ϑ
6	30	0.57735	24	7.5	0.13165
8	22.5	0.41421	26	6.923	0.12142
10	18	0.32492	28	6.428	0.11267
12	15	0.26795	30	6	0.10510
14	12.857	0.22824	32	5.625	0.09849
16	11.25	0.19891	34	5.294	0.09266
18	10	0.17632	36	5	0.08749
20	9	0.15838	38	4.737	0.08286
22	8.182	0.14378	40	4.5	0.07870

Fig 3.3 A 6-segment and a 12-segment ring, both with segment length of 1in (25mm)

Fig 3.4 Two 12-segment rings, with segment length 1in and diameter 3.732in, and with segment length 2in and diameter 7.464in

Fig 3.5 Any spacers used between the segments must be evenly distributed

You can calculate the diameter of the ring with the following formulae. This is why the tangent of the mitre angle is so useful: with this number you can calculate the diameter if you know the length of the segment.

Segment length = diameter of ring x tan ϑ

Example: What is the segment length for a 12-segment ring with a diameter of 6in?

    Angle ϑ = 180° ÷ 12 = 15°
    Tan ϑ = 0.267949
    Segment length = diameter x tan ϑ = 6 x 0.267948 =
        1.607in

Three factors determine the diameter of the ring:

- the number of segments
- the length of the segments
- the thickness of any spacers between the segments.

Three examples will help make this clearer.

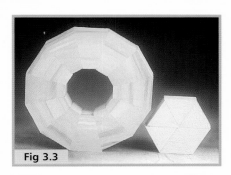
Fig 3.3

Example 1: Changing number of segments

Make two different rings with segments whose length is 1in. A 6-segment ring with a segment length of 1in will make a diameter of 1.732in. A 12-segment ring with the same segment length will make a diameter of 3.732in (Fig 3.3).

Example 2: Changing length of segments

You can change the ring diameter by varying the segment length (diameter = segment length ÷ tan ϑ). As we saw above, 12 segments 1in long make a 3.732in diameter ring; 12 segments with a length of 2in make a 7.464in ring (Fig 3.4).

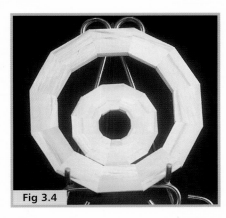
Fig 3.4

Example 3: Adding spacers to the ring

You can increase the diameter of a ring by adding spacers at equal intervals. The number of spacers must divide exactly into the number of segments to keep the ring from becoming lopsided. For example, Fig 3.5 shows a 12-segment ring with spacers every four segments. You can add spacers between all the segments only if there is an even number of segments in the ring. Adding spacers will add to the diameter of the ring; if the spacers are thin the difference will be small.

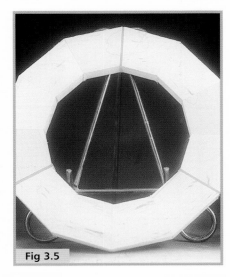
Fig 3.5

MAKING A BILL OF GOODS

A bill of goods is simply a list of how much wood you need to make a project. In segmented turning you need to take account of the different types of wood and the different widths that you must cut for some of the rings. Most of the stock you cut for rings will be about 1½in (38mm) wide, but rings that have to accommodate a large change in the shape of the bowl must be much wider: here the width of the wood might be 2–3in (50–75mm). You do not want to cut all of your stock at 3in because you would be wasting too much wood, so in your bill of goods you will list the different widths separately.

Go through the following procedure in making a bill of goods:

1 Make a drawing and divide it into rings to determine the thickness of the stock (Fig 3.6).

2 On each ring, draw a rectangle giving ½in (13mm) clearance on the inside and outside of the bowl. This will give you the inside and outside diameter of each ring (Fig 3.7).

3 Make a cutting list itemizing the diameter, width, and total segment length of each ring. Number the rings, starting at the bottom. Table 3 is a sample. Note that I round up and add 6in (150mm) of waste to make sure I have enough wood. In the example, rings 2–4 are cut from the same stock, so I add my 6in of waste only the once. This table is used to calculate your final bill of goods. It is also used in the shop when you are cutting the segments for each ring; it tells you what length to cut each segment.

4 Now make a total of the lengths needed and their width. This is the final bill of goods (Table 4).

TABLE 3: Cutting list for the bowl shown in Figs 3.6 and 3.7
(12-segment rings; all dimensions in inches)

Ring	Diameter	Segment width	Segment length	Wood type	Length required
1	3	2	0.80	padauk	10 + 6 = 16
2	3.5	1.5	0.938	maple	11 + 6 = 17
3	4	1.5	1.072	maple	13
4	4.5	1.5	1.205	maple	14
5	5	1.5	1.340	padauk	16 + 6 = 22

Fig 3.6 *A working drawing divided into layers gives you the thicknesses of the rings*

Fig 3.7 *Draw in the segments, allowing adequate clearance on the inside and outside of the bowl to allow for turning*

TABLE 4: Final bill of goods for the bowl shown in Figs 3.6 and 3.7 (all dimensions in inches)

Wood type	Width	Total length
Padauk	2	16
Padauk	1.5	22
Maple	1.5	44

Tables

Sometimes it is easier just to look up the necessary angles and measurements in a chart. I have therefore included some charts on pages 134–47 that show the length and angle of segments for different rings.

Example: For a 12-segment bowl that is 3in in diameter, what is the mitre angle and the segment length?

Go to the basic segmented ring guide on pages 135–7 and you will find that the angle for a 12-sided ring is 15°. Go to 3in diameter in the table and you will see that the segment length is 0.804in. Fill in the segment length for all the rings. You can now take your chart to the shop and cut the segments.

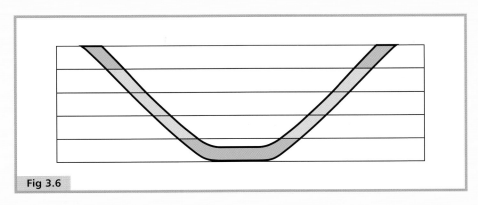

Fig 3.6

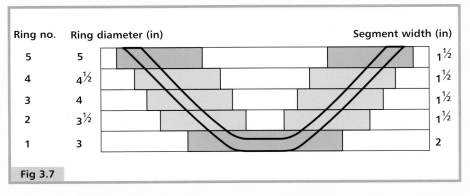

Ring no.	Ring diameter (in)		Segment width (in)
5	5		1½
4	4½		1½
3	4		1½
2	3½		1½
1	3		2

Fig 3.7

21

Vase by Hillard Gerhardt
(photo by courtesy of Hillard Gerhardt)

4
CUTTING
ACCURATE
ANGLES

AIDS TO ACCURACY

Perhaps the most crucial part of segmented turning is getting your rings to fit together with no gaps between the segments. You can make perfect rings only if you can cut very accurate angles. Once you can do this, making perfect rings is easy. There are several ways to cut accurate angles.

First of all, it is important to realize that the scale of an inexpensive mitre gauge is not accurate enough for segmented turning work (Fig 4.1). However, you can use a framing square in conjunction with your mitre gauge to achieve extremely accurate angles, as described below (pages 26–8).

There are three basic techniques for achieving accurate mitre angles:

- make a cutting board
- use a framing square
- buy a high-quality mitre gauge.

The first two techniques are very inexpensive, using equipment that you probably already have. We will look first at the high-quality mitre gauges, and then settle down with the techniques that are readily available to most turners.

HIGH-ACCURACY MITRE GAUGES

There are several manufacturers of high-quality after-market mitre gauges. The three gauges I have are very accurate and pleasant to use. They are expensive precision instruments that should be handled with care. All gauges must be set to your tablesaw; this requires a couple of minutes' set-up time. You must set the mitre gauge at 90° to the tablesaw blade, and use a square to set the fence perpendicular to the table (Fig 4.2). As a good woodworking technique you should always put a square to your mitre gauge to make sure that it is square to the blade before starting any project. It just takes a few seconds to check, and it will give you peace of mind to know that your cuts will be perfect.

Incra 5000

The Incra 5000 is a complete dual-sled mitre system that is ideal for segmented turning (Fig 4.3). The mitre gauge has positive notch settings for every single degree, and also for the half-degree marks (Fig 4.4). If you need part of a degree, there is a mechanism which allows you to 'nudge' the gauge a small amount. The second sled is used as a stop block; this allows you to

Fig 4.1 The mitre gauge supplied with your tablesaw is not accurate enough by itself

Fig 4.2 The mitre gauge must be at 90° to the blade, with the fence perpendicular to the table

Fig 4.3 The Incra 5000 system

Fig 4.4 Notches indicate degrees and half-degrees on the Incra 5000 and 3000

Fig 4.5 Cutting same-length segments on the Incra 3000 with a home-made stop block

Fig 4.6 The stop block uses fittings borrowed from a featherboard

cut any number of segments to the same length. This system allows a quick set-up and avoids the need for trial-and-error cuts.

Incra 3000

The Incra 3000 has the same mitre-gauge system as the 5000, with the same positive notch for every degree and half-degree. The difference is that it is not incorporated into a sled for the tablesaw. To cut segments of uniform length you will have to make a stop block that fits your tablesaw (Fig 4.5). This is a simple procedure. First cut a board that has two parallel slots in it, then attach it in the track with plastic inserts – I used the inserts from a store-bought featherboard (Fig 4.6). The Incra 3000 is especially well suited to go from the tablesaw to the sander; this is important for making special feature rings where the mitre angle has to be cut with a sander.

Fig 4.1

Fig 4.2

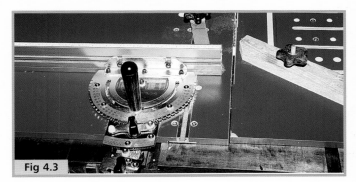
Fig 4.3

Fig 4.4

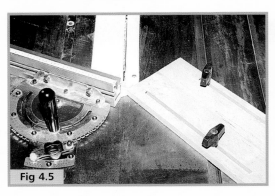
Fig 4.5

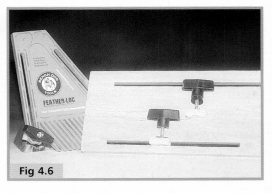
Fig 4.6

Osborne Excalibur

The Osborne Excalibur is made of heavy-duty extruded aluminium and has a sliding flip-stop (Fig 4.7). A solid triangular configuration keeps the guide absolutely rigid. The gauge has precision ball-plunger detents to locate 45, 30, 22.5 and 0°; all other degrees are located by reading an index scale. Although it does not have positive indents for every degree, you can get very good results with this gauge. It can very easily be 'nudged' to make minor adjustments to a setting. The gauge can be set for left- or right-hand cuts on either side of the blade.

USING A CARPENTER'S SQUARE

The carpenter's framing square, used with a bevel gauge, can give you any angle you choose to an accuracy of $\frac{1}{100}$°. Once you have learnt the technique it is fast and easy to use. You probably already have most of the necessary tools (Fig 4.8). You will need:

- carpenter's framing (roofing) square
- bevel gauge (sliding bevel)
- three clamps
- straightedge
- precision dial callipers.

You will also need to know the tangent of the angle. Don't panic! All the angles with their tangents are included in Table 2 on page 18.

1 Establish what angle you need to cut

You can look this up in Table 2 on page 18, or you can calculate it by dividing 180° by the number of segments in the ring and the hitting the TAN button on your calculator.

We will use for our example a 14-sided ring, for which the mitre angle is 12.857°. No mitre gauge can easily be set to this angle, but by using a framing square and a bevel gauge you can get any angle that you want to an extremely high degree of accuracy.

Example: What is the mitre angle for a 14-segment ring?

Answer: 180° ÷ 14 = 12.857°

Fig 4.7 The Osborne Excalibur

Fig 4.8 Necessary equipment for measuring angles with the carpenter's square

2 Find the tangent of the angle

You can do this either by referring to Table 2 on page 18, or by using a hand-held calculator.

Example: What is the tangent of 12.857°?

Answer: Enter 12.857 onto your calculator, if it is not already there. Hit the TAN button. 0.22824 will be displayed. That is the answer.

3 Set the framing square

The longer (horizontal) leg of the framing square is set to any convenient number of inches (or millimetres if you prefer), which we will call A. In this case we will use 20in. The longer the measurement, the more accurate the angle will be. (500mm would be suitable if you are using metric.) Measure along the lower (outer) edge of the square and place a stop block at your chosen measurement, flush with the outer edge of the square; this is measurement A.

> **DON'T MIX** metric and imperial measurements; they are not exact equivalents. Stick consistently to one system or the other.

The next step is to determine how far up the framing square you need to go to set the other stop block. I will call this vertical measurement V. The vertical measurement is determined by the following calculation (you will remember from the previous chapter that ϑ (theta) always stands for the mitre angle):

$V = \tan \vartheta \times A$

so, in our example:

$V = \tan 12.857° \times 20\text{in}$

Using a small hand-held calculator:

$\tan 12.857° = 0.22824$

so:

$V = 0.22824 \times 20\text{in} = 4.565\text{in}$

(or with metric measurements, where A = 500mm:

$V = 0.22824 \times 500\text{mm} = 114.12\text{mm}$)

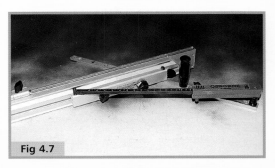

Fig 4.7

To get a perfect angle of 12.857° you must therefore set a stop block at 4.565in for the V measurement if you used 20in for A (or at 114.12mm, if A was 500mm; remember that A and V must both be in the same units).

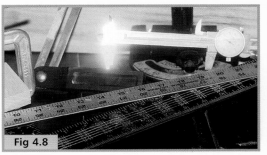

Fig 4.8

An accurate dial calliper (or vernier calliper) is necessary for precise and easy segmented turning. It must be in the same units as the framing square: either imperial or metric, but not a mixture. You will use the callipers to determine the mitre angle and the segment length.

Set the calliper to 4.565in (or 114.12mm if you are using metric). Set the calliper against the shorter leg of the framing square to measure up the outer edge of the square by this amount. Set another stop block at this measurement. Both stop blocks must be flush with the outer edge of the framing square.

Clamp a straightedge flush against the two stop blocks (Fig 4.9). We now have a triangle with the angle of 12.857° at its right-hand corner. To set our mitre gauge we need the *complement* of 12.857°, which is $90 - 12.857 = 77.143°$. This angle is found on the left side of the framing square, above the straightedge.

4 Set the bevel gauge

Place the bevel gauge on the adjacent angle formed by the straightedge and the framing square (see Fig 4.9). Carefully and accurately set your bevel gauge to this angle and, once set, check it again. Remember, this angle is not 12.857° but the adjacent angle. When you set this angle on the mitre gauge, it will leave the required angle of 12.857°.

5 Set the mitre gauge

Place an extension fence on your mitre gauge (Fig 4.10). It is important that your stock material be well supported. Use your bevel gauge to set the mitre gauge (Fig 4.11). You must be accurate. Once you have set the mitre gauge, go back and check your angle again from the framing square. Be sure that the angle is exact. If you do this accurately, you will not have to make any adjustments once you start cutting your segments. This completes the procedure to set a mitre gauge using a framing square.

USING A CUTTING BOARD: A NO-MATHS TECHNIQUE

You can use trial and error to get perfect angles using a cutting board or sled, the making of which is described in Chapter 6 (pages 39–45). With just a little practice you can get very exact angles by doing a series of six to eight test cuts. For many people this method is much faster, easier, and just as accurate as the framing-square technique. Since there are no calculations involved, it is a real blessing to those who hate maths.

Fig 4.9 The rule clamped against the stop blocks on the framing square gives the angle to which the bevel must be set

Fig 4.10 Mitre gauge fitted with an extension fence

Fig 4.11 Using the bevel gauge to set the mitre gauge

Fig 4.12 The cutting sled with its stock guide positioned correctly: the head of the stock guide pointing **IN**

Fig 4.13 The stock guide and stop block set to an arbitrary angle for the first trial cut

'Trial and error' does not mean sloppy or inferior: this is a first-class technique that will get just as good results as any other method. The only disadvantage is that the first few times you use the technique you may have to spend 20 minutes getting the correct angle. With a little practice you will be able to hit the perfect angle with about six test cuts and ten minutes' work. A few minutes' set-up time should not be a big deterrent. Remember, setting up an accurate mitre gauge or using the framing square also takes a few minutes' preparation.

The cutting sled should cut angles with the head of the stock guide angled **IN** toward the blade guard (Fig 4.12), not **OUT** away from the blade guard. As long as the head of the stock guide is pointed **IN** toward the blade guard, then the segment will be able to move safely away from the guide and stop block once it has been cut. **If the head of the stock guide were pointed OUT, the cut segment would be trapped between the stock guide and stop block. The segment would not be able to escape from the blade, and this would make a 'catch' in the segment.**

Example: Set the mitre table to cut a 12-segment ring using no maths

Start by setting your mitre support to any angle. Simply make up an angle and tighten the lock nuts so that you can make some test cuts. Just make sure that the **head** of the stock guide is pointed **IN** toward the blade guard. Set a stop block to give test blocks of uniform length; 1–2in (25–50mm) works fine (Fig 4.13).

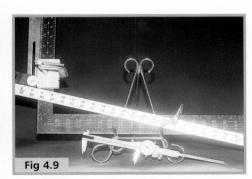
Fig 4.9

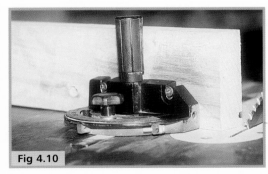
Fig 4.10

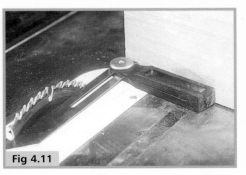
Fig 4.11

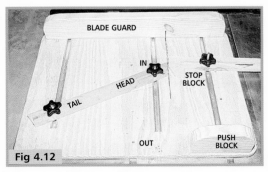
Fig 4.12

Fig 4.13

Cut three test segments. Three segments make up one fourth of a 12-segment ring; therefore three perfect segments should fit perfectly in your framing square. However, your three segments are not likely to be perfect and there is going to be a gap either on the outside or on the inside of the circle.

If your three segments have an inside gap, then move the stock guide **OUT**ward. If you have an outside gap, move the mitre fence **IN**ward (refer back to Fig 4.12 for **OUT** and **IN**).

> **SAY THIS OUT LOUD** to help you remember it:
> IN for outside gap – OUT for inside gap.

My first cut for this example produced three segments with a large gap on the inside (Fig 4.14). The correction for this is to move the head of the stock fence **OUT**.

Use a pencil to mark where your fence was on the first cut. Then make an adjustment by moving the head of the fence **OUT**. Cut three new segments, put them on the square and check your progress. If the gap is smaller than it was, this means that you have made the adjustment in the correct direction, but you have not moved it quite far enough; the correction will be to move the stock-fence head **OUT** a little further. If there is now a gap on the *outside,* you have moved it too far, and will have to move it back **IN** a little.

Adjust the fence according to the gaps of the last three segments, then cut another three segments. Continue making smaller and smaller adjustments to the fence as you come closer and closer to having no gaps in the three segments; you are close at this point. In this example I came very close on my third attempt (Fig 4.15).

Now cut a whole set of 12 segments to make a complete ring. Pull the segments together with a hose clamp (Fig 4.16). Hold the ring up to the light and see if any light comes through. In this example I used a blue pen to highlight a small gap on the outside of the 12-segment ring. Make a very tiny adjustment to the mitre fence by just barely 'bumping' it. Cut another 12 segments and pull them together with a hose clamp; you should be very close at this point (Fig 4.17). If necessary, make one more slight adjustment and do another series of cuts. By this time you should have an extremely accurately set mitre table. Use a permanent marker pen to mark the position of the mitre fence. Label the setting as '12 segments'. This will save you considerable time on future set-ups. You will still have to do a test cut or two to make sure that you are dead on, but this will get you very close, very quickly.

Fig 4.14 Testing the first trial segments against the framing square; in this case the gaps are on the inside of the circle, and the guide must be moved **OUT**

Fig 4.15 These three segments are a close fit. Now it is time to make a full-circle test

Fig 4.16 On this full-circle test there is a small gap on the outside; the correction is **IN for outside gap**

Fig 4.17 A very slight nudge **IN** made this next ring perfect

Fig 4.18 For mitre gauges and mitre saws: a gap on the **outside** means **increase** the mitre angle

Fig 4.19 A gap on the **inside** means **decrease** the mitre angle

MITRE GAUGE CORRECTIONS

If you are cutting with a mitre saw or a mitre gauge, you may need to make some minor adjustments because the gauge is off by a small amount. The correction rule is the same for both the mitre gauge and the mitre saw: **a gap on the inside means decrease the mitre angle; a gap on the outside means increase the mitre angle.**

Example: A 12-segment ring

For 12 segments the gauge should be set to 15°.

If you have set the angle to 14° there will be a gap on the outside (Fig 4.18). The solution is to increase the angle by a small amount. **A gap on the outside means increase the mitre angle.**

If you have set the angle to 16° there will be a gap on the inside (Fig 4.19). The solution is to decrease the angle by a small amount. **A gap on the inside means decrease the mitre angle.**

Fig 4.14

Fig 4.15

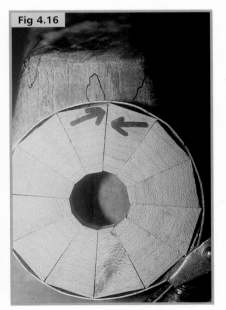

Fig 4.16

Fig 4.17

Fig 4.18

Fig 4.19

REMEMBER
IN for outside gap – OUT for inside gap.

31

Desert Night Scene by Linda Salter
(photo by Paul Tedrick)

5
SETTING UP
THE TABLESAW

WHY SET-UP MATTERS

The tablesaw is not the only way to cut segments for turning – some alternatives are discussed briefly at the end of this chapter – but it is certainly the most versatile and convenient way of doing so.

Tablesaws are wonderful pieces of equipment and can provide extremely accurate cuts. However, to achieve high accuracy a tablesaw must be properly set up. Some misalignment is bound to have occurred on the way from the factory, and when you receive your saw there is a small amount of assembly required. Proper assembly of the saw requires that you have the saw blade aligned with the tablesaw top, mitre gauge and rip fence. All errors, no matter how small, will cause a loss of accuracy in the saw's cutting.

Checking your saw for accuracy is easy, and making the proper adjustments will take only a few minutes. This investment will be repaid with years of accurate cuts. An inexpensive saw, accurately tuned, will always outperform a poorly tuned, expensive saw.

AIMS

There are seven requirements for the tablesaw to work properly. If there is any misalignment in any of these settings, the saw will not give acceptable cuts:

1 The mitre-gauge slots must be parallel to the saw blade.
2 The rip fence must be parallel to the saw blade. (There is a minor refinement to this rule: I personally like to have the distant edge of the fence slightly away from the blade to help prevent kickback.)
3 The rip fence must be at 90° to the table.
4 The blade must be at 90° to the table.
5 The vertical guide fence of the mitre gauge must be at 90° to the table.
6 The guide fence of the mitre gauge must be at 90° to the saw blade.
7 The splitter, if used, must be correctly aligned.

1 Table-top alignment

The saw blade is mounted on a non-adjustable arbor; therefore all adjustments start from the saw blade and move outward. The starting point is to set the table top parallel to the saw blade. To do this, first loosen the four bolts underneath the top (Fig 5.1). Use a simple jig with your mitre gauge to set the mitre slots parallel to the saw blade (Fig 5.2). For accurate results,

Fig 5.1 These bolts under the table top must first be loosened

Fig 5.2 A simple jig for adjusting the mitre slots parallel to the saw blade

Fig 5.3 The rod should touch the same tooth with the same amount of pressure when it is rotated to the back

Fig 5.4 Placing the fence flush against the saw blade to check for parallel

Fig 5.5 Checking the fence against a flat jig placed in the mitre slot

bring the saw blade to its full height. A small rod or pencil is clamped to the mitre gauge and is adjusted until it barely touches a tooth at the front of the saw. The saw blade is then rotated backward and the jig is moved so as to touch the same tooth in its new position (Fig 5.3). If there is a gap, or if the blade pushes on the rod, the table top must be adjusted. The saw blade should touch the rod evenly at the front and the back. Once the table is properly adjusted, retighten the four bolts that hold the table top to the saw.

2 Rip fence parallel to saw blade

Making this adjustment will depend on the type of fence that you have. You can check the parallelism in one of two ways. The first is to bring the fence up to the saw blade and check to see that the blade is flush to the fence on both sides (Fig 5.4). Another way is to cut a jig that accurately fits into the mitre slot, then bring the rip fence up to the jig and see if it is flush to the jig along its entire length (Fig 5.5).

There is a minor exception to this set-up. A lot of experienced woodworkers like the further (outfeed) end of the rip fence to be away from the saw blade by about 1⁄16in (1.5mm). This small gap helps to prevent kickback in ripping operations.

The far end of the fence must not angle in toward the saw blade. In this case the rip fence would put pressure on the stock as it leaves the cut. The stock would be pushed into the saw blade and cause a kickback.

ALWAYS unplug your saw before making any adjustments.

Fig 5.1

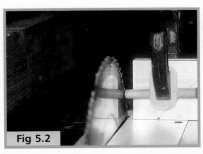
Fig 5.2

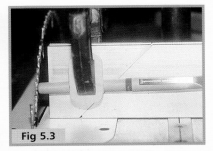
Fig 5.3

Fig 5.4

Fig 5.5

3 Rip fence at 90° to the table

Use your square to make sure that the fence is perpendicular to the table (Fig 5.6). Adjust the fence if necessary.

4 Blade at 90° to the table

For basic ripping and cross-cutting operations the blade must be at 90° to the table (Fig 5.7). Check this with the square, and use the tilt control to adjust the angle of the blade. You should have a dedicated square that lives at your tablesaw, and use it to make sure the blade is at 90° before all cutting operations. The vast majority of tablesaw cuts are done with the blade set at 90°, though for some mitre and compound-mitre cuts the blade will be adjusted away from this setting.

5 Mitre-gauge fence at 90° to the table

Use your square to make sure that the guide fence of the mitre gauge is perpendicular (Fig 5.8). Adjust if necessary.

6 Mitre-gauge fence at 90° to the saw blade

The guide fence of the mitre gauge must be at 90° to the saw blade when the mitre gauge is set to zero (Fig 5.9). Use your square to check the mitre gauge every time you set up to do an operation.

7 Aligning the splitter

I do not use a splitter myself, but if you do use one it must be carefully aligned in order to work properly. Follow the instructions provided by the manufacturer. If you are using a home-made splitter, be very careful to make sure that it is aligned properly and is securely fastened (Fig 5.10). **You must be very careful to make sure the splitter does not come apart during operation!** Splitters are most important during ripping operations.

TABLESAW MAINTENANCE

The tablesaw is a wonderful piece of equipment, but it does require a small amount of maintenance. There are three basic areas where some minimal maintenance is necessary: the saw blade, the table top, and the adjustment gears under the table.

Fig 5.6 Making sure the rip fence is square to the table

Fig 5.7 Setting the blade perpendicular to the table

Fig 5.8 The guide fence of the mitre gauge must be at 90° to the table

Fig 5.9 Setting the guide fence of the mitre gauge (set to zero) at 90° to the saw blade

Fig 5.10 A correctly aligned splitter

To function safely and provide accurate cuts, your blade must be sharp and free of sap or resin. Blades should be replaced or sharpened once they start to become dull. If possible, try to buy a high-quality tungsten-carbide blade for your saw. When it is dull you can send it back to the factory to be sharpened. You then have to decide what you are going to do while the blade is away; owning two high-quality saw blades is ideal, but expensive.

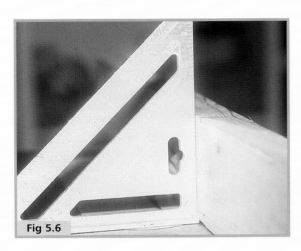

Fig 5.6

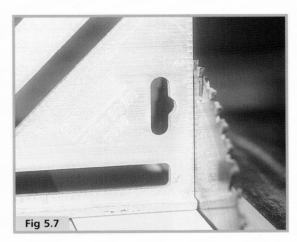

Fig 5.7

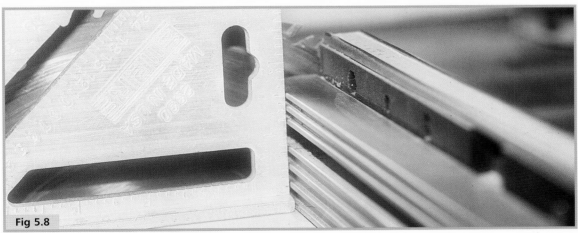

Fig 5.8

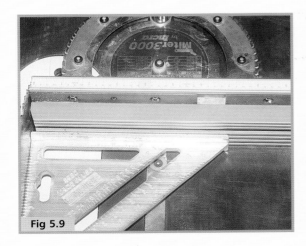

Fig 5.9

Fig 5.10

The table top should be clean and smooth. Remove any rust marks with fine-grade sandpaper, then protect the surface with paste wax. The surface of the tablesaw should be very smooth so that the stock and jigs move easily over the top. Occasionally I cannot find paste wax in my shop, so I spray the top down with WD-40. This cleans and protects the top of the saw effectively, but you must be sure to wipe the top off before placing any wood on it (Fig 5.11).

The adjustment gears underneath the table must be cleaned occasionally. There are two separate gear systems: one to raise and lower the blade, and another to tilt the blade. These gears can become clogged with sawdust. On a regular basis you must clean out the dust under the table and lubricate the gears. If the gears are not cleaned, they will become clogged and will not work properly. **Do not try to force jammed gears!** This will only result in breaking the gear mechanism, which could be very expensive to repair. Maintenance starts with dusting out the inside of the saw with a small whisk broom. An industrial vacuum cleaner is very useful for cleaning the inside of the saw (Fig 5.12). Then lightly lubricate the gears with a thin lubricant such as WD-40.

ALTERNATIVES TO THE TABLESAW

Segments can be cut easily and well with a mitre saw. A bandsaw can be used if it is properly set up and used correctly, but flexing of the blade can be a problem. I have not attempted to cut segments with a radial-arm saw. Segments could also be hand-cut using the old-fashioned handsaw and mitre box, though this would be very slow. However, you will need a tablesaw for many of the other procedures in segmented turning, so you might as well use the best saw for cutting most of the segments.

In a complicated glue-up for a feature ring, some segments will need final shaping on a sander because they are too short to be handled safely on the tablesaw.

Fig 5.11

Fig 5.12

Fig 5.11 Clean and protect the surface of your tablesaw with either paste wax or a spray lubricant

Fig 5.12 You can remove dust from the gears of the tablesaw with a small brush or a shop vacuum cleaner

6
MAKING A
CUTTING SLED

One of the most useful things you can do as a segmented turner is to make a good cutting board or sled (Fig 6.1). The use of this tablesaw accessory has already been described in Chapter 4 (pages 28–30). The sled will allow you to make the very precise and repeatable segments that are necessary for good segmented turning. It will be valuable to you even if you already have a highly accurate and expensive mitre gauge.

Expect the sled-making project to take you a good part of a weekend. The time you spend on making a good sled will be greatly repaid: your segmented cutting work will be much easier and the quality of your segments will be vastly improved. Although there is nothing really difficult in the project, there are several features of the sled that will take you some time to make correctly. Obtain your supplies in advance of making the project. You will probably have all of the wood supplies already in your shop; the only things that you may need to order are the track components. These are easily available from your woodworking supplier. You need aluminium or steel T-track, T-bolts either ¼ or ½in (6 or 13mm) in diameter, and hold-down knobs that screw onto the T-bolts (Fig 6.2).

MATERIALS REQUIRED

- 1 piece of ¾in (18 or 20mm) plywood, 27 x 21in (685 x 535mm)
- 1 piece of 2 x 4in (50 x 100mm) softwood, 26in (660mm) long
- 1 piece of 2 x 4in (50 x 100mm) softwood, 6in (150mm) long
- 3 pieces of steel or aluminium track, 18 x 0.8 x 0.4in (460 x 20 x 10mm)
- 2 pieces of hardwood the size of the track in your saw table, about 19in (480mm) long
- 1 piece of hardwood 13 x 2 x ½in (330 x 50 x 13mm) for the stop block
- 1 piece of hardwood 22 x 1½ x ½in (560 x 38 x 13mm) for the fence or stock guide
- 3 bolts and through nuts to secure the stop block and sled fence in place.
- ¾in (18–20mm) and 3in (75mm) wood screws, 8 of each

Fig 6.1 The cutting sled set up and ready to use

Fig 6.2 The track supplies can be ordered from a woodworking supplier

Fig 6.3 To make the bed of the sled you need good-quality plywood and suitable protective gear

Fig 6.4 Any cylindrical container can be used as a template for the corners

The measurements for this board do not have to be followed exactly. If your sled is a little larger or a little smaller, this will not affect its accuracy. What is important is that the runners slide smoothly and do not allow any play as the sled moves. Also, the plywood must be perfectly flat; otherwise you will have very inconsistent cuts as your stock moves over the high and low spots of the sled.

THE PLYWOOD BED

Use eye and ear protection while cutting the plywood to size (Fig 6.3). This should be good-quality plywood, preferably smooth on both sides. You will need the stock to slide easily on the top side, and you want the bottom to slide easily on the tablesaw. Minor imperfections may be sanded down.

Draw a rounded profile on all four corners. You may use a compass for this, or any round container that is handy (Fig 6.4). Cut the corners round using a bandsaw or a jigsaw, then sand them smooth with a belt sander or by hand (Fig 6.5). The round corners are nice from an aesthetic point of view, but they really become valuable if you ever drop the sled on your foot.

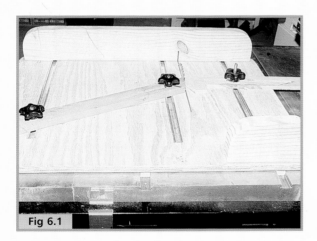
Fig 6.1

Fig 6.2

Fig 6.3

Fig 6.4

You must cut slots in the top of the sled for the steel or aluminium track to fit into. You may make these cuts for the channels using multiple passes with a tablesaw blade, or by using a straight router bit.

If you are using a router, it is best to use a straight, spiral-cutting bit. The diameter of the bit must be the same as the width of the track, or smaller. Clamp straightedges onto the sled to use as guides for the router. Place three guides to determine the width of the track and the length of the cut. Make shallow cuts; three to four passes with the router, with the bit slightly deeper each time, will allow you to do the job safely.

A tablesaw may be used to cut an exact rebate for the metal track. Mark on the plywood the positions where the three channels will be cut. Measuring from the right side (to the right of the saw blade) to the centre of each channel, the channels should be cut at 4, 11, and 23in (100, 280, and 585mm). They should be about 16in (405mm) long; place a stop mark on the tablesaw so that you will know where to stop your rebate cut. Position the saw fence carefully for each of the three grooves. Make the initial cut with the saw set to the correct depth. Then move the tablesaw fence in the appropriate direction just slightly less than the width of the blade, and repeat the cut. Continue in this manner until the rebate has been cut to the correct width.

To prevent painful splinters, use a round-over bit in a hand-held router to round over the edges of the plywood. If you do not have a round-over bit, you can get the same effect by sanding over the edges.

Use a straight chisel and mallet to square up the three corners where the saw blade made a curved exit from the wood (Fig 6.6). Test-fit the track to make sure that it fits snugly all the way to the butt joint at the end (Fig 6.7). Apply glue to the inside of the track and position all three tracks. I used epoxy glue in this case, but yellow glue (aliphatic resin) will also work. The track very likely will have screw holes in it, but this is impractical for our purposes: there is not enough plywood thickness left for the screws to have a good purchase.

BLADE GUARD AND RIGHT-HAND PUSH BLOCK

Cut your two two-by-fours to the dimensions given. The long piece will be used to make the blade guard that goes on the far side of the sled; the short piece will make the right-hand push block. Round the upper corners as you did on the plywood section (Fig 6.8), and sand them smooth with a belt sander. Round over the top edges with a round-over bit, or with sandpaper.

Fig 6.5 Rounding the corners with a belt sander

Fig 6.6 Squaring the corners of the housings

Fig 6.7 Test-fitting the track

Fig 6.8 Rounding the upper corners of the two-by-fours

The blade guard goes along the entire rear edge of the sled. It has two functions. The first is to reinforce the sled (which is weakened by the dados and the slot for the saw blade) so that it will not flex while in use. The second, most important function is to protect you from the saw blade. When you have finished cutting, pull the sled toward you so that the blade is covered by the blade guard.

You must still pay attention and not stick your hand into the saw blade, but the guard helps to remind you to be careful.

The right-hand push block is placed for two reasons also. First, it gives you a convenient place for your right hand to push the sled during operation. Second, by forcing your right hand to be in this location, it prevents it from being somewhere dangerous.

Put the T-bolts into the track before attaching the blade guard. **This is important: they cannot be put in the track once the end has been blocked off.** First try the blade guard and push block in position, then, when you are happy with their placement, attach them using both glue and screws. Apply glue to the pieces and clamp them in position, then turn the sled upside down to insert the 3in (75mm) screws.

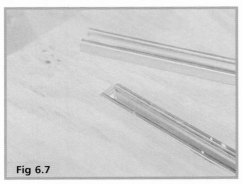

Fig 6.5

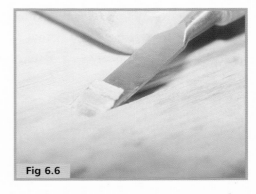

Fig 6.6

Fig 6.7

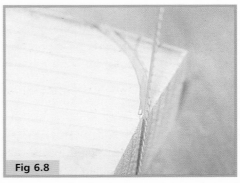

Fig 6.8

SLED RUNNERS

The two runners to go underneath the sled should be made of a stable, hard wood like maple. They should be made to fit the tracks of your saw table snugly, but without binding (Fig 6.9). If the fit is too snug your sled will not slide smoothly.

Attaching the runners

Place the two runners into the tracks of the tablesaw. Position the sled onto the tablesaw and align the front edge of the sled with the front edge of the table. Clamp the sled in position with wood clamps, and use a framing square to mark precisely the centres of the two tablesaw tracks on the top of the sled. Carefully drill four small pilot holes for screws along these two lines. Next, drill a small countersink for the head of the screw to fit into. Attach the two runners with four screws each (Fig 6.10). Do make sure that the screws are not long enough to foul the steel track.

Check the sled to make sure that it slides smoothly. If not, check whether a screw has split the runner. If the runner has been split by the screw it can expand so much that it binds in the track.

It is possible that the friction of the two tracks may be too much for the smooth operation of the sled. If this is the case, take one of the runners off and lightly sand it; then reattach the runner and test again. With just a very small amount of adjustment your new sled should be working very smoothly. You may want to lubricate the runners with paste wax or petroleum jelly.

STOP BLOCK AND STOCK GUIDE

Make the stop block from 2in (50mm)-wide stock. It should be about 13in (330mm) long. The shape of the stop block should be that of a large figure 1. The slot should run in the middle of the stem of the 1, and should be about 9in (230mm) long. Make the slot just a little wider than the T-bolt that goes in the slot (Fig 6.11). This will allow the stop block to be positioned easily at any desired location.

Make the stock guide from hardwood 1½in (38mm) wide. Start off with the length about 22in (560mm). Mark where the slots should be positioned by laying the stock guide first straight across the tracks, then slanted with the right end further toward the blade guard. Mark both locations: this will give you the length of the two slots needed in the stock guide.

Fig 6.9 *The hardwood runners must slide smoothly in the saw table*

Fig 6.10 *Having attached the two runners, check that the sled slides smoothly*

Fig 6.11 *Details of the stop block*

Fig 6.12 *The stop block in position*

Drill a hole at each end of each slot. To give a nice finish, these holes should be the same diameter as the width of the slot. Use a jigsaw to cut out the remaining part of the slot.

Attach the stock guide and stop block (Fig 6.12). This completes the construction of the cutting sled. The slot for the saw blade is made the first time you use the sled.

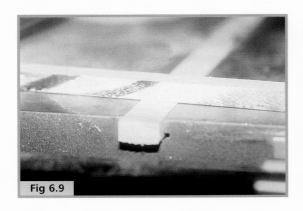

Fig 6.9

Fig 6.10

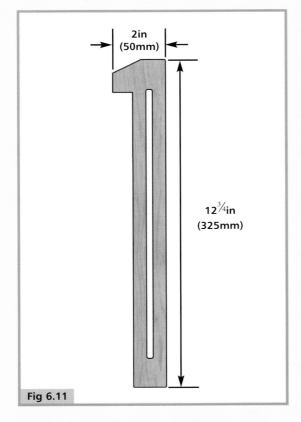

2in
(50mm)

12¾in
(325mm)

Fig 6.11

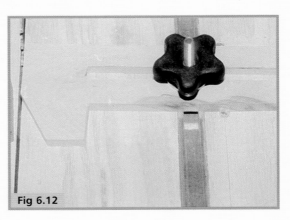

Fig 6.12

PART II
SEGMENTED TURNING PROJECTS

7
SCALLOPED
BOWL

This stave-construction bowl is a good starting point for segmented turning because of its simplicity and beauty. Another advantage of this project is that all the cuts can be made using a mitre saw (Fig 7.1).

The unique feature of this bowl is that an attractive scalloped pattern is created in the wood. This pattern is not the result of difficult and precise joinery: the scallops are developed naturally when you cut a curve into a bowl that is made from two layers of different-coloured woods.

As in all segmented turning, you will be working with kiln-dried stock. You may substitute different types of wood for this project. However, you need two highly contrasting woods for the feature ring where the scallops are developed.

BILL OF GOODS

NB: All length measurements include an allowance for wastage.

		in	mm
Scalloped ring	red oak	40 x 2 x 1	1020 x 50 x 25
Scalloped ring	walnut	40 x 2 x ½–1	1020 x 50 x 13–25
Bottom of bowl	red oak	76 x 2 x 1	1930 x 50 x 25
Top of bowl	walnut	40 x 2 x 1	1020 x 50 x 25
2 thin white layers	white oak/maple	40 x 2 x 1	1020 x 50 x 25
2 thin red layers	purpleheart/padauk	40 x 2 x 1	1020 x 50 x 25

Initial glue-up

There are two initial gluing steps to perform. The first is to glue up the red oak to make the bottom of the bowl. The second to make the 'stick' that will be used to form the scalloped ring. Yellow glue (aliphatic resin) is used for all the projects in this book.

Gluing the bottom

First cut six pieces of red oak 12 x 2 x 1in (305 x 50 x 25mm). Dry-fit these together to make a 12in (305mm) square that is 1in (25mm) thick. Glue together one section at a time.

Gluing the scallop ring

Glue the red oak strip to the walnut along the 2in (50mm) surface. The left-hand stick in Fig 7.2 is the one used in this project.

Thicknessing

After the bottom and the 'scallop stick' have set overnight it is necessary to sand both flat. The easiest way is to use a thickness sander, but hand sanding is adequate. Just make sure that both components are flat.

Mitre-saw set-up

Start by making a test ring using scrap wood. This will be a ten-segment ring, so the angle you need is 18° (180° ÷ 10 = 18°).

Set your mitre gauge to 18° (Fig 7.3). Place a piece of tape on the saw fence to use as a stop line (Fig 7.4); stop blocks on the mitre saw can be dangerous.

Fig 7.1 A mitre saw is used to cut the feature ring of this project

Fig 7.2 The feature ring is made by gluing two different-coloured woods together. The left-hand piece was used for this project

Fig 7.3 Mitre gauge set to 18° to make a 10-sided ring

Fig 7.4 Tape on the saw fence indicates the segment length

Test cuts

Using scrap timber, cut ten segments all the same length, measured against the tape on the mitre fence. To produce the necessary wedge-shaped pieces, you will have to flip the stock over each time you make a cut. Arrange the segments in a circle and pull them together with a hose clamp. Check to see if there are any gaps. To make a correction, barely move the saw in the appropriate direction. If the gap is on the **outside** of the circle, then **increase** the angle by a very small amount; if the gap is on the **inside** of the circle, slightly **decrease** the angle.

Once you have made your small adjustment, make ten more test cuts. If necessary, do another small adjustment and make another test ring.

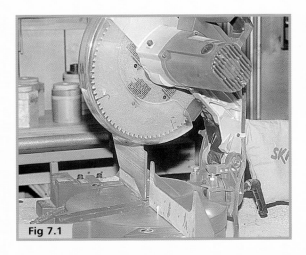

Fig 7.1

Fig 7.2

Fig 7.3

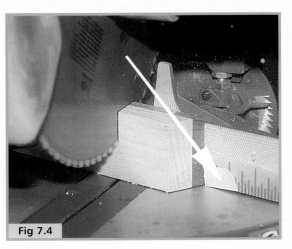

Fig 7.4

Cutting the scallop ring

Position a new piece of tape on your mitre-saw fence to cut a 3in (75mm) segment. Place the walnut and red oak stick on the mitre saw, with the walnut side facing toward you. Make the first mitre cut by just barely cutting off the right end of the stick. Now flip the stick over, set the edge against the tape stop, and make your second cut. This completes the first segment.

Now flip the stick over once more so that the walnut side is facing outward again. Barely cut off the waste end of the stick. Continue cutting all ten segments this way.

Assembling the scallop ring

Arrange the ten segments in a circle. The walnut is always on the outside of the segment, because you flipped the stick back over each time you completed a segment.

Apply a small amount of glue to each surface and press the segments together. Pull the ring together with two hose clamps, gently tapping the segments flat onto the table with a hammer or a rubber mallet (Fig 7.5). Allow the glue on this ring to set overnight.

Preparing the bottom

Sand the glued-up red oak square flat on both sides. Place the scallop ring onto it and trace the outside outline of the scallop ring onto the bottom. Use a tablesaw or bandsaw to cut the red oak square to this shape (Fig 7.6).

Sanding the scallop ring

Sand the scallop ring flat. You can easily flatten one side by hand: just lay a full sheet of 60-grit sandpaper on a flat surface and rub one side of the ring against it. Once this single side has been accurately flattened, you can glue the bottom to it. You can later turn the other side flat and parallel to the first side on the lathe.

Gluing the bottom to the scallop ring

Apply a thin layer of glue to the bottom of the ring and to the bowl bottom. Position the bottom onto the ring and clamp in place with multiple clamps (Fig 7.7).

Fig 7.5 Gently tap the glued-up feature ring to ensure flatness

Fig 7.6 The red oak square is cut to form a 10-sided bottom

Fig 7.7 Gluing the bottom to the scallop ring

Fig 7.8 Stock prepared for the top ring

Fig 7.9 Gluing the last layer of the top ring

Preparing the top ring

The top ring is made from a sandwich of regular-thickness walnut, two thin layers of white oak, and two thin layers of purpleheart (or the alternatives given in the bill of goods). The white oak and purpleheart are both cut to ¹⁄₁₆in (1.5mm) thickness on the tablesaw: cut two strips of each, 40 x 2 x ¹⁄₁₆in (1020 x 50 x 1.5mm) (Fig 7. 8).

The layers will be stacked in the order: red, white, red, white, walnut. Only one layer will be added to the stack at a time. Place the two pieces together and hold with multiple clamps. Allow the glue to set for at least 30 minutes before adding the next layer. Leave the final stack to set overnight (Fig 7.9).

Fig 7.5

Fig 7.6

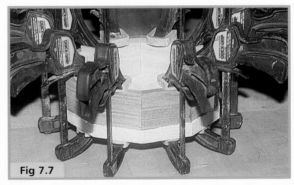
Fig 7.7

Fig 7.8

Fig 7.9

Attaching the faceplate

This project will be made using a faceplate attached to a waste block. Most hardwoods will make an acceptable waste block, but maple is ideal. **Do not use plywood: it might come apart on the lathe.** Apply glue to the bottom of the bowl and to the waste block, then press into position. Apply pressure and allow the glue to set overnight.

If the scallops are to develop evenly on the ring, it is absolutely critical that the ring be centred on the faceplate. Use a try square to mark centring lines from each side of the ring.

Centre the faceplate on the waste block in the same way, using pencil marks so you can drill pilot holes for your screws (Fig 7.10). Attach the faceplate with screws.

Turning the top of the scallop ring flat

Mount the bowl on the lathe and place your toolrest close to the top of the scallop ring. Set your lathe to a fairly slow speed of 250–500rpm. Use a bowl gouge to make the top of the ring perfectly flat. Check with a straightedge that the top is flat all the way across.

Making the top ring

Sand the five-layer stick that you made; it must be flat on all sides. Set your mitre gauge or cutting sled to 18° so that you can make a ten-sided ring. Cut ten segments from the five-layer stick, by the same method as before. Test-fit them together to make sure that the fit is perfect.

Apply a small amount of yellow glue to each section and press them together. Put an automotive hose clamp around the ring and apply some pressure, without using excessive force. Allow the glue to cure overnight, then remove the hose clamp and sand the top and bottom of the five-layer ring flat (Fig 7.11).

Gluing the top ring onto the bowl

Remove the partial bowl (this consists of the bottom and the scallop ring) from the lathe. Apply glue to the top of the scallop ring and the red layer of the five-layer ring. Position the top ring onto the scalloped ring so that the joints of the top ring fall between those of the scalloped ring (Fig 7.12). Use at least ten clamps to apply even pressure, and allow to cure overnight.

Fig 7.10 *Pencil marks squared across the waste block show where to make the centre hole for the faceplate*

Fig 7.11 *Sanding the top ring flat*

Fig 7.12 *Gluing on the top ring; note how the joints are staggered*

Fig 7.13 *Shaping the side with the bowl gouge at slow speed*

Fig 7.14 *Shaping the rim with the bowl gouge*

Turning the outside

Mount the bowl on the lathe. Set the toolrest alongside the bowl and rotate the bowl by hand to make sure that it clears the toolrest. Set your lathe to a low speed. Use your bowl gouge to turn the bowl round.

Round in the bottom somewhat and start developing a gentle curve, using the side of your bowl gouge to make a shear cut. Once you have the general shape of the bottom, you can start shaping the top of the bowl.

Use your bowl gouge to make a gentle inward curve to the side of the bowl (Fig 7.13). Cut very slowly and carefully. Leave the top of the bowl wide.

As you cut more away from the middle of the bowl you will start cutting through the walnut layer. Slowly cut the walnut away to expose the red oak layer in the middle third of the bowl. You will see a scalloped pattern start to appear where the walnut ends and the red oak begins; this is the magic part! Cut slowly and carefully to develop the full scalloped pattern. If you cut too deep you will cut through the walnut at the top, and the scalloped pattern will be broken. Notice how the rim is left wider (Fig 7.14).

Fig 7.10

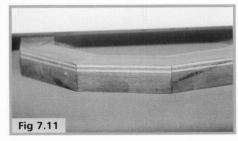
Fig 7.11

Fig 7.12

Fig 7.13

Fig 7.14

ALWAYS put on your face shield before switching on the lathe.

Turning the inside

Move your toolrest inside the bowl and use a sharp bowl gouge to cut the rim (Fig 7.15). First make light cuts to make the rim flat, then turn the bowl gouge in toward the bottom of the bowl and start cutting the inside round. Work your way down gradually, with the bevel of the gouge rubbing.

Use a round-nose scraper to cut the final junction between the side of the bowl and the bottom.

Sanding

Sand the inside and outside of the bowl at this stage. Be sure to control the dust. Hopefully you can start with about 120-grit sandpaper. If you spend more than ten minutes with the roughest paper, then you need to make smoother cuts or go to rougher sandpaper. Sand to at least 400 grit.

Applying finish

You should apply an initial finish while the turning is still on the lathe (Fig 7.16). I use Deft cellulose finish, diluted 50/50 with lacquer and applied with a paper towel (kitchen paper).

NEVER use cloth to apply finish while the turning is on the lathe: it may catch in the work and cause serious injury. Kitchen paper is safe because it tears easily.

With the lathe running slowly, run the wet paper towel over the entire surface for about 30 seconds. The paper blots up excess liquid. Allow to dry for about a minute, then apply another coat the same way. You are always applying a very thin coat. Apply as many coats as you want.

Parting off the bottom

Use your bowl gouge to finish cutting the bottom of the bowl. Carefully part away the waste block without cutting into the bottom of the bowl (Fig 7.17). Continue cutting this way until you have about a 2in (50mm) stub supporting the bowl. Then part the bottom off with a thin parting tool; you might want to have a friend support the bowl while you make the final cut. If you do not want to reverse-turn the bowl, you are almost done: just sand the bottom and apply finish.

Fig 7.15 *Shaping the inside of the rim with the bowl gouge*

Fig 7.16 *Applying finish on the lathe*

Fig 7.17 *Parting off*

Fig 7.18 *Using a bowl gouge to shape the bottom, with the bowl reverse-chucked*

Fig 7.19 *Sanding the bottom; note the decorative V-grooves*

Reverse-turning the bottom

To many people a turned base looks more finished than a sanded one. Reverse-turn the bowl using a set of 'jumbo' jaws (Fig 7.18). Apply light pressure with the jaws to the outside of the rim, and support the bottom of the turning with a live centre. Do not allow the point of the live centre to make a dent in the bottom of the bowl.

Make very fine and gentle cuts. If you like, you can cut a couple of small V-grooves in the bottom of the bowl using the sharp corner of a skew. Remove the tailstock and very lightly take off the last little bit in the centre. Sand the bottom of the bowl (Fig 7.19).

Fig 7.15

Fig 7.16

Fig 7.17

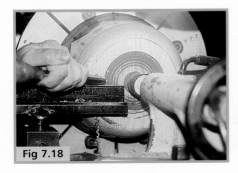

Fig 7.18

Fig 7.19

8

THREE-TRIANGLE BOWL

This beautiful little bowl will teach you a lot about segmented turning technique. The feature ring has red, white, and walnut-coloured triangles as part of the pattern. Most of the white triangle is cut away so that the walnut triangle is able to fit inside it. This actually leaves red and walnut triangles with a white line running between them.

To begin you will need three different-coloured woods: red, white, and dark (walnut). As in all of the segmented projects, you will be using kiln-dried wood. You will also be using a tablesaw to make very accurate cuts. **It is important that you pay attention and be very careful. At all times keep your fingers away from the saw blade!**

BILL OF GOODS

NB: All length measurements include an allowance for wastage.

		in	mm
Feature ring	walnut	40 x 1½ x 1	1020 x 38 x 25
Feature ring	maple	40 x 1½ x 1	1020 x 38 x 25
Feature ring	padauk	40 x 1½ x 1	1020 x 38 x 25
Thin veneer	padauk	6 x 3 x 1	150 x 75 x 25
Thin veneer	maple	6 x 3 x 1	150 x 75 x 25
Plain rings	maple	105 x 1 x 1	2670 x 25 x 25
Top walnut ring	walnut	3 x 3 x 1	75 x 75 x 25

Planning the design

Start by making a full-sized drawing (Fig 8.1). This will be your guide throughout the entire project. It will help you calculate how much wood you need and what size rings to make. The ten plain rings will be made from maple and have 12 segments. The mitre angle will therefore be 15°; the tangent of 15° is 0.26794. From your drawing you can then compile the following table:

Ring	Diameter		Segment length	
	in	mm	in	mm
1	2.50	63.5	0.670	17.018
2	2.75	69.85	0.737	26.137
3	3.36	85.344	0.900	22.86
4	3.75	95.25	1.004	25.502
5	4.0	101.6	1.072	27.229
6	4.25	107.95	1.139	28.931
7	4.5	114.3	1.206	30.632
8	4.25	107.95	1.139	28.931
9	4.0	101.6	1.072	27.229
10	3.25	82.55	0.871	22.123

Getting started

Set your mitre gauge or cutting sled to 15° and make a series of test cuts. Once you are satisfied that your gauge is set perfectly, cut the segments for all ten maple rings. Glue these rings and set them aside so that the glue can cure for at least 24 hours.

Veneer squares

We will make our own veneer for this project. Start by cutting two 3 x 3 x 1in (75 x 75 x 25mm) squares of padauk and maple. Glue the padauk squares to the maple squares.

Fig 8.1 The working drawing; make yours full size

Fig 8.2 First stage in cutting the veneer squares: maple reduced to ¹⁄₁₆in (1.5mm) thick

Fig 8.3 Second stage: padauk cut to the same thickness

Set your tablesaw fence to cut off most of the maple, leaving just ¹⁄₁₆in (1.5mm) thickness of maple on the block (Fig 8.2). Do not try to cut through the whole block in one pass. Instead, make a shallow cut on all four sides, then raise the blade about ¼in (6mm) and do the same again. Be sure to use a push stick and a featherboard while making these cuts. Sand the white side of the two blocks flat at this stage.

Reset the fence of your tablesaw to cut away most of the padauk, leaving the same thickness as you did for the maple (Fig 8.3). Sand the padauk side flat. This now leaves you with two thin squares of maple and padauk.

Initial glue-up

Attach a waste block to your faceplate. Apply glue to the white side of the veneer square and glue it to the waste block, applying pressure from the tailstock. The live centre, cushioned by a piece of scrap wood, makes a very nice glue press. Allow the glue to set for about 15 minutes and then glue on the second veneer square. Allow this glue to set overnight before turning it to a cylinder.

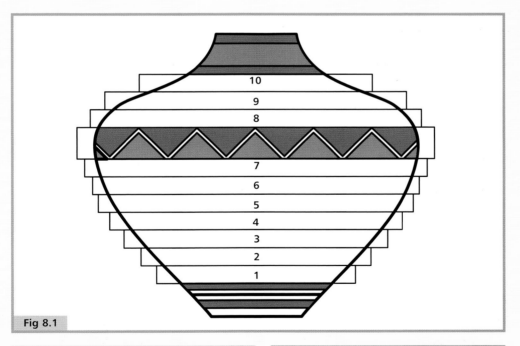

Fig 8.1

Fig 8.2

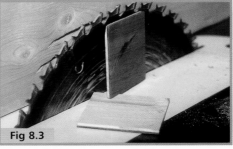

Fig 8.3

Glue ring 1 onto the veneer base and allow to cure for at least 30 minutes before adding ring 2. Be sure to make the joints of ring 2 fall in the middle of the joints of ring 1; this staggering of joints is attractive and makes the bowl stronger. A large, conical live centre can help you centre the rings while applying pressure (Fig 8.4). After 30 minutes' curing, add the next ring in the same manner. Continue in this way until the first seven rings have been assembled. Allow this glue to set overnight.

Initial turning

Turn the first seven rings glued up on the lathe. This is a small turning, so you can safely use between 500 and 800rpm. Once the outside is finished, readjust the toolrest to cut the inside of the bowl. Use your bowl gouge to make the inside cuts (Fig 8.5). Stop often to check your work. **Do not make the wall too thin, or it will break later when you are turning the upper rings.** Use a round-nose scraper to make a smooth junction between the bottom of the bowl and the side wall.

Making up the feature ring

The feature ring of this project is made from a very precise three-layer triangle stick. Start by cutting a piece of padauk 1½in (38mm) wide. Next, set the blade of your tablesaw to exactly 45° (Fig 8.6). Set the height of the blade to exactly ¼in (6mm) less than the thickness of the padauk (Fig 8.7). Set the fence of your tablesaw so that the 45° cut extends halfway into the width of the padauk.

Make your first 45° angle cut into the padauk. Be sure to use a push stick and a featherboard for safety. Next, turn the wood end for end and make another 45° cut (Fig 8.8). If you have been accurate with your cuts there should be a perfect V cut into the padauk. Now we need to make a 45° triangle out of maple or another white hardwood. The width of the triangle must match the wide part of the V-cut you have just made. Install a sacrificial fence onto your tablesaw fence. Make your first 45° cut, then flip the stick end for end and make the second. Fig 8.9 shows the cut into the sacrificial fence.

Glue the maple triangle into the V-notch of the padauk stick. Apply pressure to the centre of the maple using a waste block, which must run the entire length of the glue-up stick (Fig 8.10). Allow to set overnight.

Sand the maple and padauk stick flat on all sides. Now cut a second V, this time into the maple. This second V must be a little smaller than the first one.

Fig 8.4 Glue the rings one at a time, using the tailstock as a glue press

Fig 8.5 Cut the inside and outside of the bottom of the bowl while it is easy to reach

Fig 8.6 The stick for the feature ring needs a series of 45° cuts

Fig 8.7 The height of the tablesaw blade must be ¼in (6mm) less than the thickness of the wood

Fig 8.8 Making the second 45° cut

Fig 8.9 The finished maple triangle on the tablesaw; note the gash in the sacrificial fence

Fig 8.10 Gluing the maple triangle into the padauk

Fig 8.11 Gluing the walnut triangle into the maple and padauk

Follow the same steps as for the first V, only making the blade height ¹⁄₁₆in (1.5mm) shorter than before.

Now cut a walnut triangle to fit into the V of the maple. Glue the walnut triangle into the padauk and maple stick the same way as the first triangle, and allow to set overnight (Fig 8.11).

Fig 8.4

Fig 8.5

Fig 8.6

Fig 8.7

Fig 8.8

Fig 8.9

Fig 8.10

Fig 8.11

Initial cutting of the triangle stick

Sand the triangle stick flat and parallel on all four sides. Set your tablesaw up to cut square segments, adjusting the fence so that the offcuts are 1in (25mm) long (Fig 8.12). Cut at least 12 segments.

Mitre cuts for the triangle segments

Use a tri-square to mark the width of the maple V on the top of the block (Fig 8.13). You will be sanding the mitre angle to this line, then flipping the segment and sanding an identical angle on the other side.

Set your mitre gauge to 15° for a 12-segment ring, and install the gauge in the slot on your disc sander. Adjust the fence of the mitre gauge so that it fits close to the sanding disc without touching it. Hold the segment securely and sand the mitre angle. You are using the sander as a cutting tool, so the paper must be quite coarse: at least 60 grit. Carefully sand up to the line (Fig 8.14). This line marks the white edge of maple. If you just barely sand up to the white line, the lines will connect when you glue the segments together.

Gluing the triangle ring

Test-fit the segments together to make sure that you have a good fit (Fig 8.15). When satisfied, glue the feature ring. Bring the segments together with a hose clamp and allow the glue to cure overnight.

Completing the vase

Place the bottom of the bowl back onto the lathe. Glue the feature ring, using the same method as before (Fig 8.16). Hold in place with the tailstock. When dry, cut or sand the ring flat; a Morse-taper sanding disc in the tailstock is a very convenient way to do this (Fig 8.17). I manufacture my own discs, which are available from my website.

Add the other rings in the same way, sanding each one flat and shaping the inside before adding the next. Let each one set before proceeding (Fig 8.18).

Make a set of thin veneers for the top, in the same way as you did for the bottom. Apply glue to the veneers and centre them on the top of the bowl; allow this glue to cure for at least 30 minutes before adding the next ring.

When all rings are on, allow to cure overnight before final turning. Sand and apply finish while the bowl is still on the lathe.

Fig 8.12 Cutting the triangle stick into individual lengths

Fig 8.13 Marking the position of the white edge on the top of the block

Fig 8.14 Sanding the mitre angle

Fig 8.15 Test-fitting the segments of the feature ring

Fig 8.16 Gluing the feature ring with pressure from the tailstock

Fig 8.17 Sanding the feature ring flat before adding the next ring

Fig 8.18 Adding the upper rings one at a time

Fig 8.19 Buffing the finish

Parting off

Use a thin parting tool to part off the bowl. Sand the bottom and apply finish. A wax buffing system can put a very nice finish on your work. It is easy to use and produces a semigloss finish with an attractive lustre (Fig 8.19).

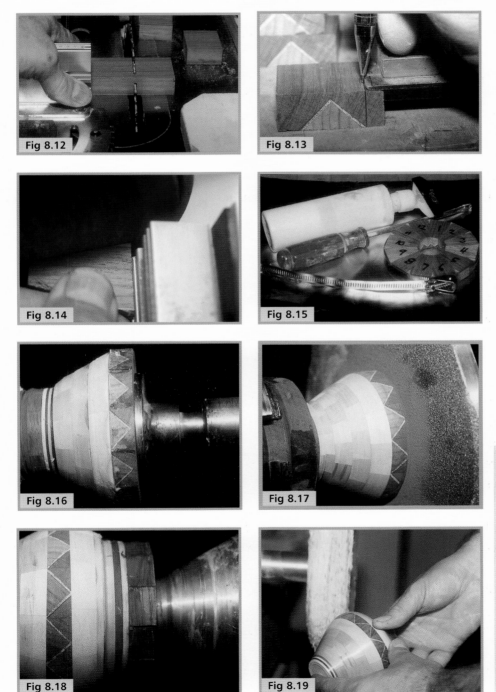

Fig 8.12

Fig 8.13

Fig 8.14

Fig 8.15

Fig 8.16

Fig 8.17

Fig 8.18

Fig 8.19

BE SURE to use a safety spacer, like the white one in Fig 8.12, to maintain a large space between the offcut and the fence. Otherwise the offcut will become wedged between the blade and the fence. This will cause a dangerous kickback.

9
30-DEGREE
BOWL

The name of this beautiful bowl comes from the fact that the zigzag pattern is created by making 30° cuts to a five-layer stick on the tablesaw.

Start by making a rough drawing of the bowl. Draw in the thickness of the rings that you want, and the pattern that you would like to make for your accent ring (Fig 9.1, page 67).

On the next page is a bill of goods that will get you started on this project. You can substitute different-coloured woods if you prefer.

BILL OF GOODS

NB: All length measurements include an allowance for wastage.

		in	mm
Base of bowl	padauk	5 x 5 x 1	127 x 127 x 25
Veneer ring at top	padauk	3 x 3 x 1	75 x 75 x 25
Feature ring and top ring	padauk	80 x 1½ x 1	2030 x 38 x 25
Feature ring	white oak/maple	40 x 1 x 1	1020 x 25 x 25
Plain rings	maple/cherry	180 x 1½ x 1	4570 x 38 x 25
Rings above feature ring	maple/cherry	40 x 3 x 1	1020 x 75 x 25

Making up the feature ring

The feature ring is made from five strips of wood that are cut on the tablesaw. The two main outside strips are white oak, and are cut 1in (25mm) wide. Both are cut at the same time to make sure that they are the same width and thickness.

Reset your tablesaw blade to cut a very thin laminate, say ⅛in (3mm). Cut three thin strips: two of red padauk and one of white oak.

Glue the five sections together. Try to have no more than ½in (13mm) between clamps (Fig 9.2). Allow this stack to set up for at least 24 hours before undoing the clamps. Call this 'stick 1'. One of the purposes of clamping your stack to a flat surface is to make sure that stick 1 will remain flat when you remove the clamps. Run stick 1 through the thickness sander to remove any excess glue from both sides (Fig 9.3).

Stick 1 must now be cut and reglued to make stick 2. Set your mitre gauge to 30° (Fig 9.4). Set your stop block to cut a 1in (25mm)-wide section from stick 1. Continue cutting 1in segments until you have used up the safe part of the stick; I used 20 segments for my bowl.

Stick 2 is now made from the segments of stick 1. Use a flat piece of sandpaper or a flat sandpaper holder to knock off any 'whiskers' of wood that might be left from your saw cut (Fig 9.5). Glue all the segments together in pairs, to make arrow-shaped pieces with a central V in them (Fig 9.6). Take great care that the central lines match up accurately. Allow the two-piece segments to set for at least an hour. Then use your hand-held sandpaper to knock off any small amount of excess glue.

Fig 9.1 Make an initial drawing to show the general concept of the 30-degree bowl

Fig 9.2 Gluing up the five strips to make the feature ring

Fig 9.3 A thickness sander does a nice job of sanding the stick flat and smooth

Fig 9.4 Cutting the segments, with the mitre gauge set to 30°

Fig 9.5 Sanding the whiskers off the segments before gluing them together

Fig 9.6 Gluing the segments together two at a time

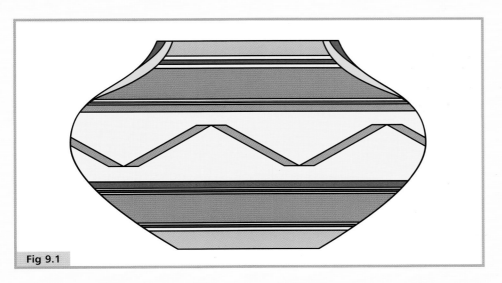

Fig 9.1

Fig 9.2

Fig 9.3

Fig 9.4

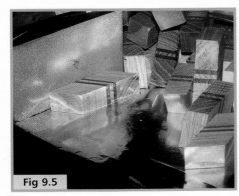

Fig 9.5

Fig 9.6

Now glue the two-piece segments into four-piece segments, and continue gluing sections together until you end up with a long zigzag-pattern stick. Sand this 'stick 2' with your thickness sander or by hand (Fig 9.7).

Use your tablesaw to cut the jagged edges off both sides of stick 2 (Fig 9.8).

Cutting the segments

Stick 2 is now cut up into V-blocks. Set your mitre gauge to exactly 90°. Carefully position stick 2 so that you cut exactly through every other joint. Each piece should have 90° joints and a V in it, as seen in Fig 9.9.

Decide how many segments you want for your ring. The more segments you use, the larger the ring will be. In this case ten segments made the size that I wanted for the feature ring, which gives a mitre angle of 18° (180° ÷ 10). Arrange the ten blocks in a test circle and check that your zigzag pattern is correct. Draw a red circle around the tops of the pieces to remind you which way up they go. Now draw in the angle that each block should have cut on it; this is just a crude estimation to show you how to position your block on the sander (Fig 9.9).

The disc sander is used as a cutting tool. You will need a coarse sandpaper to make this cut, at least 60 grit. Position the block on the sander and hold it flat against the fence of the mitre gauge (Fig 9.10). With the back of the block pressed flat against the back of the mitre fence, advance the block into the sander disc so that it starts cutting the 18° angle onto the block. Continue this sanding cut until you just barely reach the end of the block; do not cut away more material than necessary. Now flip the block over and make a second cut on the other side.

Continue cutting the correct angles with the belt sander until all ten sections have been cut. Arrange the segments into a ring and pull them together with your hose clamps (Fig 9.11).

Gluing the feature ring

Put a small amount of yellow glue on each surface. Place two hose clamps around the ring and lightly tighten. When the pieces have come together, gently hammer all the segments flat with a rubber hammer to make sure that all segments lie flat on the work table. Tighten the hose clamps.

Fig 9.7 *Sanding stick 2 flat on both sides*

Fig 9.8 *Cut the V-notches off both sides of stick 2*

Fig 9.9 *The ten V-blocks arranged in a test circle; red marks on top remind you which way to cut*

Fig 9.10 *Sanding the blocks to the mitre angle of 18°*

Fig 9.11 *Gluing the ring together; make sure all segments are flat on the workbench*

Fig 9.12 *Redraw your bowl now that you have the feature ring completed*

Redrawing the project

The initial drawing showed the general idea of what you wanted to create. Now that you have made the central ring it might be necessary to modify your drawing slightly to suit it (Fig 9.12).

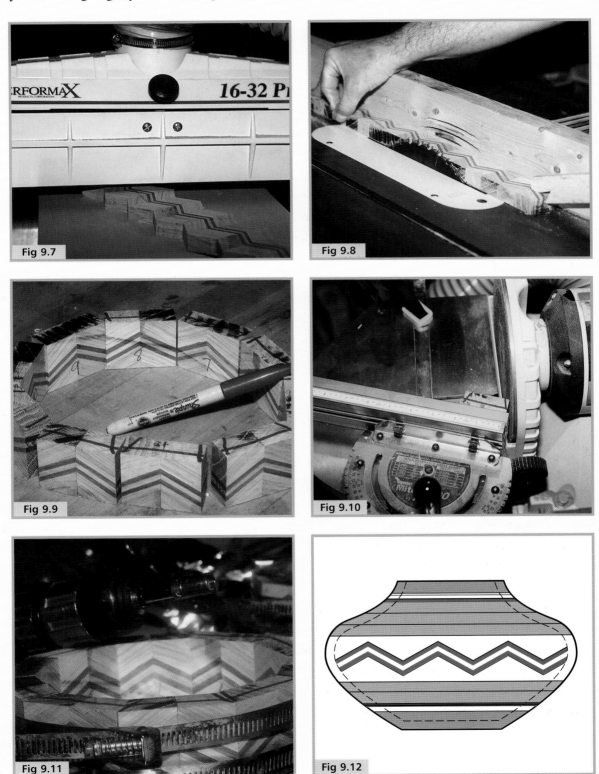

Fig 9.7

Fig 9.8

Fig 9.9

Fig 9.10

Fig 9.11

Fig 9.12

Now you can make a working drawing of the layers (Fig 9.13) and use this to create a bill of goods.

Assembling the bottom layers

Glue the bottom layer to the waste block you have already prepared. Then add four veneer layers. Apply pressure with the tailstock (Fig 9.14).

Making the rings

Cut all the segments for all of your rings at one time. This will save a lot of time and confusion. Use your drawing to make sure that you make all the rings the correct diameter. Keep your segments for each ring grouped together: I like to use plastic zip-lock bags or plastic cups for this.

Glue the rings together using a hose clamp as before. Allow all rings to set for 24 hours before working with them.

There are several ways to thickness-sand your rings; the easiest and fastest way is to use a thickness sander. Sand all rings at the same time. When all are flat on one side, flip the rings over and sand on the other side.

Assembling the first rings

Glue on the bottom rings one at a time. Allow the glue to cure for an adequate time, then sand flat before gluing the next ring. Glue the feature ring on in the same manner as the others, again making sure that the previous ring is sanded flat. Make sure that this ring is perfectly centred. Apply pressure with the tailstock and allow the glue to set overnight (Fig 9.15).

Initial turning

The bowl is now at its largest diameter. Turning the outside and the inside at this stage will make the final turning much simpler; it is more difficult to turn the inside once you have tapered the bowl down to a small opening. Do not attempt to turn the bottom narrow or thin at this time: that could cause the glue joints between rings to come apart before the project is finished.

Support the tailstock end of the bowl with a piece of scrap wood and a live centre. Always use tailstock support whenever possible.

Fig 9.13 *Sectional diagram showing width and diameter of each ring*

Fig 9.14 *Gluing the bottom layers, with pressure from the tailstock*

Fig 9.15 *The feature ring glued on and clamped by the tailstock*

Fig 9.16 *Adding further rings*

More ring stacking

Flatten the last glued ring using a Morse-taper sanding disc as in the previous project, or a very fine cut from a bowl gouge. Check with a straightedge to make sure the ring is flat. Glue the next ring, making sure it is centred. Apply even pressure to the ring segment using a tailstock pressure plate (Fig 9.16). The pressure plate I use consists of a no. 2 Morse taper with a thick steel plate attached to it.

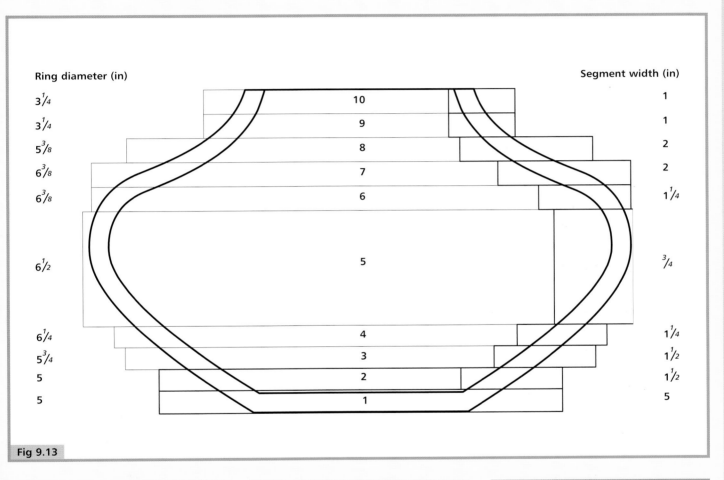

Ring diameter (in)		Segment width (in)
$3\frac{1}{4}$	10	1
$3\frac{1}{4}$	9	1
$5\frac{3}{8}$	8	2
$6\frac{3}{8}$	7	2
$6\frac{3}{8}$	6	$1\frac{1}{4}$
$6\frac{1}{2}$	5	$\frac{3}{4}$
$6\frac{1}{4}$	4	$1\frac{1}{4}$
$5\frac{3}{4}$	3	$1\frac{1}{2}$
5	2	$1\frac{1}{2}$
5	1	5

Fig 9.13

Fig 9.14

Fig 9.15

Fig 9.16

Hollowing the inside

This is a good point to start hollowing the inside. The bowl still has a large opening at the mouth and it is easy to get to the inside. A sharp scraper will cut nice shavings (Fig 9.17). Bring your toolrest as close as you can to the area that you are cutting.

Cut the inside with a bowl gouge or a boring bar. The boring bar makes easy work of the inside hollowing. Start from the tailstock end of the bowl and slowly work your way toward the bottom. Strive for a smooth continuous form on the inside of the bowl. Check often to make sure that you are not cutting the bowl too thin (Fig 9.18). Cut carefully so as to leave the inside very smooth.

Adding the final rings

Add the remaining small rings. As usual, first sand the rings flat and then apply yellow glue to both surfaces. Apply pressure with your tailstock. Be sure to check that the ring is centred and the joins are staggered.

Final cutting

Do the final external shaping of the vessel. Be sure to support the turning with a live centre. Use a sharp bowl gouge to make your external cuts. Very carefully shape the rim of the bowl.

Use your bowl gouge to shape the inside of the rim. At this point you can no longer support the bowl with the live centre, so I use a steady rest instead. The steady supports the bowl on three sides with roller-blade wheels (you can see part of one wheel in Fig 9.20).

Use a small round-nose scraper to cut the inside of the top of the vessel (Fig 9.19). Have your toolrest as close as you can to the work area. A sharp scraper supported by a close toolrest can make a very nice cut and produce beautiful shavings.

Finishing

Do your final sanding inside and out (Fig 9.20). An electric drill with hook-and-loop sanding disc on a foam pad works very well. Apply the finish of your choice. My favourite is Deft cellulose diluted 50/50 with lacquer thinner.

Fig 9.17 *Turning the inside: a sharp scraper can make beautiful, clean cuts*

Fig 9.18 *Using the boring bar; stop often to check the wall thickness*

Fig 9.19 *A round-nose scraper is a terrific tool for cutting the inside of the bowl*

Fig 9.20 *Sanding the completed bowl*

Parting off

Part off using a thin parting tool. Leave a 1in (25mm) tenon remaining, then use a handsaw to cut this last inch.

Finishing the bottom

Use your electric drill with hook-and-loop sandpaper to sand the bottom slightly concave and smooth. This is a very quick and easy procedure. Sign and date the bottom of the bowl. Apply finish to the bottom of the bowl and you have completed a very beautiful piece of artwork.

Fig 9.17

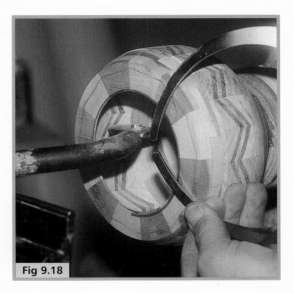

Fig 9.18

Fig 9.19

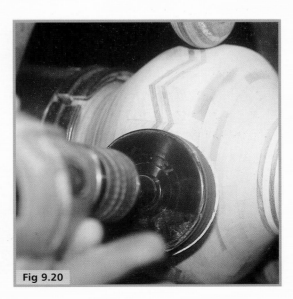

Fig 9.20

10
SUNDANCE

This project combines classic Native American pottery style with two special rings to create a unique and beautiful piece of art. I call this bowl 'Sundance' because the interplay between dark and light wood reminded me of the sun dancing across the lake close to where I live. Although the rings are fairly simple to make, the result is quite striking. This is one of my favourite segmented turning projects.

This is slightly more advanced than the previous projects. The bottom of this vase will be a ring that is solid. In your planning you will need to use stock for this ring that is wide enough not to leave a hole in the centre.

Making the drawing

The first step, as in all segmented turning, is to make a drawing (Fig 10.1). Take your time and aim to produce a beautiful vase that is well proportioned. Draw in the height of the feature in the middle, then draw in the rest of the rings.

Make a table like Table 1, listing the rings, the wood type, the width of each segment, and the diameter of each ring. On my bowl ring 12 is a little thinner than ring 15.

TABLE 1

Table 1 Ring no.	Wood	Stock width		No. of segments	Diameter of ring		Length of segment	
		in	mm		in	mm	in	mm
1	maple	1.5	38.1	12	3.2	81.3	0.857	21.768
2	maple	1	25.4	12	3.2	81.3	0.857	21.768
3	walnut	1	25.4	12	3.9	99.1	1.045	26.543
4	walnut	1	25.4	12	4.5	114.3	1.206	30.632
5	walnut	1	25.4	12	5.3	134.6	1.420	36.068
6	walnut	1	25.4	12	6	152.4	1.607	40.818
7	walnut	1	25.4	12	6.6	167.6	1.768	44.907
8	walnut	1	25.4	12	6.9	175.3	1.849	46.965
9	walnut	1	25.4	12	7.3	185.4	1.956	49.682
10	walnut	1	25.4	12	7.7	195.6	2.063	52.400
11	walnut	1	25.4	12	7.7	195.6	2.063	52.400
12	maple	1	25.4	12	7.8	198.1	1.235	31.369
13	walnut/ maple	1	25.4	20	7.8	198.1	1.235 average	31.369 average
14	walnut/ maple	1.5	38.1	20	7.8	198.1	1.235 average	31.369 average
15	maple	1.5	38.1	20	7.8	198.1	1.235	31.369
16	walnut	2.5	63.5	12	7.3	185.4	1.956	49.682
17	maple	1.75	44.5	12	4.8	121.9	0.750	19.05
18	walnut	1.75	44.5	12	4.8	121.9	0.750	19.05
19	maple	1.75	44.5	12	4.8	121.9	0.750	19.05

Use Table 1 to make a bill of goods. I usually cut my wood into 40in (1m) sections, so for every 40in of stock that I need I add 6in (150mm) of waste. For large amounts of stock I add 10% extra.

Fig 10.1 *The working drawing*

Fig 10.2 *Experiment with the amount of overlap between the black and white lines; these are the proportions I chose*

BILL OF GOODS

NB: All length measurements include an allowance for wastage.

	Stock width		Stock length	
	in	mm	in	mm
Maple	1	25.4	24	610
Maple	1.5	38.1	50	1300
Maple	1.75	44.5	40	1000
Walnut	1	25.4	253	6500
Walnut	2.5	63.5	28	700
Walnut	1.75	44.5	20	500

Overlap of segments in the feature ring

Look at the light- and dark-coloured segments in the two design rings. The dark segments are longer than the light, and this difference, combined with the staggered joints, creates the pattern of the bowl.

You will see from Table 1 that the average segment length for rings 13 and 14 is 1.235in (31.369mm). This means that two segments together will have a length of 2.470in (62.738mm). Draw two lines this length, then divide them into unequal lengths, experimenting until you have a pattern that you like; I used a measurement of 1.6in (40.64mm) dark, 0.87in (22.098mm) light (Fig 10.2).

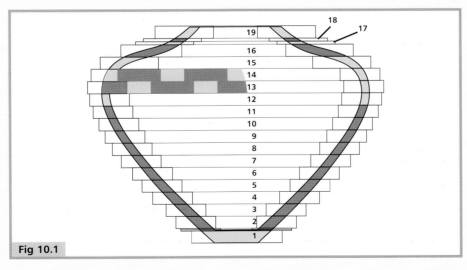

Fig 10.1

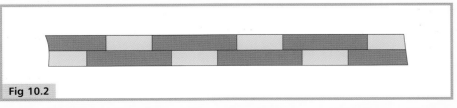

Fig 10.2

Cutting the segments

Most of the rings in this project will be composed of 12 segments. The cutting angle for 12 segments is 15° (180° ÷ 12).

The four layers of the feature ring (nos. 12–15) are each composed of 20 segments. The cutting angle for 20 segments is 9° (180° ÷ 20).

Making the accent rings

Rings 12 and 15 are all maple. There are 20 segments to each ring. Set the stop block to make 1.235in (31.369mm) segments and cut 40 segments for the two rings (Fig 10.3).

Rings 13 and 14 are each composed of 20 pieces: 10 short maple pieces and 10 long walnut pieces. Since you are making two rings, cut 20 short pieces of maple and 20 long pieces of walnut.

Dry-assemble the black and white rings, pulling them together lightly with a hose clamp. When satisfied, place a small amount of glue on each surface and press them together, using the hose clamp again (Fig 10.4). Allow these rings to set overnight before sanding (Fig 10.5).

Assembling the remaining rings

Cut and assemble the remaining rings. Be sure to set your angle to 15° to cut the 12-segment rings, and to use the correct colour of wood for each ring. Number each ring as you assemble it; I like to use a felt-tip pen to write the number on the inside of the ring, where it will not accidentally be sanded away.

All of the rings must be sanded flat and parallel on both sides. Thickness sanders are a tremendous advantage to the segmented turner: you can quickly and easily sand all of your rings parallel and flat on both sides.

Aligning the two feature rings

A home-made glue press can be helpful in assembling your rings (Figs 10.6 and 10.8). Dry-assemble first, to make sure that you understand how the rings are to be placed. The white of one ring is to be centred with the black of the other ring. Apply yellow glue to the surface of both rings, align carefully and press down on them with your full body weight. The rings will slip to some extent as you press down on them: realign and press down again. When most

Fig 10.3 Cutting the 40 maple segments for rings 12 and 15

Fig 10.4 Assembling the feature rings with a hose clamp

Fig 10.5 Thickness-sanding rings 12–15

Fig 10.6 Gluing the two feature rings together in a simple glue press

of the excess glue has been pressed out, the two rings will not slip in relation to each other.

Place the rings in the press and keep the pressure on for at least one hour.

Fig 10.3

Fig 10.4

Fig 10.5

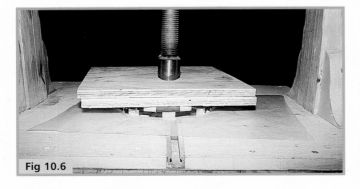

Fig 10.6

Assembling the base

Cut a 3in (75mm) circle of maple or other hardwood for the waste block to go on your faceplate. Apply glue to the waste block and to one side of ring 1. Centre the ring onto the waste block and apply pressure (Fig 10.7). You can work twice as fast by using the lathe as a second glue press.

Stacking rings

While ring 1 and the base are setting on your lathe, you can start assembling other rings in pairs on your work table. Start by dry-assembling rings 2 and 3. Place the joints of ring 2 halfway between those of ring 3. Apply glue to both rings and press together. Wipe off excess glue and re-centre ring 2 on top of ring 3. Apply hand pressure again and re-centre if necessary. Place the two rings into the glue press and allow to set for at least one hour (Fig 10.8).

While rings 2 and 3 are setting, you can go back to you lathe and glue on two layers of black veneer. Cut two squares of veneer and glue both at the same time. Apply glue to the four surfaces and glue to ring 1.

Now move back to your work table and stack the rest of your rings in pairs. Assemble each pair as before, applying pressure for one hour.

Once all your rings are stacked in pairs, you can start assembling the pairs into stacks of four (Fig 10.9). Spread glue on both rings and apply hand pressure. Re-centre the rings and then place in the glue press.

Glue a stack of four to six rings onto the base of the bowl, which is still on the lathe (Fig 10.10). Make sure that the stack is accurately centred, and apply even pressure with a pressure plate in your tailstock. This glue joint and that in the veneer layer must harden for 48 hours.

Turning the lower part

Do an initial turning of the inside and outside after the glue has cured for 48 hours. Place a block of wood on the tailstock to support the open end while you turn the outside (Fig 10.11). Leave the base wide at this time for extra strength during turning.

Place a steady rest around the bowl for support as you turn the inside (Fig 10.12). Mine is home-made from steel and roller-blade wheels; a plywood steady would work just as well.

Fig 10.7 Centring ring 1 on the waste block; hold it in place with either a live centre or a pressure plate

Fig 10.8 The glue press in action

Fig 10.9 Assembling the pairs of rings into stacks of four

Fig 10.10 Continuing assembly on the lathe

Fig 10.11 Initial turning of the outside with the bowl gouge

Fig 10.12 The steady rest in place for turning the inside

Fig 10.13 Keep the toolrest close and the bevel rubbing as you cut down to the centre of the bowl

Use careful cutting technique on the inside of the bowl. You can use either a bowl gouge or a scraper. Using a bevel-rubbing cut, you can cut all the way down to the centre of the bowl (Fig 10.13). It is important to have a toolrest that fits very close to your work area. A small round-nose scraper will allow you to develop a very delicate and smooth bottom to your bowl.

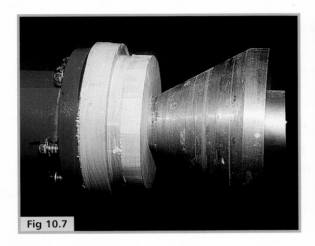
Fig 10.7

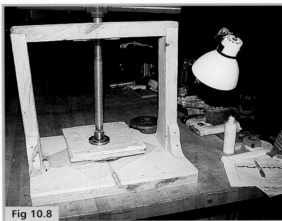
Fig 10.8

Fig 10.9

Fig 10.10

Fig 10.11

Fig 10.12

Fig 10.13

Sanding and finishing the lower part

Sand the inside of the bowl at this time. The bowl is wide open and will never be easier to sand. Feel the inside of the bowl: there should be no unevenness. If there are any cutting flaws, either recut the area or take the flaws out with 60- to 80-grit sandpaper. I usually sand the inside to about 400 grit. Apply the finish of your choice.

Adding the feature rings

Remove the bowl from the lathe and take it to your workbench. Centre the bowl onto the feature ring, apply glue and place in the press as before.

After the glue has set for 24 hours you can do some more turning. Continue to use your steady rest for support. Place a waste block on the end and support with a live centre while you cut the outside. Sand the rim flat before adding another ring.

Adding the upper rings

After turning, the bowl is ready to go back to the workbench. Add another section of rings, being careful to align the joints properly (Fig 10.14). Notice how I used ink lines to make sure the joints aligned the way I wanted them to. Allow this glue to set overnight.

Add two thin accent rings near the top of the vase. These start out as full thickness rings that you part down.

Final shaping

Use your bowl gouge to do the final shaping of the outside. Cut very carefully and develop gentle, smooth curves. Use a bowl gouge or scraper to shape the inside of the rim (Fig 10.15).

Sand the inside and outside of the top of the vase. Be very careful not to allow your hand or sandpaper to get into the wheels of your steady rest. Apply finish as desired.

Remove the steady rest and support the end of the vase with a large live centre (Fig 10.16). Gently shape the base of the bowl at this time. A bowl gouge with a long grind can give a very nice finish cut; work gently, using the side of the tool. Stop and measure the wall thickness often: there is no good time to cut through a vase!

Fig 10.14 *Ink marks aid alignment of the rings*

Fig 10.15 *Shaping the inside of the rim, in this case using a bowl gouge*

Fig 10.16 *A live centre supports the mouth of the vase while the foot is being shaped*

Fig 10.17 *Refining the foot of the vase; a skew chisel is suitable if you are confident with it*

Fig 10.18 *Sanding the bottom of the vase. There should be no flaws anywhere*

Fig 10.19 *Parting most of the way through with a thin parting tool*

Refine the bottom of the vase with whatever tool you are comfortable with (Fig 10.17). I use a skew chisel, but do not use this tool if you are not used to it: it has a tendency to give a nasty spiral kickback if you are not careful.

Make a small parting cut into the base with your thin parting tool, then sand the base to completion (Fig 10.18). Apply finish to this area.

Use your thin parting tool to cut most of the way through the base (Fig 10.19). Stop the lathe when there is about ⅛in (3mm) remaining, then use a thin saw to cut the rest of the way. (If you have somebody to support the vase, you can cut all the way through with the thin parting tool.)

Sand the bottom. Apply finish to the bottom of your vase, and you are done.

Fig 10.14

Fig 10.15

Fig 10.16

Fig 10.17

Fig 10.18

Fig 10.19

11
ORNAMENTAL BIRD HOUSE

Segmented ornamental bird houses make great gifts, and are a lot of fun to make. You will have the pleasure of learning a nice segmented turning technique, and make some beautiful presents at the same time.

The bird house is made from six pieces: body, roof, roof finial, floor, floor finial, and perch. All the dimensions are based on the width of the main body (W in Fig 11.1). A 2½in (65mm) square makes a good body for the bird house, but you could go up to 6in (150mm) square. The length of the body is 1⅓ to 1½ times the width. The height of the roof is ⅔ or ¾ the width. The width of the roof is 1½ times that of the body. The floor is slightly narrower than the roof. The top and bottom finials are about ⅓ the width of the body. The diameter of the door opening in the body is about ¼ to ⅓ of the width.

You can make bird houses from the scrap wood that is lying around your shop. I like the body, perch and finials to be made from the same wood. The roof, floor and laminates are made from a wood that contrasts with the body. The laminates in the body are made from the same wood as the roof and floor; this makes a very nice contrast. The display stand can be made from either wood. Use a brass welding rod to make the support.

Constructing the body

The bird house is made from five rings (Fig 11.2). The main body is a ring made using coopered or stave construction. The staves will be cut using your tablesaw with the blade tilted at an angle. The amount of tilt will depend on the number of staves; for this project I decide to use ten, which means that the blade needs to tilt 18° (180° ÷ 10). Tilt the tablesaw blade to the correct angle and lock it in place. An after-market tilt gauge is available which is inexpensive and fairly accurate.

Make a test ring using scrap wood. Use a mitre gauge to hold the test stick while you make the cuts. Clamp a spacer board to your tablesaw fence (Fig 11.3). This creates enough space so that the offcut does not get wedged between the blade and the fence.

Set the fence so as to leave a small space between the spacer board and the blade; this space is the width that the segment will be. To increase the width of the segment, simply move the fence further away from the blade. To decrease the width of the segment, move the fence and spacer toward the blade. You will always be left with a space no less than the width of the spacer.

Cut the first angle on one side of the test strip. Now flip the test strip over and push it up against the spacer board. Advance the mitre gauge and test strip to make the second cut. These two cuts produce the first segment or stave. Return the mitre gauge to the start position and flip the test strip so that you can make the next cut. Continue this cut-and-flip technique until you have made the necessary number of segments.

The staves for the body of my bird house are cut from a piece of maple 12 x 3 x ¾in (305 x 75 x 19mm). You may vary this to suit the scrap wood available. The ten staves are cut and test-fitted. Cut a thin veneer of walnut to go between each pair of staves.

Apply a thin layer of yellow glue to each side of one stave, and to each side of a piece of walnut veneer. Press the two together. Then add another stave and follow with another veneer. Continue doing this until all 20 pieces have been arranged into a cylinder. Adjust the elements of the cylinder so that all the pieces run straight and parallel, then apply two hose clamps to the glue-up (Fig 11.4). Allow this glue to set for at least 24 hours.

Fig 11.1 The dimensions of the bird house are multiples of its width (W)

Fig 11.2 The bird house requires just five rings

Fig 11.3 The spacer board clamped to the saw fence

Fig 11.4 The body segments glued and clamped

Fig 11.5 The body supported in the lathe by a four-jaw chuck and a live centre

Turning the body

The ends of the body should already be fairly flat. Sand the best (flattest) side perfectly flat using a belt sander. Mount the body on a four-jaw chuck and support the tailstock end with a live centre (Fig 11.5). Use a bowl gouge or a skew chisel to cut a straight cylinder 2in (50mm) in diameter. Sand and apply finish to the outside of the body. Rough-cut the inside of the body at this time. A small round-nose scraper does a nice job. Sand and apply finish to the inside.

Place electrical tape around the finished end of the body; this will protect the wood from being marred by the steel jaws. Place the taped end into the jaws and lightly tighten, then finish the inside and outside of this end in the same manner as you did the opposite end. Sand and apply finish.

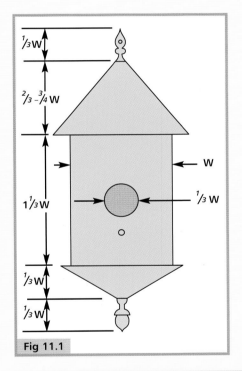
Fig 11.1

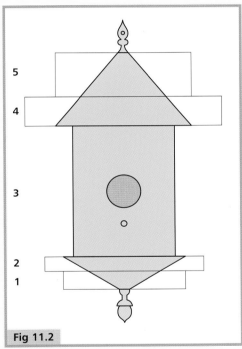
Fig 11.2

Fig 11.4

Fig 11.3

Fig 11.5

Drilling the door and perch hole

This is best done using a drill press. Note that both holes must be centred on one of the black lines. The body is held by a 2 x 4in (50 x 100mm) piece of softwood that has a V-cut down the middle. Use a ⅜–½in (10–13mm) Forstner bit to drill the hole for the door, a little above the middle of the body (Fig 11.6). Then drill the ⅛in (3mm) perch hole approximately ⅜in (10mm) below the door hole.

Now you can reduce the wall to its final thickness. The straight-edge scraper, sharpened on the side, works very well for this (Fig 11.7). Try for an even thickness of about ⅛in (3mm). Sand and apply finish to the body.

Roof and floor rings

The cylinder size determines the sizes of the four rings that are needed to make the roof and floor; remember that the roof is a little wider than the floor.

Use a mitre gauge or cutting board to cut the segments for the four rings (Fig 11.8). The stop block on the right of the cutting sled is adjusted to give the correct segment width.

Apply a small amount of glue to each side of each segment and assemble in a ring. Use a hose clamp to pull the segments together. Wipe off excess glue and allow the rings to set overnight.

Making the floor

The floor and roof are each made from two rings of different sizes, glued together. Mount the smaller ring of the floor in a four-jaw chuck.

Turn the exposed part of the floor round. You must use a light touch, whether you are using the four-jaw chuck or the glue-block technique. Turn the end of the piece round and flat using the tool of your choice (Fig 11.9).

Use callipers to measure the outside diameter of the bird house body at floor level. (This could be slightly different from the measurement at roof level.) Transfer this measurement to the floor (Fig 11.10). Cut a very shallow rebate in the floor, slightly smaller than the diameter of the body, then slightly increase the diameter until the body fits into the floor rebate. This should be an accurate fit, without being tight (Fig 11.11). An excessively snug fit might

Fig 11.6 Making the door with a Forstner bit

Fig 11.7 The inside is finished using a straight scraper with an edge on the side

Fig 11.8 Cutting the segments for the four rings that make up the roof and floor

Fig 11.9 A sharp scraper works very well for turning the floor round and flat

Fig 11.10 Marking the outside diameter of the bird house body on the floor

Fig 11.11 Test-fitting the body into the floor

cause a breakage later when the moisture level changes. Sand the top surface of the floor at this time and apply finish to it.

Drill a ⅛in (3mm) hole through the bottom of the floor. You will put the bottom finial in this hole later. It will also help you stabilize the piece when you reverse-chuck it.

Remove the floor from the four-jaw chuck and remount it from the other direction, with the chuck fitting inside the rebate you have made.

Fig 11.6

Fig 11.7

Fig 11.8

Fig 11.9

Fig 11.10

Fig 11.11

Alternatively, you can make a small jam-fit chuck and use hot-melt glue to hold the piece, as described below.

Hold the work steady with light pressure from your live centre while you shape the outside of the floor. As you approach the final shape, the live centre will have to be backed off. You might want to refine the final curve of the floor with a sharp round-nose scraper (Fig 11.12). Sand the bottom to remove all blemishes (Fig 11.13). Apply finish using kitchen paper.

Turning the roof

The roof is turned in the same manner as the floor. Start by placing the smaller ring of the roof in the four-jaw chuck. Cut the inside of the roof. Make a shallow depression with the bowl gouge (Fig 11.14). Use your callipers to measure the top diameter of the body of the bird house and transfer this measurement to the roof (Fig 11.15).

Use a sharp skew or straight scraper to cut just inside this mark to form a shallow rebate. With the same tool, slightly enlarge the rebate (Fig 11.16). Test-fit, and repeat this slow process until you have a nice fit (Fig 11.17). Like the floor, it must not be too tight. When the fit is correct, sand and apply finish to the bottom and inside of the roof.

Reverse-mount the roof so that you can cut the top. This can easily be done with a four-jaw chuck, or you can use a spigot chuck. This time, as a teaching exercise, I am going to show how to make and use a spigot chuck and hot-melt glue.

Mount a piece of scrap wood on your faceplate. Use callipers to mark the diameter of the rebate in the roof. With the skew or square-nose scraper, cut a small tenon, which must be slightly larger than the rebate in the roof. Make a slight bevel on the end of the tenon and test-fit the roof onto it. It should be too tight to fit all the way, but should barely go onto the bevelled part of the tenon. Hand-rotate the roof on the tenon; this will cause a slight burnishing of the bevelled tenon. The tenon needs to be reduced to the diameter of this burnished part.

Use your skew or scraper to reduce the tenon to this exact diameter. The fit should be snug, but not tight enough to break the roof. Now use hot-melt glue all the way around the base of the roof (Fig 11.18).

Drill a ⅛in (3mm) hole through the top of the roof for the finial. Use your bowl gouge to shape the top of the roof. Use a sharp round-nose scraper to

Fig 11.12 *Using a round-nosed scraper to refine the curve of the floor*

Fig 11.13 *Sanding the bottom of the floor*

Fig 11.14 *Use gentle cuts with the bowl gouge on the inside of the roof*

Fig 11.15 *Transferring the upper diameter of the body to the inside of the roof piece*

Fig 11.16 *Enlarging the rebate with a straight scraper that has an edge formed on the side*

Fig 11.17 *Test-fitting the roof*

Fig 11.18 *Attaching the roof to the jam-fit chuck with a hot-melt glue gun*

Fig 11.19 *Finishing the roof*

cut a gentle curve in the roof, then a sharp skew to cut the steps. This gives the illusion that the roof is made of many more rings. Sand and apply finish to the roof (Fig 11.19).

Cutting the finials and perch

Mounting the stock for the finials and perch is most easily done using a four-jaw chuck. However, it can be held by a home-made wooden chuck. To make this, first turn a dowel, then drill a hole in a waste block the same diameter as the dowel you turned. Glue the dowel into the hole and allow the glue to set. Once set, place the live centre into the indent in the end of the dowel and turn.

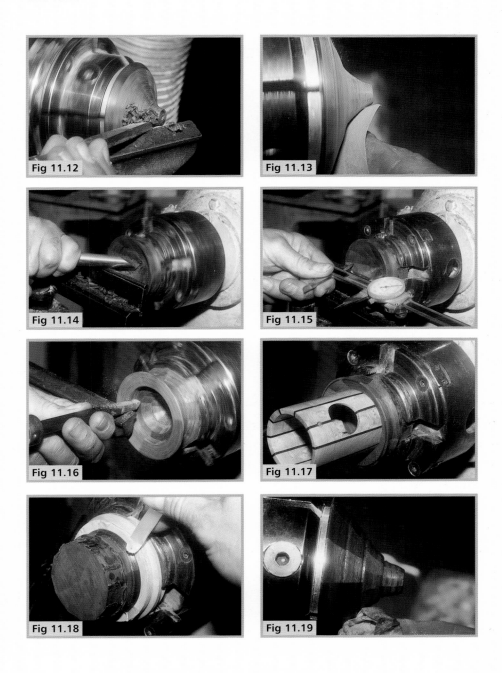

Fig 11.12

Fig 11.13

Fig 11.14

Fig 11.15

Fig 11.16

Fig 11.17

Fig 11.18

Fig 11.19

Small, delicate turnings like these have several special requirements. First, your lathe speed needs to be much higher than for large turnings: a speed of about 1000–2000rpm is indicated, if your lathe can handle it. Next, your tools must be razor-sharp.

The skew can make very detailed and clean cuts. Start by turning the stock round. Have the blade raised at an angle so that it makes a slicing action. You can lay the skew flat on the toolrest to make a scraping cut; this is not as smooth as a slicing cut, but much easier to do. Also, it is a nice way to make the stock an even diameter along the shaft.

Cutting the finials and perch is delicate work. Expect to make several attempts before you are satisfied with your results.

The floor finial

Take a piece of maple ½in (13mm) in diameter and no longer than about 4in (100mm), and turn it straight and round using a four-jaw chuck and a live centre. Make a small V-cut about ½in (13mm) from the tailstock, where the tip of the acorn will be.

Use the flat side of your skew to reduce the diameter of the bottom half of the acorn to about ⅜in (10mm), then round it over. Use the same tool to deepen the V-cut so that you can round down the tip of the acorn to a small point. The maple is now unsupported at the tailstock end.

Point the skew straight in at the middle of the acorn to make a demarcation between the acorn and its cup. Reduce the diameter of the cup to about ¹⁄₁₆in (1.5mm) larger than the lower part of the acorn. Mark off the length of the cup, about ¼in (6mm). Use your skew to round it off, leaving at least ³⁄₁₆in (5mm) thickness for the stalk.

On the side toward the headstock, make the half-bead which will fit against the bottom of the floor. Finally, use the skew to make a ⅛in (3mm) tenon that will fit into the floor of the bird house. Use callipers to make sure that you have the correct diameter (Fig 11.20). Sand and apply finish to the bottom finial.

The roof finial

Use your skew to cut a small 'genie bottle' to fit on the top of the roof. Cut a ⅛in (3mm) tenon to fit into the roof of the bird house. Sand and apply finish.

Fig 11.20 *Checking the diameter of the tenon on the finial*

Fig 11.21 *Finishing the finial* in situ

Fig 11.22 *Checking the fit of the perch tenon*

Glue the roof finial to the roof with cyanoacrylate adhesive (superglue). Apply finish again (Fig 11.21).

The perch

Use the same stock to cut a small perch for the body of the bird house. Make it as simple or as complicated as you like. Start by making a small round ball for the end of the perch. Make a small hemisphere to separate the perch from the spigot that fits into the bird house. Develop the ⅛in (3mm) tenon that fits into the bird house body; use your callipers to make sure that the tenon is a nice fit (Fig 11.22). Sand and apply finish.

Assembly

Use small amounts of cyanoacrylate glue to assemble the bird house. The fit of your parts should be very accurate, so the amount of glue used should be very small.

I drill a 1/16in (1.5mm) hole through the finial in the roof. This hole is perpendicular to the front of the house, so you cannot see it from the front. Through it I put some black nylon thread that I tie into a loop to suspend the bird house ornament.

The stand

You can make a nice stand very easily. Turn a disc about 3in (75mm) in diameter. Put a bevel on it and some concentric circles on the top. Sand and apply finish. Part it off and sand the bottom. Drill a small hole on the edge of the circle to fit some brass welding rod, which is ⅛in (3mm) in diameter. Use electrician's round-nose pliers to bend and cut the brass welding wire. Glue the wire in the hole and hang the bird house on it.

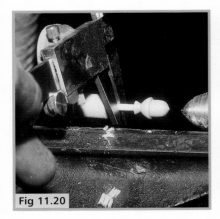

Fig 11.20

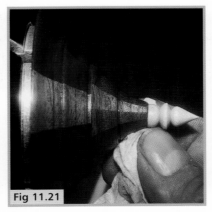

Fig 11.21

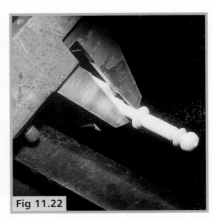

Fig 11.22

12
MOUNTAIN
BOWL

This unique bowl will give you experience in a whole new field of woodworking called 'intarsia'. Intarsia is the art of cutting thick segments of different-coloured woods very accurately so that the pieces fit together to form a picture or pattern.

The feature ring is a mountain scene made from three different woods: walnut, padauk, and maple. The pieces are be stacked and cut two at a time, then reassembled and glued. By using very accurate cuts from a scrollsaw, a beautiful mountain scene can be created. The mountain scene 'stick' is then cut into eight sections, which are mitre-cut and assembled to make the feature ring.

Getting started

Start by making an initial drawing of the bowl that you would like to make (Fig 12.1). You may have to redraw the bowl after the feature ring is completed, because the finished ring may be a slightly different size. Make the intarsia ring no more than 2in (50mm) tall; this is because the profile of the bowl must not curve in this area, and if the straight section is too tall it may be difficult to create a pleasing shape. A diameter of about 8in (about 200mm) will allow enough room for a pleasing scene. Plan where the eight mitre cuts will be made. Do not have any height changes in the scene where the joints will be: a height change at the joint will result in large jumps or gaps in the pattern when the ring is assembled.

Designing the intarsia

Make a full-size drawing that will be the pattern for your three-piece intarsia scene. Tape enough pieces of paper together to make a drawing 26¾in (680mm) long. Draw a strip 2in (50mm) tall. Mark off eight equal sections, with the thickness of the saw kerf drawn in. This will give you eight blank boxes that look like a cartoon strip. Now it is a simple matter of drawing in two layers of mountains and a sky (Fig 12.2). Draw in pencil: you may want to make several changes before you are finished. The following suggestions may help:

- Do not get too complicated: eventually you have to cut this pattern with a scrollsaw.
- Make three distinct layers that run the entire length of the drawing.
- Do not try to cut out complete circles for snow-capped peaks or clouds. It is possible to make 'drop-through' cuts that show no gaps, but this is a difficult cut and you may want to gain a little experience first.
- Make the lines at both ends of the stick come out level. The line heights A and B must be the same at each end of the stick. In this way, when the stick is bent around into a circle the two ends will match up.

Once you have a drawing that you like, ink it in with a felt-tip pen. Now make several copies on a photocopier.

Cutting the feature-ring stock

The three types of wood should be a good contrast to each other. My scrollsaw could not handle cutting detail through 2in (50mm) of hard wood. It would handle two pieces that were ¾in (19mm) thick, so that is the

Fig 12.1 The initial drawing, which may have to be revised later

Fig 12.2 An example of a drawing for the three-piece intarsia scene; make yours full size

Fig 12.3 The stock for the feature ring is all cut at once

Fig 12.4 The intarsia drawing glued to the two-part stick. The clouds and snow shown in this drawing are best omitted until you have had some practice

thickness to which I cut my stock. To make a ring the same size as mine, you will need one piece each of maple, walnut, and padauk measuring 27 x 2 x ¾in (685 x 51 x 19mm). Cut all three pieces at the same time, because they must be the exact same size (Fig 12.3).

Use hot-melt glue to join the walnut and maple. Apply glue to the edges only, and use clamps to pull the two pieces together and hold them while the glue cools. This will produce a black and white stick that measures 27 x 2 x 1½in (685 x 50 x 38mm). Use spray adhesive to attach the intarsia drawing to your stick. Be very careful in laying the pattern onto the wood (Fig 12.4).

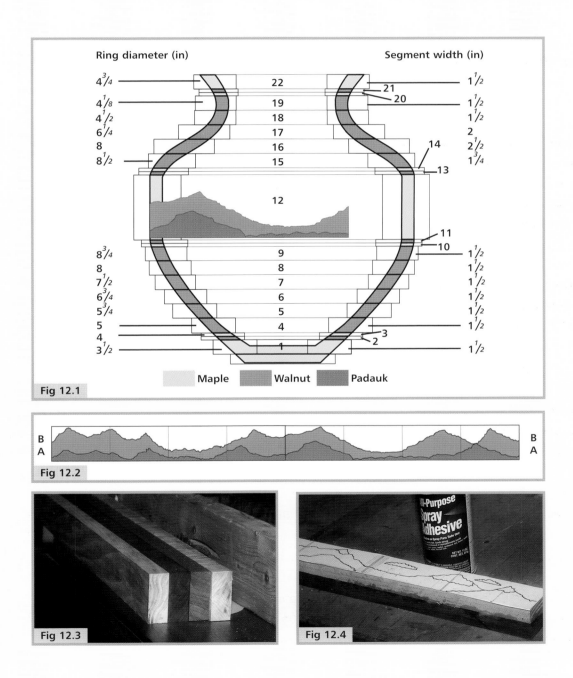

Ring diameter (in)   Segment width (in)

Ring diameter	Segment	Segment width
4³/₄	22	
	21	1½
	20	
4¹/₈	19	1½
4½	18	1½
6¼	17	2
8	16	2½
8½	15	1³/₄
	14	
	13	
	12	
	11	
	10	
8³/₄	9	1½
8	8	1½
7½	7	1½
6³/₄	6	1½
5³/₄	5	1½
5	4	1½
4	3	
	2	
3½	1	1½

Maple   Walnut   Padauk

Fig 12.1

Fig 12.2

Fig 12.3

Fig 12.4

The first cut

Put a new, sharp, thin blade on your scrollsaw. Align the table at exactly 90° to the saw blade. Make some practice cuts on scrap wood. Try not to stop, unless it is at one of the joints where a section will be cut with the tablesaw. Have a good light in position to help with visibility.

The first cut will be on the top line between the sky and the further range of mountains. Position both hands so that you can control the stick without getting cut. Make the saw blade split the line of the drawing (Fig 12.5). You may have to work from both ends so that your cut will meet in the middle.

Separate the top from the bottom of both sections. The easiest way to do this is by heating the hot-melt glue with a hairdryer or a hot-air gun. You now have four pieces: a dark top and bottom, and a light top and bottom. Test-fit the light top to the dark bottom. There should be just a very small gap between the two sections; this is normal.

Before gluing, have plenty of wood clamps at the ready. Use a brush to apply glue to all surfaces (Fig 12.6). Bring the two sections together with plenty of clamps; the clamps should not be more than 1in (25mm) apart (Fig 12.7). Allow the glue of 'stick 1' to cure for at least 24 hours.

The remaining pieces can be saved to make a second bowl with the pattern in reversed colours.

The second cut

Sand stick 1 flat and smooth to remove all excess glue. Place stick 1 on top of the padauk, and glue the two together with hot-melt glue as you did with the first two sections. Use spray adhesive to glue a second copy of the pattern to the stick. Make your second cut, which is between the two mountain ranges (Fig 12.8).

Separate the sections as before. Take the white and black top and place it on the red bottom. It should be a good fit, with a very thin kerf line which will be squeezed shut when you do the gluing. You now have a three-layer stick, with a white sky and dark and red mountains. Glue this second stick in the same manner as you did the first. Allow the glue to set for 24 hours, then sand the mountain stick flat on both sides, and on the top and bottom.

Fig 12.5 *Separating the mountain scene from the sky*

Fig 12.6 *Gluing the maple top to the walnut bottom*

Fig 12.7 *Clamping the two pieces together*

Fig 12.8 *Cutting the three-part stick to separate the two mountain ranges*

Fig 12.9 *Cut the three-tone mountain stick into eight equal pieces, starting exactly in the middle*

Fig 12.10 *Most of the mitre cut can be done on the tablesaw, but do not cut right to the corner*

Cutting the segments

The mountain stick must be cut into eight sections of exactly equal length. Divide the stick in half (Fig 12.9), then divide these in two, and in two again until you have eight equal pieces.

Cut eight pieces of scrap wood the same length as the eight mountain pieces. Set your mitre gauge to 22.5° (180° ÷ 8). Place the mitre gauge on the disc sander and cut the angle on both sides of the eight segments. You must be using at least 60-grit sandpaper or coarser. To save time, you can cut off part of the corner with your mitre gauge on the tablesaw (Fig 12.10). Do not saw all of the corner off: if you do, you will probably cut off too much from the length of the segment.

Once you are satisfied with the fit of the test pieces, cut the real segments in the same way. Check carefully that you have the segments in the correct sequence. As before, do not cut all the way up to the corner.

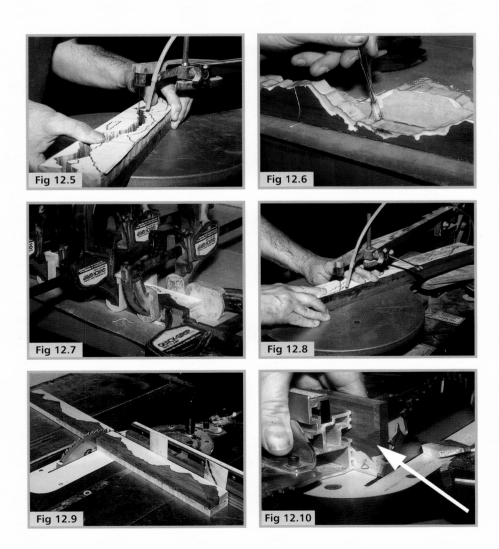

Fig 12.5

Fig 12.6

Fig 12.7

Fig 12.8

Fig 12.9

Fig 12.10

Move your mitre gauge and segments to the disc sander to complete the mitre cut (Fig 12.11). Cut just up to the edge of the segment and no further. Cut all eight sections this way.

Test-fit your segments to make sure that you have a good fit and that the segments are in the correct order.

Assembling the feature ring

Apply glue to each of the segments. Place two hose clamps around the ring and lightly tighten. Make sure that all the rings are flat on the table and that all the joints have come together properly. Tighten both hose clamps a little at a time (Fig 12.12). There should be even pressure on both clamps. Allow this ring to cure for 24 hours.

Making the plain rings

Use your drawing to make up a work chart that lists the diameter, width, length, and colour of the segments in each ring. From the chart you can easily calculate a bill of goods. I cut my stock to 40in (1m) lengths to make it easier to work with in my shop; the last column of the table shows the number of 40in lengths required.

BILL OF GOODS					
NB: All length measurements include an allowance for wastage.					
Timber	Width		Length		No. of
	in	mm	in	mm	lengths
Maple	1.5	38	130	3300	4
Walnut	1.5	38	330	8400	8
Walnut	2	51	28	710	1
Walnut	2.5	64	30	760	1

Use your work chart to get the correct segment length for the ring in question. Set your dial callipers to this length. Use a very sharp pencil to mark this length on the segment that you are about to cut (Fig 12.13). Place the work on the cutting sled so that this line is just barely left on the segment, and set your stop block to this position. Cut all of the segments for all of the rings at the same time.

Fig 12.11 *Finish the mitre cuts on the disc sander without cutting away any extra wood*

Fig 12.12 *Gluing the feature ring*

Fig 12.13 *Marking the length of each segment with a sharp pencil*

Fig 12.14 *Gluing the plain rings, using yellow glue and hose clamps*

Fig 12.15 *Thicknessing all the rings on the thickness sander*

Fig 12.16 *Glue the base and ring 1 to a waste block*

If possible, glue all of your rings at once. Twelve clamps should be enough. By the time you have used the last clamp, the first one should be ready to come off (Fig 12.14).

Allow the rings to set overnight before sanding them to thickness. If you have a thickness sander, do all the rings at the same time (Fig 12.15).

Stacking the rings

Screw a waste block of maple or other hard wood to your faceplate, and glue the one-piece base of the bowl to this. Allow this glue to set for at least 15 minutes before adding ring 1. Apply pressure to this ring with a pressure plate in the tailstock (Fig 12.16).

Fig 12.11

Fig 12.12

Fig 12.13

Fig 12.14

Fig 12.15

Fig 12.16

While this joint is curing on the lathe, you can stack some more rings at your workbench. Glue them in pairs, applying a small amount of glue to each ring. Centre the rings and press down with your full body weight. The rings will slip in relation to each other, so realign them before placing them in the glue press (Fig 12.17).

Continue stacking rings, cutting or sanding each one flat on the lathe before adding the next ring (Fig 12.18). This is especially important when you stack several rings on the workbench before gluing them on to the lathe stack. **It is much better to correct a small error than to try to figure out how to correct a big error.** Continue stacking and sanding as you build up the bottom of the vase.

If you have allowed your rings to set overnight, you can do some initial turning of the bottom rings using a sharp bowl gouge.

Initial turning of the base

A good time to turn the base is before adding the feature ring. The lower part of the bowl is still wide open so that you can easily reach the bottom. Turning the bottom at this stage will make it easier for you to centre the feature ring onto the base. The feature ring is very narrow and you do not have any room to be off-centre.

Support the open end with a piece of scrap wood and a live centre while you turn the outside (this can be seen in Fig 12.20). Blend all of the rings into a gentle, pleasing curve.

Cut the inside of the bowl with your bowl gouge. You might want to use a scraper, or a boring bar with a scraper, to cut the deepest part of the bowl. If you are using a regular scraper it is important to position the toolrest very close to the work area.

Sand or cut the last ring flat in preparation for gluing on the feature ring (Fig 12.19).

Adding the feature ring

Glue the feature ring as you do all other rings, with one minor exception. The feature ring is not as wide as other rings, so it is very important to have this ring perfectly centred when you apply pressure from the tailstock. Allow it to set for at least 24 hours before turning it (Fig 12.20).

Fig 12.17 Using the glue press to glue rings together in pairs. Make sure that they stay centred

Fig 12.18 Sand each ring flat before adding another

Fig 12.19 Sanding the last ring flat before adding the feature ring

Fig 12.20 Turning the feature ring, with support from a pressure plate in the tailstock

Fig 12.21 Finishing the top of the bowl as a separate unit

Making the top

Stack the rings for the top of the bowl as though it were a separate bowl. Cut as much of the inside and outside as you can. By building both halves at the same time you can save considerable time: while the glue from one procedure is curing, you can be working on the other half of the bowl. Sand and apply finish to the inside (Fig 12.21).

Finishing the vase

Glue the top to the bottom on the lathe. Allow the glue to set for two days. Supporting the vase with a steady rest, finish shaping the inside and outside of the top with a bowl gouge. The bowl gouge can cut the bulk of the inside of the mouth; make final finish cuts with a sharp scraper, or a scraper on a boring bar. Since you have already finished the inside of the bowl, this cut just needs to go in a very short distance.

This is quite an advanced project, and you can expect many people to ask you 'How did you do that?'

Fig 12.17

Fig 12.18

Fig 12.19

Fig 12.20

Fig 12.21

13
EASTER
SUNRISE

So far we have used simple segments to build a bowl by stacking numerous rings one upon the other. This technique is simple and produces beautiful bowls. However, compound-mitre stave construction can build a vase with far fewer rings, because the rings can be much taller. This is similar to the concept of barrel-stave construction, except that our ring will be tapered.

The disadvantage of compound-mitre construction is that it is a more complex cutting technique. Two angles are cut at the same time, one by tilting the blade of the tablesaw (blade-tilt angle), the other by setting an angle on the mitre gauge (mitre-gauge angle).

The bottom of this bowl is a starburst pattern with a cross inlaid into it (Fig 13.1).

You can do this entire project without any mathematical calculations; the compound mitre tables on pages 138–47 will give you all the necessary settings.

Planning the compound-mitre ring

Like all segmented bowls, this one starts with a drawing (Fig 13.2). The top ring is 14in (355mm) in diameter, with a slope of 38°. I decided that this ring would be 3in (75mm) tall, and consist of 14 segments. These four measurements determine the shape of the ring.

The equations for calculating mitre-gauge angle (MG) and blade tilt (BT) are included here for those who like playing with a hand-held calculator; S stands for the slope of the bowl in degrees, and N for the number of staves.

$$MG = \tan^{-1} (1/\cos S \tan (180°/N))$$
$$BT = \tan^{-1} (\sin (MG) \sin S \tan (180°/N))$$

You can solve these equations to get the two angles, or your can use the tables at the back of the book. Either way, the result should be:

Mitre gauge is set to 79.669°
Blade tilt is set to 6.743°.

Cutting the segments

The slope of the ring is 38°. Bevel both sides of the stock material so that the bottom edge of the finished ring will sit flat (Fig 13.3).

Set the blade tilt at 6.743° and the mitre gauge at 79.669°. Use a safety spacer to create a space between the cut segment and the fence of your tablesaw (Fig 13.4). Adjust the fence and spacer so that the segments are 3in (75mm) wide at the wide end.

Cut 14 segments of maple from your 5in (127mm)-wide stock. The width of the stock becomes the length of the segment. It is important to place the correct edge of the stock forward when making the cut for the segments. The leading edge slopes down onto the table (Fig 13.5). Cut 14 segments in this way (Fig 13.6).

Lay the segments down on your work area and place tape on the back to hold them together. Get a friend to help you raise the ring and tape the final segments together to check that you have a good fit (Fig 13.7).

Fig 13.1 The base of Easter Sunrise has a cross inlaid into a padauk and maple starburst

Fig 13.2 Side elevation drawing of the stave bowl

Fig 13.3 Bevelling the edges of the stock

Fig 13.4 The safety spacer clamped to the tablesaw fence

Fig 13.5 The leading edge of the stock slopes downwards

Fig 13.6 The 14 segments have a double bevel from the blade tilt and mitre gauge

Fig 13.7 Test-fit the ring together; this is a two-person job

Fig 13.8 Padauk veneers glued to the stave segments. This will make the final glue-up easier

Fig 13.9 Pulling the ring together with two hose clamps, using temporary blocks at the narrow end

Veneer strips

Cut 14 pieces of padauk veneer to go between the 14 segments. I like the veneers to be about 0.14in (3.6mm) thick, but you might prefer them thinner. Cut the veneers to length and glue to one side of each of the 14 maple segments (Fig 13.8). Allow this glue to set for at least 15 minutes before going to the next step.

Assembling the ring

Placing a hose clamp around the small end of a ring with this much slope can be difficult. To make the job easier I glue temporary blocks on the outside. You can use yellow glue or hot-melt glue for this. If you use yellow glue you should wait at least one hour for the glue to set.

Have a friend assist you in doing a test clamping of the final ring. Use two hose clamps to bring the ring together (Fig 13.9). The fit should be perfect at this time.

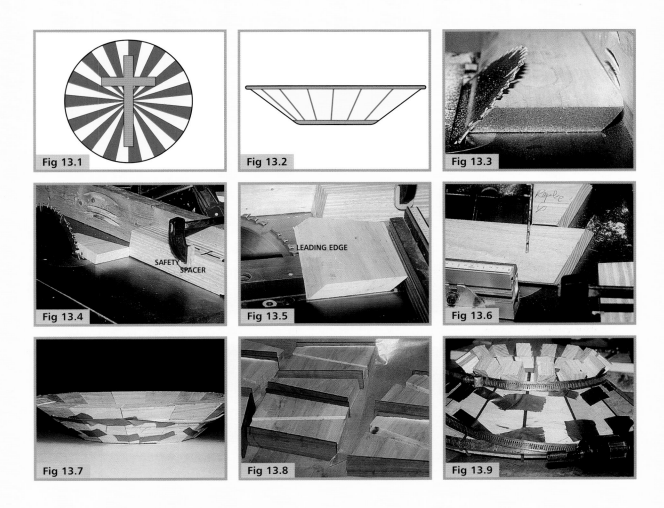

Fig 13.1

Fig 13.2

Fig 13.3

Fig 13.4

Fig 13.5

Fig 13.6

Fig 13.7

Fig 13.8

Fig 13.9

Lay the ring back down on your work table and use a brush to apply glue to each joint. Clamp up and allow to set for at least 24 hours.

Initial turning

The temporary clamping blocks need to be removed after the ring has set overnight. If you used hot-melt glue, the blocks can be twisted off with an open-ended wrench. If you used yellow glue, they will need to be turned off. You can use large 'jumbo' jaws to hold the large end of the ring, with tailstock support (Fig 13.10). Use a fairly slow speed of about 200rpm to turn the bottom. This is a large ring, so it is necessary to keep to a slow speed until it is round and balanced. Only the bottom is turned at this stage.

Making the base

The bottom of the bowl is about 7½in (190mm) in diameter. The starburst pattern is formed by a 30-segment ring using alternating padauk and maple. Use stock 4in (100mm) wide. The mitre gauge or sled is set to 6° (180° ÷ 30). Cut 15 maple and 15 padauk segments. Make sure the cut goes all the way to a fine point; this will allow the segments to come together into a solid piece.

Pull the ring together with a hose clamp, making sure that all the points come to the centre (Fig 13.11). Be careful not to break off the tips of the segments; they are fragile. Allow the glue to set for at least two hours before thickness-sanding the whole disc.

Making the cross inlay

Start by making a work jig the same thickness as the bottom of the bowl. Cut out the centre of the jig so that the starburst base can fit into it. Use hot-melt glue and wood shims to glue the starburst base firmly into the work jig (this can be seen in Fig 13.12).

The inlay rebate and the inlay itself will be cut with an inlaying kit that fits on a router. This consists of three parts: a brass base that fits onto the router, a brass collar the same thickness as the router bit, and a ⅛in (3mm) diameter router bit. This type of kit can be purchased from most woodworking supply stores.

The other piece of equipment you will need to make is the pattern template. The thickness of the pattern material must be equal to that of the brass inlay

Fig 13.10 Turn the bottom of the ring flat, using jumbo jaws and support from the tailstock

Fig 13.11 Assembling the 30 segments of the base

Fig 13.12 First stage of making the jig for routing the cross pattern. Beneath it is the bowl base installed in the work jig

Fig 13.13 Cutting the enlarged cross template from ¼in (6mm) plywood

Fig 13.14 The finished recess, and the router with the inlaying attachment in place; note the brass spacer surrounding the bit

collar – in my case, ¼in (6mm). Use a straightedge, callipers, and a fine pencil to draw a cross to your liking (Fig 13.12). However, this is not the final pattern: you must make room for the ⅛in (3mm) spacer that fits on the inlay kit (visible in Fig 13.14). Therefore you must increase the size of the pattern by ⅛in (3mm) all the way around (Fig 13.13).

Screw the inlay jig to the base of your router. There is a collar that fits on the top side of the router base, and this screws on from inside. Put on the spacer collar and insert the bit into the router.

Position the cross template over the base exactly where you want the inlay to be, and screw it to the work jig that contains the starburst base. Use four wood screws, and countersink them so that the base of the router cannot hit the screwheads. Note that the screws must not go into the starburst base itself, but into the plywood work jig that you prepared.

Set the router so that the bit extends approximately ⅜in (10mm) past the end of the brass inlay collet. Make sure the inlay attachment has its brass spacer on (Fig 13.14). Turn the router on and gently plunge it into the centre of the work area. Be careful! Wear protective eye goggles and ear muffs. Rout out the entire inside of the cross pattern.

The plywood template will guide the collar of the inlay jig. Cut a smooth, even pattern, making sure that the floor of the rebate is flat. Notice that the corners of the cross are not perfectly square; the finest detail that you can cut is determined by the radius of the router bit.

Fig 13.10

Fig 13.11

Fig 13.14

Fig 13.12

Fig 13.13

The cross inlay is made next. Before attempting this procedure on expensive wood, you should first practice on a test piece. The plunge in this procedure must be done very accurately so that there is no flaw in the final outline.

Remove the cross template from the work jig and attach it to a piece of contrasting walnut. Again make sure that the screws are countersunk so that the base of the router will not hit them. **Remove the spacer collar from the inlay attachment.** This collar must be removed to cut the walnut inlay that will fit into the rebate already cut in the starburst base (Fig 13.15).

Slowly plunge the router into the walnut while keeping the brass collar firmly pressed against the inside edge of the cross template. Slowly rout around the pattern. Be careful not to let the brass inlay collar move away from the side of the template. Cut to the full depth of the router bit.

Using a featherboard and a push stick, carefully cut a slice from the walnut on the tablesaw (Fig 13.16). The thickness of this slice should be equal to the depth of the router cut. This will cut the inlay free from the rest of the walnut stock (Fig 13.17).

Test-fit the walnut inlay into the rebate. Do not push it all the way in! You will have difficulty in getting it back out. The fit should be extremely tight. You might need to lightly sand the inlay to make it fit freely enough to slide in. Again do not push the inlay all the way in. Secure the inlay by using a small amount of yellow glue in the rebate area (Fig 13.18).

Final assembly

The accurate positioning of the base with its cross is very important. Centre the cross in the bottom of the bowl. Glue, and then apply pressure with your glue press or clamps (Fig 13.19). Allow this glue to set overnight.

Turning the bowl

It is very important to keep the cross centred when mounting the bowl to the faceplate. The following technique will ensure this. Install a faceplate and glue block on the headstock. The glue block should be at least 2in (50mm) square to give adequate gluing surface. Now use your jumbo jaws – held in a centred position by a large live centre in the tailstock – to position the bowl against the glue block (Fig 13.20). Check that everything is aligned correctly, then apply yellow glue to both surfaces and position the bowl. The tailstock

Fig 13.15 The cross shape outlined in walnut; this time the spacing collar has been removed from the inlaying attachment

Fig 13.16 Cutting the walnut inlay free on the tablesaw

Fig 13.17 The walnut cross cut free from the stock

Fig 13.18 The cross inlay finally glued into its rebate

Fig 13.19 The bottom and the outer ring united. Alignment of the pattern is critical

Fig 13.20 Using the jumbo jaws to ensure accurate alignment of the bowl with the faceplate

Fig 13.21 Applying finish on the lathe

will apply centring pressure to the jumbo jaws. Allow the glue to set for a minimum of 24 hours.

Choose a low speed when turning anything this large: try to keep between 300 and 500rpm. Use some type of live centre when turning the outside. A sharp bowl gouge is used to turn the outside.

Turning the inside of the bowl requires that you remove the live centre from the tailstock end. Use your bowl gouge to turn the top of the bowl smooth and flat, and to cut a step on the inside of the bowl. Follow this step all the way down the inside with your bowl gouge. Blend the bottom into the side wall using a round-nose scraper. Sand the bottom.

Apply finish while the bowl is still on the lathe (Fig 13.21). Part off using a thin parting tool. Sand the bottom smooth with a hook-and-loop sanding disc. If you prefer, you could reverse-turn the bottom of the bowl using a large set of jumbo jaws or a vacuum chuck. This way you could make the cross appear through on the bottom.

Compound mitring and router inlay are versatile techniques, and you may find yourself making many variations on this theme.

Fig 13.15

Fig 13.16

Fig 13.17

Fig 13.18

Fig 13.19

Fig 13.20

Fig 13.21

14
CLASSICAL
VASE

In the United States a lot of segmented turning uses the shapes of Native American pottery. However, there is a justly deserved place for classical Greek forms. In this exercise we will do a segmented vase that has its origins in classical Greek shapes.

This project uses the tablesaw to cut segments in a different manner from previous projects. Several of the tall rings, in particular, require very careful cuts. The vase will be built up from both ends, using two faceplates. This decreases the likelihood of the vase breaking during the turning.

Planning

Start by making a full-scale drawing (Fig 14.1). Indicate the approximate colours of the wood you intend to use. In this drawing the dark areas represent walnut, white stands for maple and red for padauk.

Rings 1, 3, 5, 7, 9, and 10 are simple rings. These are made with normal-thickness wood using your cutting board or mitre gauge, and there is no need to describe the process again here.

Rings 2, 4, 6, and 8 are the feature in this project. I will describe the steps in making ring 6; the others are made in the same manner.

Making ring 6

Ring 6 is the tallest, and the most difficult to make. It is a 20-segment ring, which means that the blade-tilt angle is 9° (180° ÷ 20). Because of the width of stock available, 40 segments are used, with the angle cut on one side only.

Set your saw table to 9°. Attach a sacrificial fence to the tablesaw fence. Run a section of scrap stock past the tilted blade, bevelling one side at 9°. Then use a mitre gauge set to 90° to cut off 40 sections, and arrange these in a circle. Adjust the tilt of the blade if necessary, until the segments fit accurately.

Now run your maple stock through the tablesaw in the same way, using a featherboard to hold the stock firmly against the sacrificial fence as you make the long cut (Fig 14.2). Use a push stick to keep your fingers a long way away from the saw blade. Set these pieces aside for a few minutes.

Reset your saw blade to 90°. Set your fence to make a ⅛in (3mm) cut. Cut 18ft (5.5m) of padauk 4in wide and ⅛in thick (100 x 3mm). Again use a featherboard to hold the stock firmly (Fig 14.3).

Use your mitre gauge to crosscut the padauk veneer into 5in (127mm) sections. Cut the white maple wedges in the same manner (Fig 14.4). Notice the wide gap created by the spacer, which ensures that the offcut will not become trapped and thrown between the fence and the blade. Test-assemble the 60 pieces that make up this ring (Fig 14.5).

Gluing 60 pieces together at one time can be very difficult: the glue starts to set before you are finished with the last piece. Glue groups of three together

Fig 14.1 Working drawing of the classical vase; make yours full size

Fig 14.2 Cutting the 9° segments for the even-numbered rings

Fig 14.3 Cutting the padauk veneers on the tablesaw

Fig 14.4 Crosscutting the segments to length with the mitre gauge set to 90°

Fig 14.5 Trial assembly of the 40 maple wedges and the 20 padauk veneers

first – a red segment between two white ones – then glue these 20 segments into a ring. Use four clamps to pull the final assembly together. Allow this ring to set overnight. Flatten one side of the ring on a belt sander, then set the ring aside for a while.

Fig 14.1

Fig 14.2

Fig 14.3

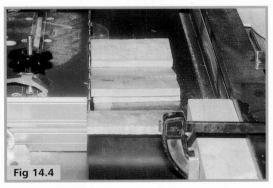

Fig 14.4

Fig 14.5

Making the bottom section

Once all the rings are made, glue rings 1 and 2 onto a waste block. Allow this to set overnight before turning. Sand and apply finish to this base section (Fig 14.6).

Add rings 3 and 4 in the same way. Shape ring 4 with the bowl gouge, using callipers to mark the diameter of the ring at both ends. Once the correct diameters have been achieved at the ends, then you can shape the middle. To cut this cove you might use either a bowl gouge or a round-nose scraper. Try to achieve a very fine cut. Cut the inside and outside of the base as you build it up. In this way you will always be able to reach the bottom easily.

Cut and sand ring 4 flat in preparation to gluing on ring 5. Apply glue to both surfaces and centre ring 5 onto ring 4.

Use a sharp bowl gouge to blend the bottom of ring 5 into the top of ring 4 (Fig 14.7). Use your callipers to mark the diameter of the top of ring 5, and reduce the top surface to this diameter. Then blend the top and bottom together with a graceful curve. Cut the inside of ring 5 using a sharp bowl gouge. It is important to leave this wall about ½in (13mm) thick to support the rest of the vase. Sand and apply finish to the inside of this ring (Fig 14.8).

Making the top section

Prepare another faceplate to be used for building the top of the vase. Glue rings 10 and 9 to the faceplate by means of a waste piece. Centre the rings on the faceplate with a live centre and allow to set overnight.

Use callipers to mark the diameters of these top two rings, and turn to shape with the bowl gouge. Drill out the inside with a regular drill bit or a Forstner bit, then shape the inside with the bowl gouge. Be sure to shape ring 9 to its final thickness, since it will not be easy to reach this area later. Sand and apply finish.

Add ring 8. Use your calipers to mark the diameter of the large end, and turn this to the correct diameter with the bowl gouge. Use the same tool to shape the rest of ring 8 and blend it into ring 9 (Fig 14.9), and to hollow out the inside of ring 8 (Fig 14.10). Use either a bowl gouge or a scraper to blend rings 8 and 9 together on the inside. Sand and apply finish to the inside of ring 8.

Fig 14.6 Assembling the base by gluing the first two rings onto a maple waste block

Fig 14.7 Starting to shape ring 5

Fig 14.8 Finishing the inside of rings 4 and 5

Fig 14.9 Blending ring 8 into ring 9. The top of the vase is built on a second faceplate

Fig 14.10 Cutting the inside of ring 8 with a sharp bowl gouge

Fig 14.11 Sanding ring 7 flat before adding ring 6

Glue ring 7 to the bottom of ring 8. Use callipers to mark the largest diameter on the bottom of ring 7. Turn ring 7 to this diameter, then blend into ring 8. At this stage the diameter of the top is getting larger with each ring. Use your parting tool to reduce the thickness of ring 7 to ¼in (6mm), then sand the surface flat (Fig 14.11).

Ring 6

Ring 6 is not only the hardest ring to build, but also the hardest to mount successfully on the vase. However, with a little patience and attention to detail this procedure can be carried out in a methodical manner.

Mount ring 6 in a four-jaw chuck and turn it to a cylinder. Cut and sand both ends flat. Cut a tenon on the small end of the ring so that you can hold it

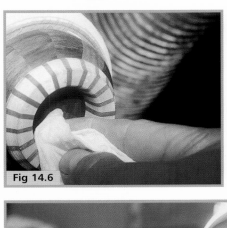

Fig 14.6

Fig 14.7

Fig 14.8

Fig 14.9

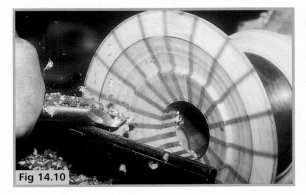

Fig 14.10

Fig 14.11

securely with a four-jaw chuck; the ring has extra length to allow for this. There are three important diameters to keep track of here. The maximum diameter of the ring is located about ¾in (about 20mm) from the top of the ring. The other two diameters to be concerned with are those of the top and bottom of the ring. First reduce the whole cylinder to the maximum diameter of the ring, then use your bowl gouge to reduce the diameters in both directions from the widest part (Fig 14.12). Bring all three diameters to the correct dimension and blend all surfaces into a smooth, continuous shape.

Before starting work on the inside of ring 6, mount a steady rest on your lathe for support. This is important because the four-jaw chuck will have a difficult time holding this large turning while you hollow out the inside.

Drill out the inside of the ring, then shape with bowl gouge or scraper. Sand the inside and apply finish. Sand the end of the ring flat in preparation for gluing to the bottom of ring 7.

Remount the top section of the vase onto the headstock. Apply glue to both surfaces and position the top of ring 6 to match up with the bottom of ring 7. **Make sure that the stripes of ring 6 match up with those of ring 8!** Apply pressure with your tailstock and allow the glue to set for two days. With the addition of this ring the vase becomes delicate and easy to break. Allowing the glue to set for two days makes it less likely that you will break the joint.

With the support of the steady rest, hollow inside the bottom of ring 6. Use a round-nose scraper to smooth the entire inside of the ring at this time. Sand and apply finish. Sand the bottom of ring 6 flat in preparation for gluing on the base.

Attaching the base

The top of the vase is held by the headstock and the steady rest. The base is supported by a large live centre that fits into the underside of the faceplate. Apply glue to both surfaces and centre the base onto the bottom of ring 6 (Fig 14.13). **Make sure that the stripes on the bottom of the vase line up with those on the top.** Allow this glue to set overnight.

Final turning

If you have been very careful and if your lathe is in alignment, then your vase should run true. Clean up the joint and do final sanding at this time. Stop and

Fig 14.12 Beginning to shape ring 6

Fig 14.13 Gluing the top and bottom together. A live centre in the tailstock serves to centre the faceplate on which the base is mounted

Fig 14.14 Parting off the top of the vase

Fig 14.15 Beginning to shape the mouth with a bowl gouge

Fig 14.16 Applying finish to the mouth of the vase

check carefully for any imperfections; this is the time to remove any small turning blemishes. Apply finish to the entire outside.

Parting off and finishing the ends

Gently take the vase off the lathe and reattach the bottom end to the headstock. Support with both headstock and tailstock while you position your steady rest in the middle. Duct tape around the middle of the vase protects the finish from the wheels of the steady rest. The faceplate at the tailstock end is supported by a large live centre. Use a thin parting tool to part off the top waste block (Fig 14.14). Back out often and widen the cut. Gently shape the top of the vase with the bowl gouge and round-nose scraper (Fig 14.15). You must use a low speed, not more than 350rpm. Shape and sand the mouth at this time. Apply finish to the top of the vase (Fig 14.16).

Use your thin parting tool to part off the base from the waste block. Have a friend support the top of the vase as you part through. Use a sanding pad with hook-and-loop sandpaper to sand the bottom of the vase. Finally, apply finish to the bottom of the vase.

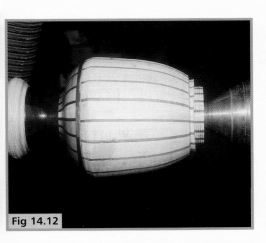

Fig 14.12

Fig 14.13

Fig 14.14

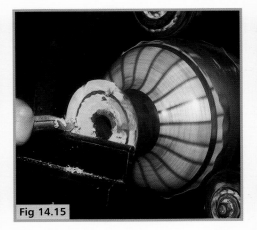

Fig 14.15

Fig 14.16

15
PEACE
BOWL

The unique feature of this bowl is the central ring with pewter inlays. I made two inlays each of the Star of David, the peace dove, and a cross. You can vary the design to suit your own taste.

I shall describe the feature ring only; all the others are plain rings made by the techniques that you learned earlier in this book.

Cutting the segments

The feature ring is made of six squares and six wedges. The mitre angle of 30° (180° ÷ 6) is cut on the wedges only. The pewter inlay will be poured into the six squares. Make a test ring to make sure that your angle is correct; in Fig 15.1 I have blacked the six wedges so that you can easily tell them from the squares.

Use your tablesaw to cut the six squares (Fig 15.2). The stock does not need to be as thick as I used. I thought thick stock would be good to dissipate the heat from the molten pewter, but this was unnecessary.

Set your mitre gauge or cutting sled to 30°. Set your stop block to the correct distance and cut your six wedges (Fig 15.3). Be sure to use a safety spacer so that the offcuts do not get wedged between the fence and the saw blade.

The six wedges will make a small circle by themselves (Fig 15.4). When the squares are added between the wedges, a much bigger circle will be created.

Routing the inlays

The six inlays are cut with a ¼in (6mm) upward-cutting spiral bit that is part of a router inlay kit. Make a jig to hold the squares while the inlay is cut into them (Fig 15.5). Design your inlays on paper and transfer the final design to ¼in (6mm) plywood.

The Star of David consists of two equilateral triangles reversed onto each other, so to make an inlay pattern for this you only need make one equilateral triangle pattern. Cut out the plywood guide and attach it to the jig that holds the ring squares (Fig 15.6).

Let the brass collar run against the plywood guide while the router bit cuts around the pattern (Fig 15.7). Now reverse and centre the pattern so that you can make the second cut (Fig 15.8). When the two triangles are cut, a Star of David is created (Fig 15.9).

You can make other patterns quite easily. The outline of a dove is pretty and easy to make (Fig 15.10). A group of three crosses makes an attractive inlay (Fig 15.11).

Fig 15.1 A test ring to check the tablesaw set-up

Fig 15.2 Cutting the six squares for the feature ring

Fig 15.3 Cutting the six wedges

Fig 15.4 The components for the feature ring

Fig 15.5 A jig to hold the squares for routing

Fig 15.6 The plywood template attached to the routing jig

Fig 15.7 First stage of routing the Star of David pattern

Fig 15.8 Moving the template into position for the second cut

Fig 15.9 The two triangle cuts make a Star of David

Pouring pewter

Pewter is an alloy of several different metals including tin, antimony, copper, and lead. For safety reasons, try to buy lead-free pewter from a hobby supply store. If you cannot, work in a well-ventilated area, preferably outside. Pewter can be melted and poured easily. I bought my melting unit at a fish-bait supply store; it was designed to melt lead fishing weights.

Fig 15.1

Fig 15.2

Fig 15.3

Fig 15.4

Fig 15.5

Fig 15.6

Fig 15.7

Fig 15.8

Fig 15.9

Make a couple of test pours before making a real pour into your ring squares. It is important to have the pewter hot enough so that it pours easily; however, you do not want it so hot that it burns the wood. A temperature of 200–300° is about right, but consult your pewter supplier for advice on this. Arrange your melting unit, pewter and squares close together on your workbench (Fig 15.12). **Wear safety glasses and a leather apron to keep the hot metal away from you.**

Safety precautions for working with molten metal

- Wear: face shield, thick leather gloves, thick leather apron that covers your shoes.
- Pour *away* from you.
- Pour the metal in a controlled motion, not too fast and not too slow.
- Make sure your work area is uncluttered, so that you cannot trip on anything.
- Do a trial run with a cold system first.

Carefully pour the hot pewter into the recess (Fig 15.13). Pour a little excess metal to allow for contraction as the metal cools. Pour pewter into all the inlays in the same manner.

Allow the pewter to cool, then use your belt sander to sand off excess metal (Fig 15.14).

Assembling the ring

For visual appeal, place thin contrasting veneers between the squares and wedges. Apply yellow glue and use two hose clamps to bring the sections together (Fig 15.15). Allow this ring to set for 24 hours before proceeding.

Making the bowl

Assemble the bowl by the standard method and shape it with your bowl gouge (Fig 15.16). When turning the bowl, use a low speed of 300–500rpm; excessive speed could throw the pewter out of the inlay. Make sure that your bowl gouge is very sharp when cutting the pewter. Take very gentle cuts; aggressive cutting will cause pieces of wood on the leading edge of the pewter to break free. Sand and apply finish in the normal way.

Fig 15.10 A pattern for the dove; the inner detail of the wing can be routed freehand

Fig 15.11 An alternative treatment for the cross pattern

Fig 15.12 All the ingredients for the pewter work. One of my test pieces is about to be melted down and reused

Fig 15.13 Pouring the molten pewter into the routed pattern

Fig 15.14 Finished inlay, with excess pewter sanded off

Fig 15.15 The ring assembled, with contrasting veneers between the segments for visual impact

Fig 15.16 Turn at a low speed to avoid damage to the inlay

Fig 15.10

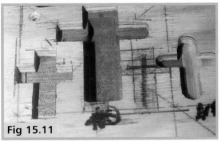

Fig 15.11

Fig 15.12

Fig 15.13

Fig 15.14

Fig 15.15

Fig 15.16

A GALLERY OF SEGMENTED TURNING

Colin Delory (no. 1)
Surrey, BC, Canada
(photo: Ron Hampton)

1 *Holly and walnut vase*

Kevin Neelley (nos. 2–5)
Lenexa, Kansas
(photos by courtesy of Kevin Neelley)

2 *Leaf-patterned vase*

3 *Bowl with zigzag band*

4 *Bowl with Native American motif*

5 *Bowl with mosaic band*

Ed Zbik (nos. 6–10)
San Diego, California
(photos by courtesy of Ed Zbik)

6 Hopi bowl

7 Dragon bowl

8 Hopi bowl

9 Greek key bowl

10 Feathers bowl

127

Richard J. Pagano (nos. 11–14)
Grafton, New York
(*photos by courtesy of Richard J. Pagano*)

12 Hopi-style jar

11 Mata Ortiz-style jar

13 Hopi-style bowl

14 Hopi-style platter

Allen Quandee
(nos. 15–17)
Cape Coral, Florida
(photos by courtesy of Allen Quandee)

15 Suspended vase

16 Vase on stand

17 Southwestern vase

Andrew C. Chen (nos. 18–19)
College Station, Texas
(photos by courtesy of Andrew C. Chen)

18 Segmented vessel

19 Segmented vessel

Hillard Gerhardt (nos. 20–22)
Cedar Crest, New Mexico
(photos by courtesy of Hillard Gerhardt)

20 Vase with zigzag motif

21 Large vase

22 Vase with Native American motifs

Delbert Dowdy
(nos. 23–24)
Wake Village, Texas
(photos: Ron Hampton)

23 Bird house

24 Segmented bowl with pierced foot

James P. Davis (nos. 25–27)
Midland, Texas
(photos: Ron Hampton)

25 Urn with feather motif

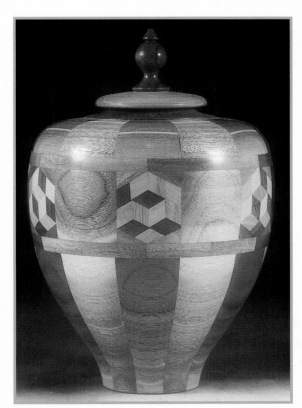

26 Urn with geometric motifs

27 Segmented bowl

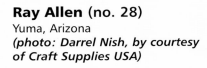

Ray Allen (no. 28)
Yuma, Arizona
*(photo: Darrel Nish, by courtesy
of Craft Supplies USA)*

28 Three segmented vessels

Curt Theobald (nos. 29–32)
Pine Bluffs, Wyoming
(photos by courtesy of Curt Theobald)

30 Dragonfly (Petroglyph series)

29 Wind River series

31 Lightning Snake

32 1600 Zuñi nested hollow forms

Linda Salter (nos. 33–34)
San Carlos, California
(photos: Paul Tedrick)

34 Desert scene

33 Desert night scene

Keith Tompkins (nos. 35–36)
Tivoli, New York
(photos by courtesy of Keith Tompkins)

35 Diamonds

36 African Flower

Explanatory note to the mathematical tables

Table A: Basic segmented ring guide (pages 135–7)

This gives data for the ordinary rings featured in nearly all the projects in this book. Choose the number of segments in the ring you wish to make, and look up this number in the first (left-hand) column. The second column shows the overall angle between the two sides of the segment, while the third indicates the angle to which each side of the segment must be cut. (The mitre gauge must be set to the *complement* of this angle; that is, 90° minus this angle.) When using a framing square to measure the angle (see pages 26–8), set the horizontal leg of the square to 20in and the vertical leg to the measurement shown in the 'V' column. The rest of the table shows the length to which each segment must be cut to make a ring of the required diameter. Look up the diameter you require in the top row, then move down the column until you come to the number corresponding to the required number of segments. For example, to make a ring of 4.25in diameter with 18 segments, a segment length of 0.749in is needed. (In practice, the segments need not be measured to this degree of accuracy; see page 18.)

Table B: Compound mitre table for tapered stave construction (pages 138–41)

This table and the next apply to projects such as the Easter Sunrise bowl (Chapter 13), where two angles are cut at the same time. The number of segments is shown down the left-hand side of the table, and the slope of the bowl side, in degrees, is indicated along the top (0° indicates a horizontal surface, 90° a vertical one). Where these two rows meet, you will find the mitre-gauge angle (MG) and the blade-tilt angle (BT) for a ring of these specifications (see pages 105–6).

Table C: Framing square compound mitre table (pages 142–7)

Determine the slope of the bowl side first, then look up the relevant section of the table, which shows the mitre-gauge angle (MG) and blade-tilt angle (BT) for any given number of segments. The 'V' column in each case shows the distance to be set on the vertical arm of the framing square when the horizontal arm is set to 20in (see pages 26–8).

The tables were prepared by James P. Davis of Midland, Texas, and are reproduced here with his permission.

Table A: Basic segmented ring guide

Ring diameter (segment width)

Number of sides or segments	Segment angle	Mitre angle	V (inches)	3.00	3.25	3.50	3.75	4.00	4.25	4.50	4.75	5.00	5.25	5.50	5.75	6.00	6.25	6.50	6.75	7.00	7.25	7.50	7.75	8.00	8.25	8.50	8.75	9.00	9.25	9.50	9.75
4	90.00	45	20.000	3.000	3.250	3.500	3.750	4.000	4.250	4.500	4.750	5.000	5.250	5.500	5.750	6.000	6.250	6.500	6.750	7.000	7.250	7.500	7.750	8.000	8.250	8.500	8.750	9.000	9.250	9.500	9.750
5	72.00	36.00	14.531	2.180	2.361	2.543	2.725	2.906	3.088	3.269	3.451	3.633	3.814	3.996	4.178	4.359	4.541	4.723	4.904	5.086	5.267	5.449	5.631	5.812	5.994	6.176	6.357	6.539	6.721	6.902	7.084
6	60.00	30.00	11.547	1.732	1.876	2.021	2.165	2.309	2.454	2.598	2.742	2.887	3.031	3.175	3.320	3.464	3.608	3.753	3.897	4.041	4.186	4.330	4.474	4.619	4.763	4.907	5.052	5.196	5.340	5.485	5.629
7	51.43	25.71	9.631	1.445	1.565	1.686	1.806	1.926	2.047	2.167	2.287	2.408	2.528	2.649	2.769	2.889	3.010	3.130	3.251	3.371	3.491	3.612	3.732	3.853	3.973	4.093	4.214	4.334	4.455	4.575	4.695
8	45.00	22.50	8.284	1.243	1.346	1.450	1.553	1.657	1.760	1.864	1.968	2.071	2.175	2.278	2.382	2.485	2.589	2.692	2.796	2.899	3.003	3.107	3.210	3.314	3.417	3.521	3.624	3.728	3.831	3.935	4.039
9	40.00	20.00	7.279	1.092	1.183	1.274	1.365	1.456	1.547	1.638	1.729	1.820	1.911	2.002	2.093	2.184	2.275	2.366	2.457	2.548	2.639	2.730	2.821	2.912	3.003	3.094	3.185	3.276	3.367	3.458	3.549
10	36.00	18.00	6.498	0.975	1.056	1.137	1.218	1.300	1.381	1.462	1.543	1.625	1.706	1.787	1.868	1.950	2.031	2.112	2.193	2.274	2.356	2.437	2.518	2.599	2.681	2.762	2.843	2.924	3.006	3.087	3.168
11	32.73	16.36	5.873	0.881	0.954	1.028	1.101	1.175	1.248	1.321	1.395	1.468	1.542	1.615	1.688	1.762	1.835	1.909	1.982	2.055	2.129	2.202	2.276	2.349	2.422	2.496	2.569	2.643	2.716	2.789	2.863
12	30.000	15.000	5.359	0.804	0.871	0.938	1.005	1.072	1.139	1.206	1.273	1.340	1.407	1.474	1.541	1.608	1.675	1.742	1.809	1.876	1.943	2.010	2.077	2.144	2.211	2.278	2.345	2.412	2.479	2.546	2.613
13	27.69	13.85	4.930	0.739	0.801	0.863	0.924	0.986	1.048	1.109	1.171	1.232	1.294	1.356	1.417	1.479	1.540	1.602	1.664	1.725	1.787	1.849	1.910	1.972	2.033	2.095	2.157	2.218	2.280	2.342	2.403
14	25.71	12.86	4.565	0.685	0.742	0.799	0.856	0.913	0.970	1.027	1.084	1.141	1.198	1.255	1.312	1.369	1.427	1.484	1.541	1.598	1.655	1.712	1.769	1.826	1.883	1.940	1.997	2.054	2.111	2.168	2.225
15	24.00	12.00	4.251	0.638	0.691	0.744	0.797	0.850	0.903	0.957	1.010	1.063	1.116	1.169	1.222	1.275	1.328	1.382	1.435	1.488	1.541	1.594	1.647	1.700	1.754	1.807	1.860	1.913	1.966	2.019	2.072
16	22.50	11.25	3.978	0.597	0.646	0.696	0.746	0.796	0.845	0.895	0.945	0.995	1.044	1.094	1.144	1.193	1.243	1.293	1.343	1.392	1.442	1.492	1.542	1.591	1.641	1.691	1.740	1.790	1.840	1.890	1.939
17	21.18	10.59	3.739	0.561	0.608	0.654	0.701	0.748	0.794	0.841	0.888	0.935	0.981	1.028	1.075	1.122	1.168	1.215	1.262	1.309	1.355	1.402	1.449	1.495	1.542	1.589	1.636	1.682	1.729	1.776	1.823
18	20.00	10.00	3.527	0.529	0.573	0.617	0.661	0.705	0.749	0.793	0.838	0.882	0.926	0.970	1.014	1.058	1.102	1.146	1.190	1.234	1.278	1.322	1.367	1.411	1.455	1.499	1.543	1.587	1.631	1.675	1.719
19	18.95	9.47	3.337	0.501	0.542	0.584	0.626	0.667	0.709	0.751	0.793	0.834	0.876	0.918	0.960	1.001	1.043	1.085	1.126	1.168	1.210	1.252	1.293	1.335	1.377	1.418	1.460	1.502	1.544	1.585	1.627
20	18.00	9.00	3.168	0.475	0.515	0.554	0.594	0.634	0.673	0.713	0.752	0.792	0.832	0.871	0.911	0.950	0.990	1.029	1.069	1.109	1.148	1.188	1.227	1.267	1.307	1.346	1.386	1.425	1.465	1.505	1.544
21	17.14	8.57	3.015	0.452	0.490	0.528	0.565	0.603	0.641	0.678	0.716	0.754	0.791	0.829	0.867	0.904	0.942	0.980	1.017	1.055	1.093	1.130	1.168	1.206	1.243	1.281	1.319	1.357	1.394	1.432	1.470
22	16.36	8.18	2.876	0.431	0.467	0.503	0.539	0.575	0.611	0.647	0.683	0.719	0.755	0.791	0.827	0.863	0.899	0.935	0.971	1.006	1.042	1.078	1.114	1.150	1.186	1.222	1.258	1.294	1.330	1.366	1.402
23	15.65	7.83	2.749	0.412	0.447	0.481	0.515	0.550	0.584	0.618	0.653	0.687	0.721	0.756	0.790	0.825	0.859	0.893	0.928	0.962	0.996	1.031	1.065	1.100	1.134	1.168	1.203	1.237	1.271	1.306	1.340
24	15.00	7.50	2.633	0.395	0.428	0.461	0.494	0.527	0.560	0.592	0.625	0.658	0.691	0.724	0.757	0.790	0.823	0.856	0.889	0.922	0.954	0.987	1.020	1.053	1.086	1.119	1.152	1.185	1.218	1.251	1.284
25	14.40	7.20	2.527	0.379	0.411	0.442	0.474	0.505	0.537	0.568	0.600	0.632	0.663	0.695	0.726	0.758	0.790	0.821	0.853	0.884	0.916	0.947	0.979	1.011	1.042	1.074	1.105	1.137	1.169	1.200	1.232
26	13.85	6.92	2.428	0.364	0.395	0.425	0.455	0.486	0.516	0.546	0.577	0.607	0.637	0.668	0.698	0.729	0.759	0.789	0.820	0.850	0.880	0.911	0.941	0.971	1.002	1.032	1.062	1.093	1.123	1.154	1.184
27	13.33	6.67	2.338	0.351	0.380	0.409	0.438	0.468	0.497	0.526	0.555	0.584	0.614	0.643	0.672	0.701	0.731	0.760	0.789	0.818	0.847	0.877	0.906	0.935	0.964	0.994	1.023	1.052	1.081	1.110	1.140
28	12.86	6.43	2.253	0.338	0.366	0.394	0.423	0.451	0.479	0.507	0.535	0.563	0.592	0.620	0.648	0.676	0.704	0.732	0.761	0.789	0.817	0.845	0.873	0.901	0.930	0.958	0.986	1.014	1.042	1.070	1.099
29	12.41	6.21	2.175	0.326	0.353	0.381	0.408	0.435	0.462	0.489	0.517	0.544	0.571	0.598	0.625	0.653	0.680	0.707	0.734	0.761	0.788	0.816	0.843	0.870	0.897	0.924	0.952	0.979	1.006	1.033	1.060
30	12.00	6.00	2.102	0.315	0.342	0.368	0.394	0.420	0.447	0.473	0.499	0.526	0.552	0.578	0.604	0.631	0.657	0.683	0.709	0.736	0.762	0.788	0.815	0.841	0.867	0.893	0.920	0.946	0.972	0.998	1.025
31	11.61	5.81	2.034	0.305	0.330	0.356	0.381	0.407	0.432	0.458	0.483	0.508	0.534	0.559	0.585	0.610	0.636	0.661	0.686	0.712	0.737	0.763	0.788	0.814	0.839	0.864	0.890	0.915	0.941	0.966	0.991
32	11.25	5.63	1.970	0.295	0.320	0.345	0.369	0.394	0.419	0.443	0.468	0.492	0.517	0.542	0.566	0.591	0.616	0.640	0.665	0.689	0.714	0.739	0.763	0.788	0.813	0.837	0.862	0.886	0.911	0.936	0.960
33	10.91	5.45	1.910	0.286	0.310	0.334	0.358	0.382	0.406	0.430	0.454	0.477	0.501	0.525	0.549	0.573	0.597	0.621	0.645	0.668	0.692	0.716	0.740	0.764	0.788	0.812	0.836	0.859	0.883	0.907	0.931
34	10.59	5.29	1.853	0.278	0.301	0.324	0.347	0.371	0.394	0.417	0.440	0.463	0.486	0.510	0.533	0.556	0.579	0.602	0.625	0.649	0.672	0.695	0.718	0.741	0.764	0.788	0.811	0.834	0.857	0.880	0.903
35	10.29	5.14	1.800	0.270	0.293	0.315	0.338	0.360	0.383	0.405	0.428	0.450	0.473	0.495	0.518	0.540	0.563	0.585	0.608	0.630	0.653	0.675	0.698	0.720	0.743	0.765	0.788	0.810	0.833	0.855	0.878
36	10.00	5.00	1.750	0.262	0.284	0.306	0.328	0.350	0.372	0.394	0.416	0.437	0.459	0.481	0.503	0.525	0.547	0.569	0.591	0.612	0.634	0.656	0.678	0.700	0.722	0.744	0.766	0.787	0.809	0.831	0.853
37	9.73	4.86	1.702	0.255	0.277	0.298	0.319	0.340	0.362	0.383	0.404	0.426	0.447	0.468	0.489	0.511	0.532	0.553	0.575	0.596	0.617	0.638	0.660	0.681	0.702	0.723	0.745	0.766	0.787	0.809	0.830
38	9.47	4.74	1.657	0.249	0.269	0.290	0.311	0.331	0.352	0.373	0.394	0.414	0.435	0.456	0.476	0.497	0.518	0.539	0.559	0.580	0.601	0.621	0.642	0.663	0.684	0.704	0.725	0.746	0.766	0.787	0.808
39	9.23	4.62	1.615	0.242	0.262	0.283	0.303	0.323	0.343	0.363	0.383	0.404	0.424	0.444	0.464	0.484	0.505	0.525	0.545	0.565	0.585	0.605	0.626	0.646	0.666	0.686	0.706	0.727	0.747	0.767	0.787
40	9.00	4.50	1.574	0.236	0.256	0.275	0.295	0.315	0.334	0.354	0.374	0.394	0.413	0.433	0.453	0.472	0.492	0.512	0.531	0.551	0.571	0.590	0.610	0.630	0.649	0.669	0.689	0.708	0.728	0.748	0.767
41	8.78	4.39	1.535	0.230	0.250	0.269	0.288	0.307	0.326	0.345	0.365	0.384	0.403	0.422	0.441	0.461	0.480	0.499	0.518	0.537	0.557	0.576	0.595	0.614	0.633	0.653	0.672	0.691	0.710	0.729	0.749
42	8.57	4.29	1.499	0.225	0.244	0.262	0.281	0.300	0.318	0.337	0.356	0.375	0.393	0.412	0.431	0.450	0.468	0.487	0.506	0.525	0.543	0.562	0.581	0.600	0.618	0.637	0.656	0.674	0.693	0.712	0.731
43	8.37	4.19	1.464	0.220	0.238	0.256	0.274	0.293	0.311	0.329	0.348	0.366	0.384	0.403	0.421	0.439	0.457	0.476	0.494	0.512	0.531	0.549	0.567	0.586	0.604	0.622	0.640	0.659	0.677	0.695	0.714
44	8.18	4.09	1.430	0.215	0.232	0.250	0.268	0.286	0.304	0.322	0.340	0.358	0.375	0.393	0.411	0.429	0.447	0.465	0.483	0.501	0.519	0.536	0.554	0.572	0.590	0.608	0.626	0.644	0.662	0.679	0.697
45	8.00	4.00	1.399	0.210	0.227	0.245	0.262	0.280	0.297	0.315	0.332	0.350	0.367	0.385	0.402	0.420	0.437	0.455	0.472	0.489	0.507	0.524	0.542	0.559	0.577	0.594	0.612	0.629	0.647	0.664	0.682
46	7.83	3.91	1.368	0.205	0.222	0.239	0.257	0.274	0.291	0.308	0.325	0.342	0.359	0.376	0.393	0.410	0.428	0.445	0.462	0.479	0.496	0.513	0.530	0.547	0.564	0.581	0.599	0.616	0.633	0.650	0.667
47	7.66	3.83	1.339	0.201	0.218	0.234	0.251	0.268	0.285	0.301	0.318	0.335	0.351	0.368	0.385	0.402	0.418	0.435	0.452	0.469	0.485	0.502	0.519	0.536	0.552	0.569	0.586	0.602	0.619	0.636	0.653
48	7.50	3.75	1.311	0.197	0.213	0.229	0.246	0.262	0.279	0.295	0.311	0.328	0.344	0.360	0.377	0.393	0.410	0.426	0.442	0.459	0.475	0.492	0.508	0.524	0.541	0.557	0.574	0.590	0.606	0.623	0.639

135

Table A (continued)

Number of sides or segments	Segment angle	Mitre angle	V (inches)	Ring diameter																											
				10.00	10.25	10.50	10.75	11.00	11.25	11.50	11.75	12.00	12.25	12.50	12.75	13.00	13.25	13.50	13.75	14.00	14.25	14.50	14.75	15.00	15.25	15.50	15.75	16.00	16.25	16.50	16.75
				Segment width																											
4	90.00	45	20.000	10.000	10.250	10.500	10.750	11.000	11.250	11.500	11.750	12.000	12.250	12.500	12.750	13.000	13.250	13.500	13.750	14.000	14.250	14.500	14.750	15.000	15.250	15.500	15.750	16.000	16.250	16.500	16.750
5	72.00	36.00	14.531	7.265	7.447	7.629	7.810	7.992	8.174	8.355	8.537	8.719	8.900	9.082	9.263	9.445	9.627	9.808	9.990	10.172	10.353	10.535	10.717	10.898	11.080	11.261	11.443	11.625	11.806	11.988	12.170
6	60.00	30.00	11.547	5.774	5.918	6.062	6.207	6.351	6.495	6.640	6.784	6.928	7.073	7.217	7.361	7.506	7.650	7.794	7.939	8.083	8.227	8.372	8.516	8.660	8.805	8.949	9.093	9.238	9.382	9.526	9.671
7	51.43	25.71	9.631	4.816	4.936	5.057	5.177	5.297	5.418	5.538	5.659	5.779	5.899	6.020	6.140	6.260	6.381	6.501	6.622	6.742	6.862	6.983	7.103	7.224	7.344	7.464	7.585	7.705	7.826	7.946	8.066
8	45.00	22.50	8.284	4.142	4.246	4.349	4.453	4.556	4.660	4.763	4.867	4.971	5.074	5.178	5.281	5.385	5.488	5.592	5.695	5.799	5.903	6.006	6.110	6.213	6.317	6.420	6.524	6.627	6.731	6.835	6.938
9	40.00	20.00	7.279	3.640	3.731	3.822	3.913	4.004	4.095	4.186	4.277	4.368	4.459	4.550	4.641	4.732	4.823	4.914	5.005	5.096	5.187	5.278	5.369	5.460	5.551	5.642	5.733	5.824	5.915	6.006	6.097
10	36.00	18.00	6.498	3.249	3.330	3.412	3.493	3.574	3.655	3.737	3.818	3.899	3.980	4.061	4.143	4.224	4.305	4.386	4.468	4.549	4.630	4.711	4.793	4.874	4.955	5.036	5.117	5.199	5.280	5.361	5.442
11	32.73	16.36	5.873	2.936	3.010	3.083	3.156	3.230	3.303	3.377	3.450	3.524	3.597	3.670	3.744	3.817	3.891	3.964	4.037	4.111	4.184	4.258	4.331	4.404	4.478	4.551	4.625	4.698	4.771	4.845	4.918
12	30.00	15.00	5.359	2.679	2.746	2.813	2.880	2.947	3.014	3.081	3.148	3.215	3.282	3.349	3.416	3.483	3.550	3.617	3.684	3.751	3.818	3.885	3.952	4.019	4.086	4.153	4.220	4.287	4.354	4.421	4.488
13	27.69	13.85	4.930	2.465	2.526	2.588	2.650	2.711	2.773	2.834	2.896	2.958	3.019	3.081	3.143	3.204	3.266	3.327	3.389	3.451	3.512	3.574	3.636	3.697	3.759	3.820	3.882	3.944	4.005	4.067	4.129
14	25.71	12.86	4.565	2.282	2.339	2.397	2.454	2.511	2.568	2.625	2.682	2.739	2.796	2.853	2.910	2.967	3.024	3.081	3.138	3.195	3.252	3.310	3.367	3.424	3.481	3.538	3.595	3.652	3.709	3.766	3.823
15	24.00	12.00	4.251	2.126	2.179	2.232	2.285	2.338	2.391	2.444	2.498	2.551	2.604	2.657	2.710	2.763	2.816	2.870	2.923	2.976	3.029	3.082	3.135	3.188	3.241	3.295	3.348	3.401	3.454	3.507	3.560
16	22.50	11.25	3.978	1.989	2.039	2.089	2.138	2.188	2.238	2.287	2.337	2.387	2.437	2.486	2.536	2.586	2.636	2.685	2.735	2.785	2.835	2.884	2.934	2.984	3.033	3.083	3.133	3.183	3.232	3.282	3.332
17	21.18	10.59	3.739	1.869	1.916	1.963	2.010	2.056	2.103	2.150	2.196	2.243	2.290	2.337	2.383	2.430	2.477	2.524	2.570	2.617	2.664	2.711	2.757	2.804	2.851	2.897	2.944	2.991	3.038	3.084	3.131
18	20.00	10.00	3.527	1.763	1.807	1.851	1.896	1.940	1.984	2.028	2.072	2.116	2.160	2.204	2.248	2.292	2.336	2.380	2.424	2.469	2.513	2.557	2.601	2.645	2.689	2.733	2.777	2.821	2.865	2.909	2.953
19	18.95	9.47	3.337	1.669	1.710	1.752	1.794	1.836	1.877	1.919	1.961	2.002	2.044	2.086	2.128	2.169	2.211	2.253	2.294	2.336	2.378	2.420	2.461	2.503	2.545	2.586	2.628	2.670	2.712	2.753	2.795
20	18.00	9.00	3.168	1.584	1.623	1.663	1.703	1.742	1.782	1.821	1.861	1.901	1.940	1.980	2.019	2.059	2.099	2.138	2.178	2.217	2.257	2.297	2.336	2.376	2.415	2.455	2.495	2.534	2.574	2.613	2.653
21	17.14	8.57	3.015	1.507	1.545	1.583	1.620	1.658	1.696	1.733	1.771	1.809	1.846	1.884	1.922	1.959	1.997	2.035	2.072	2.110	2.148	2.186	2.223	2.261	2.299	2.336	2.374	2.412	2.449	2.487	2.525
22	16.36	8.18	2.876	1.438	1.474	1.510	1.546	1.582	1.618	1.653	1.689	1.725	1.761	1.797	1.833	1.869	1.905	1.941	1.977	2.013	2.049	2.085	2.121	2.157	2.193	2.229	2.265	2.300	2.336	2.372	2.408
23	15.65	7.83	2.749	1.374	1.409	1.443	1.478	1.512	1.546	1.581	1.615	1.649	1.684	1.718	1.752	1.787	1.821	1.856	1.890	1.924	1.959	1.993	2.027	2.062	2.096	2.130	2.165	2.199	2.234	2.268	2.302
24	15.00	7.50	2.633	1.317	1.349	1.382	1.415	1.448	1.481	1.514	1.547	1.580	1.613	1.646	1.679	1.711	1.744	1.777	1.810	1.843	1.876	1.909	1.942	1.975	2.008	2.041	2.074	2.106	2.139	2.172	2.205
25	14.40	7.20	2.527	1.263	1.295	1.326	1.358	1.390	1.421	1.453	1.484	1.516	1.548	1.579	1.611	1.642	1.674	1.705	1.737	1.769	1.800	1.832	1.863	1.895	1.927	1.958	1.990	2.021	2.053	2.084	2.116
26	13.85	6.92	2.428	1.214	1.245	1.275	1.305	1.336	1.366	1.396	1.427	1.457	1.487	1.518	1.548	1.578	1.609	1.639	1.670	1.700	1.730	1.761	1.791	1.821	1.852	1.882	1.912	1.943	1.973	2.003	2.034
27	13.33	6.67	2.338	1.169	1.198	1.227	1.256	1.286	1.315	1.344	1.373	1.403	1.432	1.461	1.490	1.519	1.549	1.578	1.607	1.636	1.666	1.695	1.724	1.753	1.782	1.812	1.841	1.870	1.899	1.929	1.958
28	12.86	6.43	2.253	1.127	1.155	1.183	1.211	1.239	1.268	1.296	1.324	1.352	1.380	1.408	1.437	1.465	1.493	1.521	1.549	1.577	1.606	1.634	1.662	1.690	1.718	1.746	1.775	1.803	1.831	1.859	1.887
29	12.41	6.21	2.175	1.088	1.115	1.142	1.169	1.196	1.224	1.251	1.278	1.305	1.332	1.359	1.387	1.414	1.441	1.468	1.495	1.523	1.550	1.577	1.604	1.631	1.659	1.686	1.713	1.740	1.767	1.794	1.822
30	12.00	6.00	2.102	1.051	1.077	1.104	1.130	1.156	1.182	1.209	1.235	1.261	1.288	1.314	1.340	1.366	1.393	1.419	1.445	1.471	1.498	1.524	1.550	1.577	1.603	1.629	1.655	1.682	1.708	1.734	1.760
31	11.61	5.81	2.034	1.017	1.042	1.068	1.093	1.119	1.144	1.169	1.195	1.220	1.246	1.271	1.297	1.322	1.347	1.373	1.398	1.424	1.449	1.475	1.500	1.525	1.551	1.576	1.602	1.627	1.652	1.678	1.703
32	11.25	5.63	1.970	0.985	1.010	1.034	1.059	1.083	1.108	1.133	1.157	1.182	1.207	1.231	1.256	1.280	1.305	1.330	1.354	1.379	1.404	1.428	1.453	1.477	1.502	1.527	1.551	1.576	1.600	1.625	1.650
33	10.91	5.45	1.910	0.955	0.979	1.003	1.027	1.050	1.074	1.098	1.122	1.146	1.170	1.194	1.217	1.241	1.265	1.289	1.313	1.337	1.361	1.385	1.408	1.432	1.456	1.480	1.504	1.528	1.552	1.576	1.599
34	10.59	5.29	1.853	0.927	0.950	0.973	0.996	1.019	1.042	1.066	1.089	1.112	1.135	1.158	1.181	1.205	1.228	1.251	1.274	1.297	1.320	1.344	1.367	1.390	1.413	1.436	1.459	1.483	1.506	1.529	1.552
35	10.29	5.14	1.800	0.900	0.923	0.945	0.968	0.990	1.013	1.035	1.058	1.080	1.103	1.125	1.148	1.170	1.193	1.215	1.238	1.260	1.283	1.305	1.328	1.350	1.373	1.395	1.418	1.440	1.463	1.485	1.508
36	10.00	5.00	1.750	0.875	0.897	0.919	0.941	0.962	0.984	1.006	1.028	1.050	1.072	1.094	1.115	1.137	1.159	1.181	1.203	1.225	1.247	1.269	1.290	1.312	1.334	1.356	1.378	1.400	1.422	1.444	1.465
37	9.73	4.86	1.702	0.851	0.872	0.894	0.915	0.936	0.958	0.979	1.000	1.021	1.043	1.064	1.085	1.106	1.128	1.149	1.170	1.192	1.213	1.234	1.255	1.277	1.298	1.319	1.341	1.362	1.383	1.404	1.426
38	9.47	4.74	1.657	0.829	0.849	0.870	0.891	0.911	0.932	0.953	0.974	0.994	1.015	1.036	1.056	1.077	1.098	1.119	1.139	1.160	1.181	1.202	1.222	1.243	1.264	1.284	1.305	1.326	1.347	1.367	1.388
39	9.23	4.62	1.615	0.807	0.827	0.848	0.868	0.888	0.908	0.928	0.949	0.969	0.989	1.009	1.029	1.049	1.070	1.090	1.110	1.130	1.150	1.171	1.191	1.211	1.231	1.251	1.271	1.292	1.312	1.332	1.352
40	9.00	4.50	1.574	0.787	0.807	0.826	0.846	0.866	0.885	0.905	0.925	0.944	0.964	0.984	1.003	1.023	1.043	1.062	1.082	1.102	1.121	1.141	1.161	1.181	1.200	1.220	1.240	1.259	1.279	1.299	1.318
41	8.78	4.39	1.535	0.768	0.787	0.806	0.825	0.845	0.864	0.883	0.902	0.921	0.940	0.960	0.979	0.998	1.017	1.036	1.056	1.075	1.094	1.113	1.132	1.152	1.171	1.190	1.209	1.228	1.248	1.267	1.286
42	8.57	4.29	1.499	0.749	0.768	0.787	0.806	0.824	0.843	0.862	0.881	0.899	0.918	0.937	0.955	0.974	0.993	1.012	1.030	1.049	1.068	1.087	1.105	1.124	1.143	1.162	1.180	1.199	1.218	1.237	1.255
43	8.37	4.19	1.464	0.732	0.750	0.769	0.787	0.805	0.823	0.842	0.860	0.878	0.897	0.915	0.933	0.951	0.970	0.988	1.006	1.025	1.043	1.061	1.080	1.098	1.116	1.134	1.153	1.171	1.189	1.208	1.226
44	8.18	4.09	1.430	0.715	0.733	0.751	0.769	0.787	0.805	0.822	0.840	0.858	0.876	0.894	0.912	0.930	0.948	0.966	0.983	1.001	1.019	1.037	1.055	1.073	1.091	1.109	1.126	1.144	1.162	1.180	1.198
45	8.00	4.00	1.399	0.699	0.717	0.734	0.752	0.769	0.787	0.804	0.822	0.839	0.857	0.874	0.892	0.909	0.927	0.944	0.961	0.979	0.996	1.014	1.031	1.049	1.066	1.084	1.101	1.119	1.136	1.154	1.171
46	7.83	3.91	1.368	0.684	0.701	0.718	0.735	0.752	0.770	0.787	0.804	0.821	0.838	0.855	0.872	0.889	0.906	0.923	0.941	0.958	0.975	0.992	1.009	1.026	1.043	1.060	1.077	1.094	1.112	1.129	1.146
47	7.66	3.83	1.339	0.669	0.686	0.703	0.720	0.736	0.753	0.770	0.787	0.803	0.820	0.837	0.854	0.870	0.887	0.904	0.920	0.937	0.954	0.971	0.987	1.004	1.021	1.038	1.054	1.071	1.088	1.105	1.121
48	7.50	3.75	1.311	0.655	0.672	0.688	0.705	0.721	0.737	0.754	0.770	0.787	0.803	0.819	0.836	0.852	0.868	0.885	0.901	0.918	0.934	0.950	0.967	0.983	1.000	1.016	1.032	1.049	1.065	1.081	1.098

Ring diameter / Segment width

Number of sides or segments	Segment angle	Mitre angle	V (inches)	17.00	17.25	17.50	17.75	18.00	18.25	18.50	18.75	19.00	19.25	19.50	19.75	20.00	20.25	20.50	20.75	21.00	21.25	21.50	21.75	22.00	22.25	22.50	22.75	23.00	23.25	23.50	23.75
4	90.00	45	20.000	12.351	12.533	12.714	12.896	13.078	13.259	13.441	13.623	13.804	13.986	14.168	14.349	14.531	14.712	14.894	15.076	15.257	15.439	15.621	15.802	15.984	16.166	16.347	16.529	16.710	16.892	17.074	17.255
5	72.00	36.00	11.547	9.815	9.959	10.104	10.248	10.392	10.537	10.681	10.825	10.970	11.114	11.258	11.403	11.547	11.691	11.836	11.980	12.124	12.269	12.413	12.557	12.702	12.846	12.990	13.135	13.279	13.423	13.568	13.712
6	60.00	30.00	9.631	8.187	8.307	8.428	8.548	8.668	8.789	8.909	9.030	9.150	9.270	9.391	9.511	9.631	9.752	9.872	9.993	10.113	10.233	10.354	10.474	10.595	10.715	10.835	10.956	11.076	11.197	11.317	11.437
7	51.43	25.71	8.284	7.042	7.145	7.249	7.352	7.456	7.559	7.663	7.767	7.870	7.974	8.077	8.181	8.284	8.388	8.491	8.595	8.698	8.802	8.906	9.009	9.113	9.216	9.320	9.423	9.527	9.630	9.734	9.838
8	45.00	22.50	7.279	6.187	6.278	6.369	6.460	6.551	6.642	6.733	6.824	6.915	7.006	7.097	7.188	7.279	7.370	7.461	7.552	7.643	7.734	7.825	7.916	8.007	8.098	8.189	8.280	8.371	8.462	8.553	8.644
9	40.00	20.00	6.498	5.524	5.605	5.686	5.767	5.849	5.930	6.011	6.092	6.173	6.255	6.336	6.417	6.498	6.580	6.661	6.742	6.823	6.905	6.986	7.067	7.148	7.229	7.311	7.392	7.473	7.554	7.636	7.717
10	36.00	18.00	5.873	4.992	5.065	5.138	5.212	5.285	5.359	5.432	5.505	5.579	5.652	5.726	5.799	5.873	5.946	6.019	6.093	6.166	6.240	6.313	6.386	6.460	6.533	6.607	6.680	6.753	6.827	6.900	6.974
11	32.73	16.36	5.359	4.555	4.622	4.689	4.756	4.823	4.890	4.957	5.024	5.091	5.158	5.225	5.292	5.359	5.426	5.493	5.560	5.627	5.694	5.761	5.828	5.895	5.962	6.029	6.096	6.163	6.230	6.297	6.364
12	30.00	15.00	4.930	4.190	4.252	4.313	4.375	4.437	4.498	4.560	4.621	4.683	4.745	4.806	4.868	4.930	4.991	5.053	5.114	5.176	5.238	5.299	5.361	5.423	5.484	5.546	5.607	5.669	5.731	5.792	5.854
13	27.69	13.85	4.565	3.880	3.937	3.994	4.051	4.108	4.165	4.223	4.280	4.337	4.394	4.451	4.508	4.565	4.622	4.679	4.736	4.793	4.850	4.907	4.964	5.021	5.078	5.135	5.193	5.250	5.307	5.364	5.421
14	25.71	12.86	4.251	3.613	3.667	3.720	3.773	3.826	3.879	3.932	3.985	4.039	4.092	4.145	4.198	4.251	4.304	4.357	4.411	4.464	4.517	4.570	4.623	4.676	4.729	4.783	4.836	4.889	4.942	4.995	5.048
15	24.00	12.00	3.978	3.382	3.431	3.481	3.531	3.580	3.630	3.680	3.730	3.779	3.829	3.879	3.929	3.978	4.028	4.078	4.127	4.177	4.227	4.277	4.326	4.376	4.426	4.476	4.525	4.575	4.625	4.674	4.724
16	22.50	11.25	3.739	3.178	3.225	3.271	3.318	3.365	3.412	3.458	3.505	3.552	3.598	3.645	3.692	3.739	3.785	3.832	3.879	3.926	3.972	4.019	4.066	4.113	4.159	4.206	4.253	4.299	4.346	4.393	4.440
17	21.18	10.59	3.527	2.998	3.042	3.086	3.130	3.174	3.218	3.262	3.306	3.350	3.394	3.438	3.482	3.527	3.571	3.615	3.659	3.703	3.747	3.791	3.835	3.879	3.923	3.967	4.011	4.056	4.100	4.144	4.188
18	20.00	10.00	3.337	2.837	2.879	2.920	2.962	3.004	3.045	3.087	3.129	3.171	3.212	3.254	3.296	3.337	3.379	3.421	3.463	3.504	3.546	3.588	3.629	3.671	3.713	3.755	3.796	3.838	3.880	3.921	3.963
19	18.95	9.47	3.168	2.693	2.732	2.772	2.811	2.851	2.891	2.930	2.970	3.009	3.049	3.088	3.128	3.168	3.207	3.247	3.286	3.326	3.366	3.405	3.445	3.484	3.524	3.564	3.603	3.643	3.682	3.722	3.762
20	18.00	9.00	3.015	2.562	2.600	2.638	2.675	2.713	2.751	2.788	2.826	2.864	2.901	2.939	2.977	3.015	3.052	3.090	3.128	3.165	3.203	3.241	3.278	3.316	3.354	3.391	3.429	3.467	3.504	3.542	3.580
21	17.14	8.57	2.876	2.444	2.480	2.516	2.552	2.588	2.624	2.660	2.696	2.732	2.768	2.804	2.840	2.876	2.912	2.947	2.983	3.019	3.055	3.091	3.127	3.163	3.199	3.235	3.271	3.307	3.343	3.379	3.415
22	16.36	8.18	2.749	2.337	2.371	2.405	2.440	2.474	2.508	2.543	2.577	2.611	2.646	2.680	2.715	2.749	2.783	2.818	2.852	2.886	2.921	2.955	2.989	3.024	3.058	3.093	3.127	3.161	3.196	3.230	3.264
23	15.65	7.83	2.633	2.238	2.271	2.304	2.337	2.370	2.403	2.436	2.468	2.501	2.534	2.567	2.600	2.633	2.666	2.699	2.732	2.765	2.798	2.831	2.863	2.896	2.929	2.962	2.995	3.028	3.061	3.094	3.127
24	15.00	7.50	2.527	2.148	2.179	2.211	2.242	2.274	2.306	2.337	2.369	2.400	2.432	2.463	2.495	2.527	2.558	2.590	2.621	2.653	2.684	2.716	2.748	2.779	2.811	2.842	2.874	2.906	2.937	2.969	3.000
25	14.40	7.20	2.428	2.064	2.095	2.125	2.155	2.186	2.216	2.246	2.277	2.307	2.337	2.368	2.398	2.428	2.459	2.489	2.520	2.550	2.580	2.611	2.641	2.671	2.702	2.732	2.762	2.793	2.823	2.853	2.884
26	13.85	6.92	2.338	1.987	2.016	2.045	2.075	2.104	2.133	2.162	2.192	2.221	2.250	2.279	2.308	2.338	2.367	2.396	2.425	2.455	2.484	2.513	2.542	2.571	2.601	2.630	2.659	2.688	2.718	2.747	2.776
27	13.33	6.67	2.253	1.915	1.944	1.972	2.000	2.028	2.056	2.084	2.113	2.141	2.169	2.197	2.225	2.253	2.282	2.310	2.338	2.366	2.394	2.422	2.451	2.479	2.507	2.535	2.563	2.591	2.620	2.648	2.676
28	12.86	6.43	2.175	1.849	1.876	1.903	1.930	1.958	1.985	2.012	2.039	2.066	2.094	2.121	2.148	2.175	2.202	2.230	2.257	2.284	2.311	2.338	2.365	2.393	2.420	2.447	2.474	2.501	2.529	2.556	2.583
29	12.41	6.21	2.102	1.787	1.813	1.839	1.866	1.892	1.918	1.944	1.971	1.997	2.023	2.050	2.076	2.102	2.128	2.155	2.181	2.207	2.233	2.260	2.286	2.312	2.339	2.365	2.391	2.417	2.444	2.470	2.496
30	12.00	6.00	2.034	1.729	1.754	1.780	1.805	1.830	1.856	1.881	1.907	1.932	1.958	1.983	2.008	2.034	2.059	2.085	2.110	2.135	2.161	2.186	2.212	2.237	2.263	2.288	2.313	2.339	2.364	2.390	2.415
31	11.61	5.81	1.970	1.674	1.699	1.724	1.748	1.773	1.797	1.822	1.847	1.871	1.896	1.921	1.945	1.970	1.994	2.019	2.044	2.068	2.093	2.118	2.142	2.167	2.191	2.216	2.241	2.265	2.290	2.315	2.339
32	11.25	5.63	1.910	1.623	1.647	1.671	1.695	1.719	1.743	1.767	1.790	1.814	1.838	1.862	1.886	1.910	1.934	1.958	1.981	2.005	2.029	2.053	2.077	2.101	2.125	2.148	2.172	2.196	2.220	2.244	2.268
33	10.91	5.45	1.853	1.575	1.598	1.622	1.645	1.668	1.691	1.714	1.737	1.761	1.784	1.807	1.830	1.853	1.876	1.900	1.923	1.946	1.969	1.992	2.015	2.039	2.062	2.085	2.108	2.131	2.154	2.178	2.201
34	10.59	5.29	1.800	1.530	1.553	1.575	1.598	1.620	1.643	1.665	1.688	1.710	1.733	1.755	1.778	1.800	1.823	1.845	1.868	1.890	1.913	1.935	1.958	1.980	2.003	2.025	2.048	2.070	2.093	2.115	2.138
35	10.29	5.14	1.750	1.487	1.509	1.531	1.553	1.575	1.597	1.619	1.640	1.662	1.684	1.706	1.728	1.750	1.772	1.794	1.815	1.837	1.859	1.881	1.903	1.925	1.947	1.968	1.990	2.012	2.034	2.056	2.078
36	10.00	5.00	1.702	1.447	1.468	1.489	1.511	1.532	1.553	1.575	1.596	1.617	1.638	1.660	1.681	1.702	1.724	1.745	1.766	1.787	1.809	1.830	1.851	1.872	1.894	1.915	1.936	1.958	1.979	2.000	2.021
37	9.73	4.86	1.657	1.409	1.429	1.450	1.471	1.492	1.512	1.533	1.554	1.574	1.595	1.616	1.637	1.657	1.678	1.699	1.719	1.740	1.761	1.782	1.802	1.823	1.844	1.864	1.885	1.906	1.927	1.947	1.968
38	9.47	4.74	1.615	1.372	1.393	1.413	1.433	1.453	1.473	1.493	1.514	1.534	1.554	1.574	1.594	1.615	1.635	1.655	1.675	1.695	1.715	1.736	1.756	1.776	1.796	1.816	1.837	1.857	1.877	1.897	1.917
39	9.23	4.62	1.574	1.338	1.358	1.377	1.397	1.417	1.436	1.456	1.476	1.495	1.515	1.535	1.554	1.574	1.594	1.613	1.633	1.653	1.672	1.692	1.712	1.731	1.751	1.771	1.790	1.810	1.830	1.849	1.869
40	9.00	4.50	1.535	1.305	1.324	1.344	1.363	1.382	1.401	1.420	1.440	1.459	1.478	1.497	1.516	1.535	1.555	1.574	1.593	1.612	1.631	1.651	1.670	1.689	1.708	1.727	1.747	1.766	1.785	1.804	1.823
41	8.78	4.39	1.499	1.274	1.293	1.311	1.330	1.349	1.368	1.386	1.405	1.424	1.443	1.461	1.480	1.499	1.518	1.536	1.555	1.574	1.592	1.611	1.630	1.649	1.667	1.686	1.705	1.724	1.742	1.761	1.780
42	8.57	4.29	1.464	1.244	1.263	1.281	1.299	1.317	1.336	1.354	1.372	1.391	1.409	1.427	1.446	1.464	1.482	1.500	1.519	1.537	1.555	1.574	1.592	1.610	1.628	1.647	1.665	1.683	1.702	1.720	1.738
43	8.37	4.19	1.430	1.216	1.234	1.252	1.270	1.287	1.305	1.323	1.341	1.359	1.377	1.395	1.413	1.430	1.448	1.466	1.484	1.502	1.520	1.538	1.556	1.573	1.591	1.609	1.627	1.645	1.663	1.681	1.699
44	8.18	4.09	1.399	1.189	1.206	1.224	1.241	1.259	1.276	1.294	1.311	1.329	1.346	1.364	1.381	1.399	1.416	1.433	1.451	1.468	1.486	1.503	1.521	1.538	1.556	1.573	1.591	1.608	1.626	1.643	1.661
45	8.00	4.00	1.368	1.163	1.180	1.197	1.214	1.231	1.248	1.265	1.283	1.300	1.317	1.334	1.351	1.368	1.385	1.402	1.419	1.436	1.454	1.471	1.488	1.505	1.522	1.539	1.556	1.573	1.590	1.607	1.625
46	7.83	3.91	1.339	1.138	1.155	1.171	1.188	1.205	1.222	1.238	1.255	1.272	1.289	1.305	1.322	1.339	1.356	1.372	1.389	1.406	1.423	1.439	1.456	1.473	1.489	1.506	1.523	1.540	1.556	1.573	1.590
47	7.66	3.83	1.311	1.114	1.131	1.147	1.163	1.180	1.196	1.213	1.229	1.245	1.262	1.278	1.294	1.311	1.327	1.344	1.360	1.376	1.393	1.409	1.426	1.442	1.458	1.475	1.491	1.507	1.524	1.540	1.557
48	7.50	3.75																													

Table B: Compound mitre table

Tapered stave construction, two angles cut at the same time

No. of sides	Slope	0°	1	2	3	4	5	6	7	8	9	10	11	12	13	14	15	16	17	18	19	20	21	22
4	MG	45.0000	45.0044	45.0175	45.0393	45.0699	45.1092	45.1574	45.2143	45.2802	45.3549	45.4385	45.5312	45.6329	45.7437	45.8637	45.9930	46.1315	46.2795	46.4370	46.6267	46.7808	46.9674	47.1638
	BT	0.0000	0.7071	1.4141	2.1208	2.8273	3.5333	4.2388	4.9436	5.6476	6.3508	7.0530	7.7541	8.4540	9.1526	9.8497	10.5453	11.2392	11.9313	12.6214	13.3355	13.9954	14.6791	15.3602
5	MG	54.0000	54.0041	54.0166	54.0374	54.0664	54.1038	54.1495	54.2036	54.2660	54.3369	54.4161	54.5038	54.5999	54.7045	54.8177	54.9394	55.0696	55.2086	55.3362	55.6271	55.6776	55.8815	56.0343
	BT	0.0000	0.5878	1.1754	1.7628	2.3499	2.9365	3.5225	4.1078	4.6923	5.2758	5.8583	6.4395	7.0195	7.5981	8.1751	8.7504	9.3239	9.8955	10.4650	11.0472	11.5975	12.1601	12.7201
6	MG	60.0000	60.0038	60.0151	60.0340	60.0605	60.0945	60.1361	60.1853	60.2420	60.3064	60.3783	60.4579	60.5451	60.6399	60.7424	60.8526	60.9704	61.0959	61.2291	61.4733	61.5188	61.6752	61.8394
	BT	0.0000	0.5000	0.9998	1.4995	1.9988	2.4976	2.9959	3.4935	3.9902	4.4861	4.9809	5.4746	5.9670	6.4580	6.9476	7.4355	7.9216	8.4060	8.8883	9.3776	9.8466	10.3222	10.7954
7	MG	64.2857	64.2891	64.2994	64.3164	64.3403	64.3710	64.4085	64.4529	64.5041	64.5621	64.6270	64.6986	64.7772	64.8625	64.9547	65.0538	65.1597	65.2724	65.3920	65.6109	65.6517	65.7919	65.9388
	BT	0.0000	0.4339	0.8676	1.3012	1.7344	2.1672	2.5994	3.0310	3.4619	3.8919	4.3209	4.7489	5.1757	5.6011	6.0252	6.4478	6.8687	7.2879	7.7053	8.1266	8.5340	8.9452	9.3541
8	MG	67.5000	67.5031	67.5123	67.5278	67.5494	67.5771	67.6111	67.6512	67.6974	67.7498	67.8084	67.8732	67.9441	68.0211	68.1043	68.1937	68.2892	68.3908	68.4985	68.6956	68.7323	68.8584	68.9906
	BT	0.0000	0.3827	0.7652	1.1476	1.5297	1.9113	2.2925	2.6731	3.0530	3.4321	3.8102	4.1874	4.5635	4.9384	5.3120	5.6842	6.0549	6.4240	6.7914	7.1611	7.5208	7.8825	8.2421
9	MG	70.0000	70.0028	70.0112	70.0252	70.0449	70.0701	70.1009	70.1374	70.1794	70.2270	70.2803	70.3391	70.4034	70.4734	70.5489	70.6299	70.7166	70.8087	70.9064	71.0850	71.1183	71.2325	71.3521
	BT	0.0000	0.3420	0.6839	1.0256	1.3671	1.7082	2.0488	2.3889	2.7283	3.0670	3.4049	3.7418	4.0777	4.4126	4.7462	5.0785	5.4095	5.7390	6.0669	6.3961	6.7177	7.0404	7.3611
10	MG	72.0000	72.0026	72.0103	72.0231	72.0410	72.0641	72.0923	72.1256	72.1640	72.2076	72.2562	72.3099	72.3687	72.4326	72.5016	72.5756	72.6647	72.7388	72.8280	72.9910	73.0213	73.1254	73.2245
	BT	0.0000	0.3090	0.6179	0.9267	1.2352	1.5433	1.8510	2.1583	2.4649	2.7708	3.0760	3.3803	3.6837	3.9861	4.2873	4.5874	4.8862	5.1836	5.4796	5.7762	6.0669	6.3581	6.6475
11	MG	73.6364	73.6387	73.6458	73.6576	73.6741	73.6953	73.7212	73.7519	73.7872	73.8272	73.8719	73.9213	73.9754	74.0341	74.0975	74.1655	74.2382	74.3154	74.3973	74.5470	74.5748	74.6704	74.7706
	BT	0.0000	0.2817	0.5634	0.8448	1.1261	1.4070	1.6876	1.9676	2.2471	2.5260	2.8042	3.0815	3.3581	3.6336	3.9082	4.1816	4.4538	4.7248	4.9945	5.2643	5.5295	5.7947	6.0582
12	MG	75.0000	75.0022	75.0087	75.0196	75.0349	75.0545	75.0785	75.1068	75.1395	75.1765	75.2178	75.2635	75.3135	75.3677	75.4263	75.4892	75.5563	75.6277	75.7033	75.8416	75.8673	75.9556	76.0480
	BT	0.0000	0.2588	0.5175	0.7761	1.0345	1.2926	1.5503	1.8075	2.0643	2.3204	2.5759	2.8307	3.0847	3.3377	3.5899	3.8410	4.0910	4.3398	4.5874	4.8349	5.0785	5.3220	5.5639
14	MG	77.1429	77.1448	77.1504	77.1599	77.1731	77.1902	77.2110	77.2355	77.2639	77.2960	77.3318	77.3714	77.4148	77.4618	77.5126	77.5671	77.6253	77.6871	77.7527	77.8724	77.8947	77.9711	78.0512
	BT	0.0000	0.2225	0.4450	0.6673	0.8894	1.1113	1.3328	1.5540	1.7747	1.9949	2.2145	2.4335	2.6517	2.8692	3.0859	3.3016	3.5164	3.7302	3.9429	4.1553	4.3648	4.5739	4.7816
16	MG	78.7500	78.7517	78.7567	78.7650	78.7767	78.7917	78.8101	78.8317	78.8567	78.8850	78.9166	78.9516	78.9898	79.0313	79.0760	79.1240	79.1753	79.2298	79.2876	79.3930	79.4126	79.4800	79.5505
	BT	0.0000	0.1951	0.3901	0.5850	0.7798	0.9743	1.1685	1.3624	1.5558	1.7489	1.9414	2.1333	2.3246	2.5153	2.7052	2.8943	3.0825	3.2699	3.4562	3.6421	3.8259	4.0091	4.1910
18	MG	80.0000	80.0015	80.0060	80.0134	80.0239	80.0373	80.0537	80.0731	80.0954	80.1207	80.1489	80.1801	80.2143	80.2513	80.2913	80.3342	80.3800	80.4287	80.4803	80.5744	80.5920	80.6521	80.7150
	BT	0.0000	0.1736	0.3472	0.5207	0.6940	0.8672	1.0400	1.2126	1.3848	1.5566	1.7279	1.8988	2.0690	2.2387	2.4077	2.5759	2.7434	2.9101	3.0760	3.2413	3.4049	3.5678	3.7297
20	MG	81.0000	81.0013	81.0054	81.0121	81.0216	81.0337	81.0485	81.0660	81.0862	81.1090	81.1345	81.1627	81.1936	81.2270	81.2632	81.3019	81.3433	81.3872	81.4338	81.5188	81.5347	81.5889	81.6457
	BT	0.0000	0.1564	0.3128	0.4691	0.6252	0.7812	0.9369	1.0924	1.2475	1.4023	1.5566	1.7105	1.8638	2.0167	2.1689	2.3204	2.4713	2.6215	2.7708	2.9196	3.0670	3.2137	3.3595
22	MG	81.8182	81.8194	81.8231	81.8292	81.8378	81.8489	81.8624	81.8784	81.8967	81.9176	81.9408	81.9665	81.9946	82.0251	82.0581	82.0934	82.1311	82.1712	82.2136	82.2911	82.3055	82.3550	82.4067
	BT	0.0000	0.1423	0.2846	0.4268	0.5688	0.7107	0.8524	0.9938	1.1349	1.2757	1.4161	1.5561	1.6956	1.8346	1.9730	2.1109	2.2481	2.3847	2.5205	2.6559	2.7899	2.9234	3.0560
24	MG	82.5000	82.5011	82.5045	82.5102	82.5181	82.5282	82.5406	82.5553	82.5722	82.5913	82.6127	82.6363	82.6621	82.6901	82.7204	82.7528	82.7874	82.8242	82.8632	82.9344	82.9476	82.9930	83.0406
	BT	0.0000	0.1305	0.2610	0.3914	0.5217	0.6518	0.7818	0.9115	1.0409	1.1700	1.2988	1.4271	1.5551	1.6826	1.8095	1.9360	2.0618	2.1871	2.3116	2.4357	2.5587	2.6811	2.8027
26	MG	83.0769	83.0780	83.0811	83.0863	83.0936	83.1030	83.1145	83.1280	83.1437	83.1613	83.1811	83.2029	83.2268	83.2527	83.2807	83.3106	83.3427	83.3767	83.4127	83.4785	83.4907	83.5327	83.5767
	BT	0.0000	0.1205	0.2410	0.3614	0.4818	0.6019	0.7219	0.8417	0.9612	1.0804	1.1993	1.3179	1.4360	1.5538	1.6710	1.7878	1.9040	2.0196	2.1346	2.2492	2.3627	2.4757	2.5880
28	MG	83.5714	83.5724	83.5753	83.5802	83.5870	83.5957	83.6064	83.6189	83.6335	83.6499	83.6683	83.6886	83.7108	83.7349	83.7609	83.7887	83.8185	83.8501	83.8836	83.9448	83.9562	83.9952	84.0360
	BT	0.0000	0.1120	0.2239	0.3357	0.4475	0.5591	0.6706	0.7818	0.8928	1.0036	1.1140	1.2242	1.3339	1.4432	1.5521	1.6606	1.7685	1.8759	1.9828	2.0891	2.1946	2.2996	2.4038
30	MG	84.0000	84.0009	84.0036	84.0082	84.0145	84.0227	84.0326	84.0444	84.0580	84.0733	84.0905	84.1095	84.1302	84.1527	84.1770	84.2030	84.2308	84.2604	84.2917	84.3488	84.3594	84.3959	84.4340
	BT	0.0000	0.1045	0.2090	0.3134	0.4178	0.5220	0.6260	0.7299	0.8335	0.9369	1.0400	1.1428	1.2453	1.3474	1.4490	1.5503	1.6510	1.7513	1.8510	1.9503	2.0488	2.1468	2.2441
32	MG	84.3750	84.3759	84.3784	84.3827	84.3886	84.3963	84.4056	84.4167	84.4294	84.4438	84.4599	84.4777	84.4972	84.5183	84.5411	84.5655	84.5916	84.6193	84.6487	84.7023	84.7122	84.7464	84.7822
	BT	0.0000	0.0980	0.1960	0.2939	0.3918	0.4895	0.5870	0.6844	0.7816	0.8786	0.9752	1.0716	1.1677	1.2634	1.3588	1.4537	1.5482	1.6422	1.7357	1.8288	1.9211	2.0130	2.1043
34	MG	84.7059	84.7067	84.7091	84.7131	84.7187	84.7259	84.7347	84.7451	84.7571	84.7707	84.7859	84.8026	84.8209	84.8408	84.8623	84.8853	84.9099	84.9360	84.9636	85.0141	85.0235	85.0557	85.0894
	BT	0.0000	0.0923	0.1845	0.2767	0.3688	0.4608	0.5526	0.6443	0.7358	0.8270	0.9180	1.0088	1.0992	1.1893	1.2790	1.3684	1.4573	1.5458	1.6339	1.7215	1.8084	1.8949	1.9808
36	MG	85.0000	85.0008	85.0030	85.0068	85.0121	85.0189	85.0273	85.0371	85.0484	85.0613	85.0756	85.0914	85.1087	85.1275	85.1478	85.1696	85.1928	85.2174	85.2436	85.2913	85.3001	85.3306	85.3624
	BT	0.0000	0.0872	0.1743	0.2613	0.3483	0.4352	0.5220	0.6086	0.6950	0.7812	0.8672	0.9529	1.0383	1.1234	1.2082	1.2926	1.3766	1.4602	1.5433	1.6260	1.7082	1.7899	1.8710

No. of sides	Slope	45	44	43	42	41	40	39	38	37	36	35	34	33	32	31	30	29	28	27	26	25	24	23°
4	MG	54.7356	54.2710	53.8200	53.3823	52.9578	52.5463	52.1476	51.7615	51.3879	51.0266	50.6773	50.3400	48.5572	49.7005	49.3979	49.1066	48.8264	48.5572	48.2988	48.0510	47.8137	47.5869	47.3703
	BT	30.0000	29.4193	28.8322	28.2388	27.6393	27.0340	26.4231	25.8068	25.1853	24.5588	23.9275	23.2915	22.2087	22.0064	21.3576	20.7048	20.0483	19.3882	18.7246	18.0577	17.3877	16.7147	16.0388
5	MG	62.8085	62.2070	62.0156	61.6342	61.2628	60.9013	60.5496	60.2079	59.8759	59.5536	59.2411	58.9381	57.3199	58.3610	58.0867	57.8217	57.5661	57.3199	57.0828	56.8550	56.6362	56.4266	56.2260
	BT	24.5588	24.0987	23.6325	23.1603	22.6823	22.1988	21.7098	21.2155	20.7161	20.2118	19.7027	19.1890	18.4210	18.1484	17.6218	17.0911	16.5567	16.0185	15.4768	14.9317	14.4834	13.8319	13.2774
6	MG	67.7923	67.4463	67.1082	66.7780	66.4557	66.1413	65.8349	65.5364	65.2459	64.9634	64.6888	64.4221	62.9889	63.9127	63.6698	63.4349	63.2080	62.9889	62.7777	62.5743	62.3789	62.1912	62.0114
	BT	20.7048	20.3240	19.9378	19.5461	19.1492	18.7472	18.3403	17.9285	17.5121	17.0911	16.6658	16.2361	15.6501	15.3646	14.9229	14.4775	14.0285	13.5760	13.1202	12.6612	12.1991	11.7340	11.2661
7	MG	71.1950	70.8931	70.5977	70.3087	70.0264	69.7506	69.4814	69.2189	68.9631	68.7140	68.4716	68.2360	66.9646	67.7850	67.5697	67.3611	67.1594	66.9646	66.7765	66.5953	66.4209	66.2554	66.0927
	BT	17.8666	17.5418	17.2120	16.8774	16.5381	16.1943	15.8460	15.4933	15.1364	14.7754	14.4104	14.0415	13.5700	13.2926	12.9127	12.5295	12.1429	11.7532	11.3604	10.9646	10.5660	10.1646	9.7606
8	MG	73.6751	73.4080	73.1465	72.8906	72.6402	72.3955	72.1564	71.9231	71.6955	71.4737	71.2577	71.0476	69.9111	70.6450	70.4526	70.2661	70.0856	69.9111	69.7426	69.5801	69.4236	69.2732	69.1289
	BT	15.6999	15.4165	15.1288	14.8367	14.5404	14.2400	13.9356	13.6272	13.3150	12.9991	12.6796	12.3565	11.9625	11.7002	11.3672	11.0311	10.6920	10.3499	10.0050	9.6575	9.3073	8.9546	8.5995
9	MG	75.5672	75.3282	75.0940	74.8647	74.6402	74.4206	74.2060	73.9964	73.7919	73.5925	73.3982	73.2091	72.1843	72.8464	72.6729	72.5048	72.3419	72.1843	72.0321	71.8853	71.7439	71.6079	71.4773
	BT	13.9954	13.7442	13.4889	13.2297	12.9667	12.7000	12.4296	12.1557	11.8783	11.5975	11.3134	11.0260	10.6875	10.4422	10.1458	9.8466	9.5446	9.2399	8.9327	8.6230	8.3109	7.9965	7.6799
10	MG	77.0607	76.8446	76.6327	76.4251	76.2218	76.0029	75.8285	75.6385	75.4530	75.2721	75.0958	74.9240	73.9925	74.5946	74.4369	74.2840	74.1358	73.9925	73.8540	73.7203	73.5915	73.4676	73.3486
	BT	12.6214	12.3957	12.1663	11.9333	11.6968	11.4570	11.2138	10.9674	10.7178	10.4650	10.2093	9.9507	9.6537	9.4249	9.1579	8.8883	8.6162	8.3416	8.0647	7.7855	7.5040	7.2205	6.9350
11	MG	78.2706	78.0734	77.8801	77.6906	77.5050	77.3224	77.1457	76.9721	76.8026	76.6371	76.4758	76.3187	75.4657	76.0172	75.8728	75.7328	75.5950	75.4657	75.3387	75.2162	75.0980	74.9844	74.8752
	BT	11.4911	11.2861	11.0778	10.8662	10.6514	10.4335	10.2125	9.9886	9.7617	9.5320	9.2995	9.0643	8.7997	8.5861	8.3432	8.0980	7.8504	7.6005	7.3485	7.0943	6.8382	6.5800	6.3200
12	MG	79.2714	79.0902	78.9125	78.7383	78.5676	78.4005	78.2371	78.0773	77.9212	77.7689	77.6204	77.4757	76.6894	77.1979	77.0648	76.9357	76.8105	76.6894	76.5723	76.4592	76.3503	76.2454	76.1446
	BT	10.5453	10.3576	10.1668	9.9730	9.7762	9.5766	9.3741	9.1689	8.9609	8.7504	8.5373	8.3216	8.0828	7.8831	7.6604	7.4355	7.2084	6.9792	6.7479	6.5147	6.2797	6.0428	5.8042
14	MG	80.8319	80.6761	80.5232	80.3732	80.2263	80.0824	79.9416	79.8039	79.6694	79.5380	79.4099	79.2850	78.6060	79.0452	78.9303	78.8188	78.7107	78.6060	78.5047	78.4070	78.3127	78.2220	78.1348
	BT	9.0529	8.8922	8.7289	8.5629	8.3944	8.2234	8.0500	7.8741	7.6960	7.5155	7.3328	7.1480	6.9478	6.7720	6.5809	6.3880	6.1931	5.9965	5.7980	5.5979	5.3961	5.1928	4.9879
16	MG	81.9937	81.8571	81.7229	81.5914	81.4625	81.3362	81.2125	81.0917	80.9735	80.8581	80.7456	80.6359	80.0388	80.4251	80.3240	80.2260	80.1309	80.0388	79.9497	79.8637	79.7807	79.7008	79.6241
	BT	7.9292	7.7888	7.6459	7.5009	7.3535	7.2040	7.0522	6.8984	6.7426	6.5847	6.4248	6.2630	6.0905	5.9340	5.7668	5.5978	5.4272	5.2550	5.0813	4.9060	4.7293	4.5512	4.3718
18	MG	82.8929	82.7713	82.6518	82.5347	82.4199	82.3074	82.1973	82.0895	81.9843	81.8814	81.7811	81.6833	81.1508	81.4954	81.4053	81.3178	81.2330	81.1508	81.0713	80.9946	80.9205	80.8492	80.7807
	BT	7.0530	6.9282	6.8014	6.6725	6.5415	6.4086	6.2738	6.1371	5.9986	5.8583	5.7162	5.5724	5.4206	5.2798	5.1311	4.9809	4.8292	4.6761	4.5216	4.3657	4.2085	4.0501	3.8905
20	MG	83.6098	83.5002	83.3926	83.2870	83.1835	83.0821	82.9829	82.8858	82.7909	82.6982	82.6077	82.5195	82.0391	82.3500	82.2687	82.1898	82.1132	82.0391	81.9674	81.8981	81.8313	81.7669	81.7051
	BT	6.3508	6.2386	6.1244	6.0084	5.8907	5.7711	5.6498	5.5268	5.4021	5.2758	5.1479	5.0185	4.8830	4.7551	4.6213	4.4861	4.3495	4.2117	4.0726	3.9322	3.7907	3.6481	3.5043
22	MG	84.1949	84.0952	83.9972	83.9012	83.8070	83.7147	83.6244	83.5360	83.4496	83.3652	83.2829	83.2026	82.7651	83.0482	82.9742	82.9023	82.8326	82.7651	82.6997	82.6366	82.5758	82.5171	82.4608
	BT	5.7756	5.6735	5.5698	5.4644	5.3573	5.2487	5.1384	5.0266	4.9132	4.7984	4.6822	4.5645	4.4420	4.3251	4.2034	4.0805	3.9563	3.8309	3.7044	3.5768	3.4481	3.3184	3.1877
24	MG	84.6815	84.5901	84.5003	84.4121	84.3257	84.2411	84.1582	84.0771	83.9978	83.9204	83.8448	83.7711	83.3696	83.6294	83.5615	83.4955	83.4316	83.3696	83.3096	83.2517	83.1958	83.1419	83.0902
	BT	5.2957	5.2022	5.1072	5.0105	4.9124	4.8128	4.7117	4.6093	4.5054	4.4001	4.2936	4.1857	4.0739	3.9662	3.8547	3.7420	3.6281	3.5132	3.3972	3.2802	3.1622	3.0433	2.9234
26	MG	85.0927	85.0082	84.9253	84.8439	84.7641	84.6859	84.6094	84.5345	84.4612	84.3897	84.3199	84.2518	83.8807	84.1209	84.0581	83.9972	83.9380	83.8807	83.8253	83.7718	83.7201	83.6704	83.6225
	BT	4.8894	4.8031	4.7154	4.6262	4.5356	4.4437	4.3504	4.2558	4.1599	4.0628	3.9644	3.8649	3.7620	3.6622	3.5593	3.4552	3.3501	3.2440	3.1369	3.0289	2.9200	2.8101	2.6995
28	MG	85.4448	85.3663	85.2893	85.2137	85.1395	85.0669	84.9958	84.9262	84.8581	84.7916	84.7268	84.6635	84.3187	84.5418	84.4835	84.4269	84.3719	84.3187	84.2672	84.2174	84.1694	84.1231	84.0787
	BT	4.5409	4.4608	4.3793	4.2966	4.2125	4.1271	4.0405	3.9527	3.8636	3.7734	3.6821	3.5896	3.4944	3.4015	3.3059	3.2092	3.1116	3.0131	2.9136	2.8133	2.7121	2.6102	2.5074
30	MG	85.7496	85.6763	85.6044	85.5338	85.4646	85.3968	85.3304	85.2654	85.2018	85.1398	85.0792	85.0201	84.6980	84.9065	84.8520	84.7991	84.7478	84.6980	84.6499	84.6035	84.5586	84.5154	84.4739
	BT	4.2388	4.1640	4.0880	4.0107	3.9322	3.8526	3.7717	3.6898	3.6067	3.5225	3.4372	3.3509	3.2623	3.1753	3.0861	2.9959	2.9048	2.8128	2.7200	2.6263	2.5319	2.4367	2.3408
32	MG	86.0161	85.9474	85.8800	85.8138	85.7489	85.6853	85.6230	85.5620	85.5024	85.4442	85.3874	85.3320	85.0299	85.2254	85.1743	85.1247	85.0766	85.0299	84.9848	84.9412	84.8991	84.8586	84.8196
	BT	3.9743	3.9042	3.8329	3.7605	3.6870	3.6123	3.5365	3.4596	3.3817	3.3028	3.2229	3.1420	3.0590	2.9773	2.8937	2.8091	2.7237	2.6375	2.5504	2.4626	2.3741	2.2848	2.1949
34	MG	86.2512	86.1865	86.1230	86.0607	85.9996	85.9397	85.8811	85.8237	85.7676	85.7128	85.6593	85.6071	85.3226	85.5067	85.4586	85.4119	85.3666	85.3226	85.2801	85.2391	85.1995	85.1613	85.1246
	BT	3.7408	3.6749	3.6078	3.5397	3.4704	3.4001	3.3288	3.2565	3.1832	3.1089	3.0337	2.9575	2.8796	2.8026	2.7238	2.6442	2.5638	2.4827	2.4008	2.3181	2.2348	2.1508	2.0661
36	MG	86.4600	86.3989	86.3389	86.2801	86.2223	86.1658	86.1104	86.0562	86.0032	85.9514	85.9008	85.8515	85.5828	85.7567	85.7113	85.6671	85.6243	85.5828	85.5426	85.5038	85.4664	85.4304	85.3957
	BT	3.5333	3.4710	3.4077	3.3433	3.2779	3.2115	3.1442	3.0759	3.0066	2.9365	2.8654	2.7935	2.7200	2.6472	2.5728	2.4976	2.4217	2.3450	2.2677	2.1896	2.1109	2.0315	1.9516

Table B (continued)

No. of sides	Slope	46°	47	48	49	50	51	52	53	54	55	56	57	58	59	60	61	62	63	64	65	66	67	68
4	MG	55.2139	55.7061	56.2123	56.7328	57.2676	57.8170	58.3810	58.9598	59.5536	60.1624	60.7864	61.4256	62.0800	62.7498	63.4349	64.1354	64.8513	65.5824	66.3287	67.0902	67.8666	68.6579	69.4637
4	BT	30.5740	31.1409	31.7007	32.2531	32.7978	33.3344	33.8629	34.3829	34.8941	35.3963	35.8891	36.3723	36.8456	37.3087	37.7612	38.2030	38.6336	39.0528	39.4603	39.8557	40.2388	40.6091	40.9665
5	MG	63.2200	63.6415	64.0732	64.5150	64.9668	65.4288	65.9008	66.3829	66.8750	67.3772	67.8892	68.4111	68.9429	69.4843	70.0054	70.5960	71.1660	71.7452	72.3336	72.9309	73.5370	74.1517	74.7747
5	BT	25.0126	25.4599	25.9005	26.3343	26.7610	27.1805	27.5926	27.9971	28.3938	28.7825	29.1630	29.5352	29.8988	30.2537	30.5997	30.9366	31.2641	31.5821	31.8905	32.1890	32.4775	32.7558	33.0236
6	MG	68.1462	68.5079	68.8773	69.2545	69.6394	70.0320	70.4321	70.8398	71.2549	71.6775	72.1073	72.5444	72.9886	73.4398	73.8979	74.3628	74.8344	75.3125	75.7970	76.2878	76.7847	77.2875	77.7961
6	BT	21.0799	21.4492	21.8126	22.1699	22.5210	22.8657	23.2040	23.5355	23.8603	24.1782	24.4890	24.7926	25.0889	25.3777	25.6689	25.9324	26.1980	26.4555	26.7050	26.9462	27.1791	27.4034	27.6191
7	MG	71.5034	71.8181	72.1392	72.4665	72.8001	73.1398	73.4856	73.8374	74.1952	74.5588	74.9282	75.3033	75.6839	76.0701	76.4616	76.8584	77.2604	77.6675	78.0794	78.4962	78.9176	79.3435	79.7738
7	BT	18.1864	18.5011	18.8105	19.1145	19.4129	19.7058	19.9930	20.2743	20.5497	20.8190	21.0821	21.3390	21.5895	21.8335	22.0709	22.3017	22.5256	22.7427	22.9528	23.1558	23.3516	23.5402	23.7214
8	MG	73.9475	74.2254	74.5086	74.7971	75.0908	75.3897	75.6936	76.0026	76.3165	76.6353	76.9588	77.2871	77.6199	77.9573	78.2991	78.6452	78.9955	79.3500	79.7084	80.0707	80.4369	80.8066	81.1799
8	BT	15.9787	16.2529	16.5223	16.7870	17.0468	17.3016	17.5512	17.7957	18.0350	18.2688	18.4972	18.7201	18.9373	19.1489	19.3546	19.5544	19.7483	19.9362	20.1179	20.2935	20.4628	20.6257	20.7823
9	MG	75.8110	76.0594	76.3124	76.5701	76.8322	77.0987	77.3697	77.6449	77.9244	78.2080	78.4957	78.7875	79.0831	79.3826	79.6859	79.9928	80.3033	80.6173	80.9346	81.2553	81.5791	81.9060	82.2358
9	BT	14.2426	14.4857	14.7244	14.9589	15.1889	15.4145	15.6354	15.8518	16.0634	16.2701	16.4720	16.6690	16.8609	17.0477	17.2294	17.4058	17.5769	17.7427	17.9030	18.0578	18.2070	18.3506	18.4886
10	MG	77.2810	77.5055	77.7340	77.9666	78.2031	78.4435	78.6878	78.9359	79.1877	79.4431	79.7021	79.9646	80.2305	80.4998	80.7724	81.0481	81.2069	81.6088	81.8936	82.1812	82.4716	82.7647	83.0603
10	BT	12.8435	13.0617	13.2761	13.4866	13.6931	13.8955	14.0937	14.2878	14.4775	14.6629	14.8439	15.0204	15.1924	15.3398	15.5225	15.6805	15.8337	15.9820	16.1255	16.2641	16.3976	16.5261	16.6495
11	MG	78.4715	78.6761	78.8844	79.0963	79.3118	79.5307	79.7530	79.9788	80.2078	80.4401	80.6756	80.9142	81.1558	81.4004	81.6479	81.8982	82.1513	82.4070	82.6654	82.9262	83.1895	83.4551	83.7230
11	BT	11.6926	11.8907	12.0853	12.2763	12.4636	12.6472	12.8270	13.0030	13.1750	13.3431	13.5072	13.6671	13.8230	13.9746	14.1220	14.2651	14.4039	14.5382	14.6681	14.7935	14.9144	15.0307	15.1423
12	MG	79.4560	79.6440	79.8353	80.0298	80.2276	80.4285	80.6325	80.8396	81.0496	81.1626	81.4785	81.6971	81.9185	82.1426	82.3693	82.5985	82.8302	83.0643	83.3007	83.5393	83.7802	84.0231	84.2681
12	BT	10.7299	10.9113	11.0894	11.2242	11.4356	11.6036	11.7682	11.9292	12.0865	12.2403	12.3903	12.5366	12.6791	12.8178	12.9525	13.0833	13.2102	13.3330	13.4517	13.5663	13.6767	13.7829	13.8849
14	MG	80.9907	81.1522	81.3166	81.4837	81.6536	81.8260	82.0011	82.1788	82.3589	82.5415	82.7265	82.9139	83.1035	83.2954	83.4895	83.6856	83.8839	84.0841	84.2863	84.4903	84.6961	84.9037	85.1130
14	BT	9.2109	9.3661	9.5185	9.6680	9.8146	9.9583	10.0990	10.2366	10.3711	10.5025	10.6307	10.7557	10.8774	10.9958	11.1109	11.2226	11.3309	11.4357	11.5370	11.6348	11.7290	11.8196	11.9067
16	MG	82.1329	82.2745	82.4186	82.5650	82.7138	82.8649	83.0182	83.1737	83.3314	83.4912	83.6531	83.8170	83.9828	84.1506	84.3203	84.4917	84.6650	84.8399	85.0166	85.1948	85.3746	85.5558	85.7385
16	BT	8.0673	8.2030	8.3361	8.4668	8.5949	8.7205	8.8433	8.9635	9.0810	9.1958	9.3077	9.4169	9.5231	9.6265	9.7270	9.8244	9.9189	10.0104	10.0988	10.1841	10.2663	10.3454	10.4213
18	MG	83.0168	83.1428	83.2710	83.4013	83.5336	83.6680	83.8044	83.9427	84.0829	84.2249	84.3688	84.5144	84.6618	84.8109	84.9616	85.1139	85.2678	85.4232	85.5800	85.7383	85.8978	86.0588	86.2209
18	BT	7.1757	7.2962	7.4145	7.5305	7.6443	7.7557	7.8648	7.9716	8.0759	8.1777	8.2771	8.3740	8.4683	8.5600	8.6492	8.7357	8.8195	8.9007	8.9791	9.0548	9.1277	9.1978	9.2652
20	MG	83.7214	83.8349	83.9504	84.0677	84.1869	84.3079	84.4306	84.5551	84.6813	84.8092	84.9387	85.0697	85.2024	85.3365	85.4721	85.6091	85.7475	85.8872	86.0283	86.1706	86.3141	86.4587	86.6045
20	BT	6.4612	6.5695	6.6759	6.7803	6.8826	6.9829	7.0810	7.1770	7.2707	7.3623	7.4517	7.5388	7.6236	7.7060	7.7862	7.8639	7.9393	8.0122	8.0827	8.1507	8.2163	8.2793	8.3398
22	MG	84.2964	84.3997	84.5047	84.6114	84.7198	84.8298	84.9414	85.0546	85.1694	85.2856	85.4033	85.5225	85.6430	85.7649	85.8881	86.0126	86.1384	86.2654	86.3935	86.5228	86.6532	86.7846	86.9170
22	BT	5.8758	5.9743	6.0710	6.1658	6.2588	6.3499	6.4390	6.5262	6.6114	6.6946	6.7758	6.8549	6.9319	7.0068	7.0796	7.1502	7.2187	7.2849	7.3489	7.4107	7.4702	7.5275	7.5824
24	MG	84.7746	84.8694	84.9657	85.0635	85.1629	85.2638	85.3661	85.4699	85.5751	85.6816	85.7895	85.8987	86.0092	86.1209	86.2239	86.3480	86.4632	86.5796	86.6970	86.8154	86.9349	87.0553	87.1766
24	BT	5.3876	5.4778	5.5664	5.6533	5.7385	5.8220	5.9037	5.9835	6.0616	6.1378	6.2122	6.2847	6.3552	6.4239	6.4905	6.5552	6.6179	6.6786	6.7372	6.7938	6.8483	6.9008	6.9511
26	MG	85.1787	85.2662	85.3551	85.4454	85.5372	85.6303	85.7248	85.8206	85.9177	86.0161	86.1157	86.2165	86.3184	86.4216	86.5258	86.6311	86.7374	86.8448	86.9531	87.0624	87.1726	87.2837	87.3957
26	BT	4.9742	5.0575	5.1392	5.2194	5.2980	5.3750	5.4504	5.5241	5.5962	5.6665	5.7351	5.8020	5.8671	5.9304	5.9919	6.0516	6.1094	6.1654	6.2195	6.2717	6.3220	6.3703	6.4168
28	MG	85.5246	85.6059	85.6885	85.7724	85.8576	85.9441	86.0318	86.1208	86.2110	86.3023	86.3948	86.4884	86.5831	86.6788	86.7756	86.8733	86.9721	87.0717	87.1723	87.2738	87.3761	87.4792	87.5831
28	BT	4.6196	4.6970	4.7729	4.8473	4.9203	4.9918	5.0617	5.1302	5.1970	5.2623	5.3260	5.3881	5.4485	5.5073	5.5644	5.6198	5.6735	5.7254	5.7756	5.8241	5.8707	5.9156	5.9587
30	MG	85.8242	85.9000	85.9771	86.0554	86.1350	86.2157	86.2976	86.3807	86.4648	86.5501	86.6364	86.7237	86.8121	86.9014	86.9918	87.0830	87.1751	87.2681	87.3620	87.4567	87.5521	87.6483	87.7453
30	BT	4.3122	4.3844	4.4552	4.5247	4.5928	4.6595	4.7248	4.7886	4.8510	4.9119	4.9714	5.0293	5.0857	5.1405	5.1938	5.2455	5.2955	5.3440	5.3909	5.4361	5.4796	5.5215	5.5617
32	MG	86.0860	86.1572	86.2295	86.3029	86.3775	86.4532	86.5300	86.6078	86.6867	86.7667	86.8476	86.9295	87.0123	87.0961	87.1807	87.2662	87.3526	87.4398	87.5277	87.6165	87.7060	87.7961	87.8870
32	BT	4.0431	4.1108	4.1772	4.2423	4.3061	4.3687	4.4299	4.4897	4.5482	4.6053	4.6610	4.7153	4.7681	4.8195	4.8694	4.9179	4.9648	5.0102	5.0542	5.0965	5.1373	5.1766	5.2142
34	MG	86.3170	86.3839	86.4520	86.5211	86.5913	86.6626	86.7348	86.8081	86.8824	86.9576	87.0338	87.1108	87.1888	87.2676	87.3473	87.4278	87.5090	87.5911	87.6739	87.7574	87.8416	87.9264	88.0119
34	BT	3.8057	3.8693	3.9318	3.9931	4.0531	4.1120	4.1696	4.2259	4.2809	4.3347	4.3871	4.4381	4.4879	4.5362	4.5832	4.6288	4.6730	4.7157	4.7570	4.7969	4.8353	4.8722	4.9076
36	MG	86.5221	86.5854	86.6497	86.7150	86.7813	86.8486	86.9168	86.9860	87.0562	87.1272	87.1991	87.2719	87.3456	87.4200	87.4952	87.5712	87.6480	87.7255	87.8036	87.8825	87.9620	88.0421	88.1229
36	BT	3.5945	3.6546	3.7136	3.7715	3.8282	3.8838	3.9382	3.9913	4.0433	4.0940	4.1435	4.1918	4.2387	4.2844	4.3288	4.3718	4.4135	4.4539	4.4929	4.5305	4.5668	4.6016	4.6351

No. of sides	Slope	69°	70	71	72	73	74	75	76	77	78	79	80	81	82	83	84	85	86	87	88	89	90
4	MG	70.2839	71.1183	71.9664	72.8280	73.7026	74.5898	75.4892	76.4002	77.3223	78.2549	79.1973	80.1489	81.1090	82.0769	83.0517	84.0326	85.0189	86.0097	87.0041	88.0012	89.0002	90.0000
	BT	41.3106	41.6411	41.9578	42.2602	42.5482	42.8213	43.0795	43.3224	43.5497	43.7612	43.9568	44.1360	44.2989	44.4451	44.5745	44.6870	44.7824	44.8606	44.9215	44.9651	44.9913	45.0000
5	MG	75.4060	76.0451	76.6919	77.3461	78.0075	78.6756	79.3503	80.0311	80.7178	81.4100	82.1073	82.8094	83.5158	84.2262	84.9400	85.6570	86.3767	87.0987	87.8224	88.5475	89.2735	90.0000
	BT	33.2809	33.5275	33.7632	33.9878	34.2013	34.4034	34.5940	34.7729	34.9401	35.0955	35.2388	35.3701	35.4891	35.5959	35.6903	35.7723	35.8418	35.8987	35.9430	35.9746	35.9937	36.0000
6	MG	78.3302	78.8298	79.3345	79.8842	80.4187	80.9578	81.5012	82.0487	82.6001	83.1551	83.7134	84.2749	84.8392	85.4061	85.9752	86.5464	87.1193	87.6937	88.2693	88.8457	89.4227	90.0000
	BT	27.8261	28.0243	28.2136	28.3938	28.5648	28.7266	28.8791	29.0222	29.1557	29.2797	29.3941	29.4987	29.5936	29.6786	29.7537	29.8190	29.8742	29.9195	29.9547	29.9799	29.9950	30.0000
7	MG	80.2083	80.6469	81.0894	81.5357	81.9855	82.4388	82.8953	83.3548	83.8172	84.2823	84.7499	85.2198	85.6918	86.1656	86.6412	87.1183	87.5966	88.0760	88.5562	89.0371	89.5185	90.0000
	BT	23.8952	24.0615	24.2202	24.3713	24.5146	24.6501	24.7777	24.8975	25.0092	25.1128	25.2084	25.2958	25.3751	25.4461	25.5088	25.5632	25.6093	25.6471	25.6765	25.6975	25.7101	25.7143
8	MG	81.5566	81.9366	82.3197	82.7059	83.0949	83.4866	83.8809	84.2776	84.6767	85.0778	85.4810	85.8859	86.2926	86.7007	87.1102	87.5208	87.9325	88.3450	88.7581	89.1718	89.5858	90.0000
	BT	20.9324	21.0759	21.2129	21.3432	21.4668	21.5836	21.6937	21.7968	21.8931	21.9823	22.0646	22.1399	22.2081	22.2692	22.3232	22.3701	22.4097	22.4422	22.4675	22.4855	22.4964	22.5000
9	MG	82.5686	82.9040	83.2421	83.5827	83.9258	84.2710	84.6185	84.9679	85.3193	85.6725	86.0273	86.3836	86.7412	87.1002	87.4602	87.8212	88.1831	88.5456	88.9087	89.2722	89.6361	90.0000
	BT	18.6208	18.7472	18.8678	18.9826	19.0914	19.1942	19.2910	19.3818	19.4464	19.5449	19.6173	19.6835	19.7435	19.7972	19.8446	19.8858	19.9207	19.9492	19.9714	19.9873	19.9968	20.0000
10	MG	83.3583	83.6588	83.9615	84.2664	84.5733	84.8822	85.1930	85.5055	85.8196	86.1353	86.4523	86.7707	87.0902	87.4108	87.7324	88.0548	88.3779	88.7016	89.0258	89.3503	89.6751	90.0000
	BT	16.7677	16.8808	16.9886	17.0911	17.1884	17.2803	17.3668	17.4479	17.5235	17.5936	17.6583	17.7174	17.7709	17.8189	17.8613	17.8980	17.9292	17.9547	17.9745	17.9880	17.9972	18.0000
11	MG	83.9931	84.2652	84.5394	84.8154	85.0933	85.3729	85.6541	85.9368	86.2210	86.5065	86.7933	87.0811	87.3701	87.6599	87.9506	88.2420	88.5341	88.8266	89.1196	89.4129	89.7064	90.0000
	BT	15.2493	15.3516	15.4492	15.5419	15.6299	15.7130	15.7912	15.8645	15.9329	15.9963	16.0548	16.1082	16.1566	16.2000	16.2383	16.2715	16.2996	16.3227	16.3406	16.3534	16.3611	16.3636
12	MG	84.5150	84.7638	85.0144	85.2667	85.5206	85.7760	86.0329	86.2911	86.5506	86.8114	87.0732	87.3360	87.5998	87.8644	88.1297	88.3957	88.6622	88.9292	89.1966	89.4642	89.7321	90.0000
	BT	13.9827	14.0761	14.1652	14.2499	14.3302	14.4061	14.4775	14.5444	14.6069	14.6648	14.7181	14.7669	14.8111	14.8506	14.8856	14.9159	14.9416	14.9626	14.9790	14.9906	14.9977	15.0000
14	MG	85.3239	85.5363	85.7502	85.9655	86.1822	86.4001	86.6193	86.8395	87.0608	87.2831	87.5063	87.7303	87.9551	88.1806	88.4067	88.6333	88.8604	89.0878	89.3156	89.5436	89.7718	90.0000
	BT	11.9900	12.0697	12.1457	12.2179	12.2864	12.3511	12.4119	12.4690	12.5222	12.5715	12.6170	12.6585	12.6962	12.7299	12.7597	12.7855	12.8074	12.8253	12.8392	12.8492	12.8552	12.8571
16	MG	85.9226	86.1080	86.2947	86.4826	86.6716	86.8617	87.0529	87.2450	87.4380	87.6318	87.8264	88.0217	88.2177	88.4143	88.6113	88.8089	89.0068	89.2050	89.4036	89.6023	89.8011	90.0000
	BT	10.4940	10.5635	10.6297	10.6927	10.7524	10.8088	10.8619	10.9117	10.9580	11.0011	11.0407	11.0769	11.1097	11.1391	11.1651	11.1876	11.2066	11.2222	11.2344	11.2431	11.2483	11.2500
18	MG	86.3843	86.5488	86.7145	86.8811	87.0488	87.2175	87.3870	87.5574	87.7286	87.9005	88.0730	88.2462	88.4200	88.5942	88.7690	88.9441	89.1196	89.2953	89.4713	89.6474	89.8237	90.0000
	BT	9.3297	9.3913	9.4500	9.5059	9.5589	9.6089	9.6559	9.7000	9.7412	9.7793	9.8144	9.8466	9.8756	9.9017	9.9247	9.9447	9.9616	9.9754	9.9862	9.9938	9.9985	10.0000
20	MG	86.7514	86.8993	87.0482	87.1980	87.3487	87.5002	87.6526	87.8057	87.9595	88.1139	88.2690	88.4246	88.5807	88.7372	88.8942	89.0515	89.2091	89.3670	89.5251	89.6833	89.8416	90.0000
	BT	8.3977	8.4531	8.5059	8.5561	8.6037	8.6486	8.6909	8.7305	8.7675	8.8017	8.8333	8.8622	8.8883	8.9117	8.9324	8.9503	8.9655	8.9779	8.9876	8.9945	8.9986	9.0000
22	MG	87.0504	87.1847	87.3200	87.4560	87.5929	87.7305	87.8689	88.0079	88.1475	88.2878	88.4285	88.5698	88.7115	88.8537	88.9962	89.1390	89.2821	89.4254	89.5689	89.7125	89.8562	90.0000
	BT	7.6350	7.6853	7.7333	7.7788	7.8220	7.8628	7.9012	7.9372	7.9707	8.0018	8.0305	8.0567	8.0804	8.1017	8.1204	8.1367	8.1505	8.1618	8.1705	8.1768	8.1806	8.1818
24	MG	87.2988	87.4218	87.5457	87.6703	87.7957	87.9217	88.0484	88.1758	88.3037	88.4321	88.5610	88.6904	88.8202	88.9503	89.0808	89.2116	89.3426	89.4738	89.6052	89.7368	89.8684	90.0000
	BT	6.9993	7.0453	7.0892	7.1310	7.1705	7.2079	7.2430	7.2760	7.3067	7.3352	7.3614	7.3854	7.4071	7.4266	7.4438	7.4587	7.4713	7.4816	7.4897	7.4954	7.4989	7.5000
26	MG	87.5084	87.6219	87.7362	87.8512	87.9668	88.0831	88.2000	88.3174	88.4354	88.5539	88.6728	88.7921	88.9118	89.0319	89.1522	89.2728	89.3937	89.5147	89.6359	89.7572	89.8786	90.0000
	BT	6.4612	6.5037	6.5442	6.5827	6.6192	6.6537	6.6861	6.7165	6.7448	6.7711	6.7953	6.8144	6.8374	6.8554	6.8712	6.8850	6.8966	6.9061	6.9135	6.9188	6.9220	6.9231
28	MG	87.6877	87.7931	87.8992	88.0059	88.1132	88.2211	88.3296	88.4386	88.5481	88.6580	88.7684	88.8791	88.9902	89.1016	89.2133	89.3252	89.4374	89.5497	89.6621	89.7747	89.8873	90.0000
	BT	6.0000	6.0394	6.0770	6.1127	6.1466	6.1785	6.2086	6.2368	6.2631	6.2875	6.3100	6.3305	6.3491	6.3657	6.3805	6.3932	6.4040	6.4128	6.4197	6.4246	6.4276	6.4286
30	MG	87.8429	87.9412	88.0402	88.1397	88.2399	88.3406	88.4418	88.5435	88.6456	88.7481	88.8511	88.9544	89.0580	89.1620	89.2661	89.3706	89.4752	89.5799	89.6848	89.7898	89.8949	90.0000
	BT	5.6002	5.6369	5.6720	5.7053	5.7369	5.7668	5.7948	5.8211	5.8457	5.8684	5.8894	5.9085	5.9259	5.9414	5.9551	5.9670	5.9771	5.9853	5.9917	5.9963	5.9991	6.0000
32	MG	87.9785	88.0707	88.1634	88.2567	88.3506	88.4449	88.5398	88.6351	88.7308	88.8269	88.9234	89.0202	89.1173	89.2147	89.3123	89.4102	89.5082	89.6064	89.7047	89.8031	89.9015	90.0000
	BT	5.2503	5.2848	5.3176	5.3489	5.3785	5.4064	5.4327	5.4574	5.4804	5.5017	5.5213	5.5393	5.5555	5.5701	5.5829	5.5941	5.6035	5.6113	5.6173	5.6216	5.6241	5.6250
34	MG	88.0980	88.1847	88.2720	88.3598	88.4481	88.5369	88.6261	88.7158	88.8059	88.8963	88.9871	89.0781	89.1695	89.2611	89.3530	89.4451	89.5373	89.6297	89.7221	89.8147	89.9073	90.0000
	BT	4.9416	4.9740	5.0049	5.0343	5.0622	5.0885	5.1132	5.1364	5.1581	5.1781	5.1966	5.2135	5.2288	5.2425	5.2545	5.2650	5.2739	5.2812	5.2868	5.2909	5.2933	5.2941
36	MG	88.2042	88.2861	88.3685	88.4514	88.5347	88.6186	88.7028	88.7875	88.8725	88.9579	89.0436	89.1296	89.2159	89.3024	89.3891	89.4760	89.5631	89.6503	89.7377	89.8251	89.9125	90.0000
	BT	4.6671	4.6978	4.7270	4.7547	4.7810	4.8058	4.8292	4.8511	4.8715	4.8905	4.9079	4.9238	4.9383	4.9512	4.9626	4.9725	4.9809	4.9878	4.9931	4.9969	4.9992	5.0000

Table C: Framing square compound mitre table

Bowl slope 90° — Bevel angle 0°

Sides	MG°	V	BT°	V
4	90.000	0.000	45.000	20.000
5	90.000	0.000	36.000	14.531
6	90.000	0.000	30.000	11.547
7	90.000	0.000	25.714	9.631
8	90.000	0.000	22.500	8.284
9	90.000	0.000	20.000	7.279
10	90.000	0.000	18.000	6.498
11	90.000	0.000	16.364	5.873
12	90.000	0.000	15.000	5.359
14	90.000	0.000	12.857	4.565
16	90.000	0.000	11.250	3.978
18	90.000	0.000	10.000	3.527
20	90.000	0.000	9.000	3.168
22	90.000	0.000	8.182	2.876
24	90.000	0.000	7.500	2.633
26	90.000	0.000	6.923	2.428
28	90.000	0.000	6.429	2.253
30	90.000	0.000	6.000	2.102
32	90.000	0.000	5.625	1.970
34	90.000	0.000	5.294	1.853
36	90.000	0.000	5.000	1.750

Bowl slope 89 — Bevel angle 1

Sides	MG°	V	BT°	V
4	89.000	0.349	44.991	19.994
5	89.274	0.254	35.994	14.527
6	89.518	0.168	29.995	11.545
7	89.518	0.168	25.710	9.630
8	89.586	0.145	22.496	8.283
9	89.636	0.127	19.997	7.278
10	89.675	0.113	17.997	6.497
11	89.706	0.102	16.361	5.872
12	89.732	0.094	14.998	5.358
14	89.772	0.080	12.855	4.564
16	89.801	0.069	11.248	3.978
18	89.824	0.062	9.998	3.526
20	89.842	0.055	8.999	3.167
22	89.856	0.050	8.181	2.875
24	89.868	0.046	7.499	2.633
26	89.879	0.042	6.922	2.428
28	89.887	0.039	6.428	2.253
30	89.895	0.037	5.999	2.102
32	89.902	0.034	5.624	1.970
34	89.907	0.032	5.293	1.853
36	89.913	0.031	4.999	1.750

Bowl slope 88 — Bevel angle 3

Sides	MG°	V	BT°	V
4	88.001	0.698	44.965	19.976
5	88.548	0.507	35.975	14.517
6	89.037	0.336	29.980	11.538
7	89.037	0.336	25.697	9.624
8	89.172	0.289	22.486	8.278
9	89.272	0.254	19.987	7.274
10	89.350	0.227	17.989	6.494
11	89.413	0.205	16.353	5.869
12	89.464	0.187	16.353	5.869
14	89.544	0.159	12.849	4.562
16	89.602	0.139	11.243	3.976
18	89.647	0.123	9.994	3.524
20	89.683	0.111	8.994	3.166
22	89.713	0.100	8.177	2.874
24	89.737	0.092	7.495	2.631
26	89.757	0.085	6.919	2.427
28	89.775	0.079	6.425	2.252
30	89.790	0.073	5.996	2.101
32	89.803	0.069	5.622	1.969
34	89.815	0.065	5.291	1.852
36	89.825	0.061	4.997	1.749

Bowl slope 87 — Bevel angle 3

Sides	MG°	V	BT°	V
4	87.004	1.047	44.922	19.945
5	87.822	0.760	35.943	14.500
6	88.269	0.604	29.955	11.526
7	88.556	0.504	25.676	9.615
8	88.758	0.434	22.467	8.271
9	88.909	0.381	19.971	7.268
10	89.026	0.340	17.974	6.489
11	89.120	0.307	16.341	5.864
12	89.197	0.280	14.979	5.351
14	89.316	0.239	12.839	4.558
16	89.404	0.208	11.234	3.973
18	89.471	0.185	9.986	3.522
20	89.525	0.166	8.988	3.163
22	89.569	0.150	8.171	2.872
24	89.605	0.138	7.490	2.629
26	89.636	0.127	6.914	2.425
28	89.662	0.118	6.420	2.250
30	89.685	0.110	5.992	2.099
32	89.705	0.103	5.617	1.967
34	89.722	0.097	5.287	1.851
36	89.738	0.092	4.993	1.747

Bowl slope 86 — Bevel angle 4

Sides	MG°	V	BT°	V
4	86.010	1.395	44.861	19.903
5	87.099	1.014	35.899	14.477
6	87.694	0.805	29.919	11.510
7	88.076	0.672	25.647	9.603
8	88.345	0.578	22.442	8.261
9	88.546	0.508	19.949	7.259
10	88.702	0.453	17.955	6.481
11	88.827	0.410	16.323	5.857
12	88.929	0.374	14.963	5.345
14	89.088	0.318	12.825	4.553
16	89.205	0.278	11.222	3.968
18	89.295	0.246	9.975	3.518
20	89.367	0.221	8.978	3.160
22	89.425	0.201	8.162	2.868
24	89.474	0.184	7.482	2.627
26	89.515	0.169	6.906	2.422
28	89.550	0.157	6.413	2.248
30	89.580	0.147	5.985	2.097
32	89.606	0.137	5.611	1.965
34	89.630	0.129	5.281	1.849
36	89.650	0.122	4.988	1.745

Bowl slope 85 — Bevel angle 5

Sides	MG°	V	BT°	V
4	85.019	1.743	44.782	19.849
5	86.377	1.266	35.842	14.447
6	87.119	1.006	29.874	11.489
7	87.597	0.839	25.609	9.586
8	87.932	0.722	22.410	8.247
9	88.183	0.634	19.921	7.248
10	88.378	0.566	17.929	6.471
11	88.534	0.512	16.300	5.848
12	88.662	0.467	14.942	5.337
14	88.860	0.398	12.807	4.547
16	89.007	0.347	11.207	3.963
18	89.120	0.307	9.962	3.513
20	89.209	0.276	8.965	3.155
22	89.282	0.251	8.150	2.864
24	89.343	0.229	7.471	2.623
26	89.394	0.212	6.897	2.419
28	89.437	0.196	6.404	2.245
30	89.475	0.183	5.977	2.094
32	89.508	0.172	5.604	1.962
34	89.537	0.162	5.274	1.846
36	89.563	0.153	4.981	1.743

Bowl slope 84 — Bevel angle 6

Sides	MG°	V	BT°	V
4	84.033	2.091	44.687	19.783
5	85.657	1.519	35.772	14.410
6	86.546	1.207	29.819	11.463
7	87.118	1.007	25.563	9.567
8	87.521	0.866	22.370	8.231
9	87.821	0.761	19.886	7.234
10	88.055	0.679	17.898	6.459
11	88.242	0.614	16.271	5.838
12	88.396	0.560	14.916	5.328
14	88.633	0.477	12.786	4.539
16	88.809	0.416	11.188	3.956
18	88.944	0.369	9.945	3.507
20	89.052	0.331	8.950	3.150
22	89.139	0.301	8.137	2.859
24	89.212	0.275	7.459	2.618
26	89.273	0.254	6.885	2.415
28	89.325	0.236	6.393	2.241
30	89.371	0.220	5.967	2.090
32	89.410	0.206	5.594	1.959
34	89.445	0.194	5.265	1.843
36	89.476	0.183	4.973	1.740

Bowl slope 83 — Bevel angle 7

Sides	MG°	V	BT°	V
4	83.052	2.437	44.575	19.705
5	84.940	1.771	35.690	14.366
6	85.975	1.407	0.000	0.000
7	86.641	1.174	25.509	9.543
8	87.110	1.010	22.323	8.212
9	87.460	0.887	19.845	7.218
10	87.732	0.792	17.861	6.445
11	87.951	0.716	16.238	5.825
12	88.130	0.653	14.886	5.316
14	88.407	0.556	12.760	4.529
16	88.611	0.485	11.165	3.947
18	88.769	0.430	9.925	3.499
20	88.894	0.386	8.932	3.143
22	88.996	0.350	8.120	2.854
24	89.081	0.321	7.444	2.613
26	89.152	0.296	6.871	2.410
28	89.213	0.275	6.380	2.236
30	89.266	0.256	5.955	2.086
32	89.312	0.240	5.583	1.955
34	89.353	0.226	5.255	1.839
36	89.389	0.213	4.963	1.737

Bowl slope 82 — Bevel angle 8

Sides	MG°	V	BT°	V
4	82.077	2.783	44.445	19.616
5	84.226	2.022	35.596	14.316
6	85.406	1.607	29.679	11.398
7	86.166	1.340	25.446	9.516
8	86.701	1.153	22.269	8.190
9	87.100	1.013	19.797	7.199
10	87.411	0.904	17.819	6.429
11	87.660	0.817	16.200	5.811
12	87.864	0.746	14.851	5.303
14	88.181	0.635	12.730	4.518
16	88.414	0.554	11.139	3.938
18	88.594	0.491	9.902	3.491
20	88.737	0.441	8.912	3.136
22	88.854	0.400	8.102	2.847
24	88.950	0.366	7.427	2.607
26	89.032	0.338	6.855	2.404
28	89.102	0.314	6.366	2.231
30	89.162	0.293	5.941	2.081
32	89.215	0.274	5.570	1.950
34	89.261	0.258	5.242	1.835
36	89.302	0.244	4.951	1.733

Bowl slope 81 — Bevel angle 9

Sides	MG°	V	BT°	V
4	79.197	3.816	43.957	19.285
5	82.107	2.773	35.239	14.129
6	83.713	2.203	29.394	11.267
7	84.750	1.838	25.208	9.415
8	85.481	1.581	22.065	8.107
9	86.027	1.389	19.617	7.128
10	86.452	1.240	17.658	6.367
11	86.793	1.121	16.055	5.756
12	87.073	1.023	14.718	5.254
14	87.506	0.871	12.617	4.477
16	87.826	0.759	11.041	3.902
18	88.073	0.673	9.814	3.460
20	88.269	0.604	8.833	3.108
22	88.429	0.549	8.030	2.822
24	88.561	0.502	7.361	2.584
26	88.673	0.463	6.795	2.383
28	88.768	0.430	6.310	2.212
30	88.851	0.401	5.889	2.063
32	88.923	0.376	5.521	1.933
34	88.987	0.354	5.197	1.819
36	89.044	0.334	4.908	1.717

Bowl slope 80 — Bevel angle 10

Sides	MG°	V	BT°	V
4	80.149	3.473	44.445	19.616
5	82.809	2.523	35.596	14.316
6	84.275	2.005	29.679	11.398
7	85.220	1.672	25.446	9.516
8	85.886	1.439	22.269	8.190
9	86.384	1.264	19.797	7.199
10	86.771	1.128	17.819	6.429
11	87.081	1.020	16.200	5.811
12	87.336	0.931	14.851	5.303
14	87.730	0.793	12.730	4.518
16	88.022	0.691	11.139	3.938
18	88.246	0.612	9.902	3.491
20	88.425	0.550	8.912	3.136
22	88.570	0.499	8.102	2.847
24	88.690	0.457	7.427	2.607
26	88.792	0.422	6.855	2.404
28	88.879	0.391	6.366	2.231
30	88.954	0.365	5.941	2.081
32	89.020	0.342	5.570	1.950
34	89.078	0.322	5.242	1.835
36	89.130	0.304	4.951	1.733

Bowl slope 79 — Bevel angle 11

Sides	MG°	V	BT°	V
4	79.197	3.816	43.957	19.285
5	82.107	2.773	35.239	14.129
6	83.713	2.203	29.394	11.267
7	84.750	1.838	25.208	9.415
8	85.481	1.581	22.065	8.107
9	86.027	1.389	19.617	7.128
10	86.452	1.240	17.658	6.367
11	86.793	1.121	16.055	5.756
12	87.073	1.023	14.718	5.254
14	87.506	0.871	12.617	4.477
16	87.826	0.759	11.041	3.902
18	88.073	0.673	9.814	3.460
20	88.269	0.604	8.833	3.108
22	88.429	0.549	8.030	2.822
24	88.561	0.502	7.361	2.584
26	88.673	0.463	6.795	2.383
28	88.768	0.430	6.310	2.212
30	88.851	0.401	5.889	2.063
32	88.923	0.376	5.521	1.933
34	88.987	0.354	5.197	1.819
36	89.044	0.334	4.908	1.717

Bowl slope 78 — Bevel angle 12

Sides	MG°	V	BT°	V
4	78.255	4.158	43.761	19.153
5	81.410	3.021	35.095	14.054
6	83.155	2.401	29.280	11.214
7	84.282	2.002	25.113	9.374
8	85.078	1.722	21.982	8.073
9	85.672	1.513	19.545	7.100
10	86.135	1.351	17.594	6.342
11	86.507	1.221	15.996	5.734
12	86.811	1.114	14.665	5.234
14	87.283	0.949	12.572	4.460
16	87.632	0.827	11.001	3.888
18	87.900	0.733	9.779	3.447
20	88.114	0.659	8.802	3.097
22	88.288	0.598	8.002	2.811
24	88.432	0.547	7.335	2.575
26	88.554	0.505	6.771	2.375
28	88.658	0.469	6.288	2.204
30	88.748	0.437	5.868	2.056
32	88.827	0.410	5.502	1.926
34	88.896	0.385	5.178	1.812
36	88.958	0.364	4.890	1.711

Bowl slope 77 — Bevel angle 13

Sides	MG°	V	BT°	V
4	77.322	4.499	43.550	19.012
5	80.718	3.269	34.940	13.973
6	82.600	2.598	29.156	11.157
7	83.817	2.167	25.009	9.330
8	84.677	1.864	21.893	8.037
9	85.319	1.638	19.466	7.069
10	85.820	1.462	17.523	6.315
11	86.221	1.321	15.933	5.710
12	86.551	1.206	14.607	5.212
14	87.061	1.027	12.522	4.442
16	87.438	0.895	10.958	3.872
18	87.729	0.793	9.741	3.433
20	87.959	0.713	8.767	3.085
22	88.148	0.647	7.971	2.800
24	88.304	0.592	7.307	2.564
26	88.435	0.546	6.745	2.365
28	88.548	0.507	6.263	2.195
30	88.646	0.473	5.846	2.048
32	88.731	0.443	5.480	1.919
34	88.806	0.417	5.158	1.805
36	88.873	0.394	4.872	1.705

Bowl slope 76 — Bevel angle 14

Sides	MG°	V	BT°	V
4	76.400	4.838	43.322	18.862
5	80.031	3.515	34.773	13.886
6	82.049	2.793	29.022	11.096
7	83.355	2.330	24.897	9.283
8	84.278	2.004	21.797	7.998
9	84.968	1.761	19.382	7.036
10	85.505	1.572	17.448	6.286
11	85.937	1.421	15.865	5.684
12	86.291	1.296	14.544	5.189
14	86.840	1.104	12.469	4.423
16	87.245	0.962	10.912	3.856
18	87.557	0.853	9.700	3.419
20	87.806	0.766	8.731	3.071
22	88.008	0.696	7.937	2.788
24	88.176	0.637	7.276	2.554
26	88.317	0.587	6.716	2.355
28	88.439	0.545	6.237	2.186
30	88.543	0.509	5.821	2.039
32	88.635	0.477	5.457	1.911
34	88.716	0.448	5.136	1.798
36	88.787	0.423	4.851	1.697

Bowl slope	Sides	MG°	V	BT°	V
75°	4	75.489	5.176	43.080	18.702
	5	79.350	3.761	34.594	13.794
	6	81.501	2.989	28.879	11.031
	7	82.895	2.493	24.778	9.232
Bevel angle *15°*	8	83.881	2.144	21.694	7.956
	9	84.618	1.884	19.291	7.000
	10	85.193	1.682	17.367	6.255
	11	85.654	1.520	15.791	5.656
	12	86.033	1.387	14.478	5.164
	14	86.619	1.181	12.412	4.402
	16	87.053	1.030	10.862	3.838
	18	87.387	0.913	9.656	3.403
	20	87.653	0.820	8.691	3.057
	22	87.869	0.744	7.901	2.776
	24	88.048	0.681	7.243	2.542
	26	88.200	0.629	6.686	2.345
	28	88.330	0.583	6.209	2.176
	30	88.442	0.544	5.795	2.030
	32	88.540	0.510	5.433	1.902
	34	88.626	0.480	5.113	1.790
	36	88.703	0.453	4.829	1.690

Bowl slope	Sides	MG°	V	BT°	V
74	4	74.590	5.513	42.821	18.534
	5	78.676	4.005	34.403	13.696
	6	80.958	3.183	28.727	10.962
	7	82.439	2.655	24.650	9.178
Bevel angle *16*	8	83.487	2.283	21.584	7.912
	9	84.271	2.006	19.194	6.962
	10	84.882	1.791	17.280	6.222
	11	85.373	1.619	15.713	5.627
	12	85.776	1.477	14.406	5.137
	14	86.400	1.258	12.351	4.379
	16	86.862	1.097	10.809	3.818
	18	87.217	0.972	9.609	3.386
	20	87.500	0.873	8.649	3.042
	22	87.731	0.793	7.863	2.762
	24	87.922	0.726	7.208	2.529
	26	88.083	0.669	6.654	2.333
	28	88.221	0.621	6.179	2.165
	30	88.341	0.579	5.767	2.020
	32	88.445	0.543	5.406	1.893
	34	88.537	0.511	5.088	1.781
	36	88.619	0.482	4.806	1.682

Bowl slope	Sides	MG°	V	BT°	V
73	4	73.703	5.847	42.548	18.358
	5	78.007	4.248	34.201	13.593
	6	80.419	3.376	28.565	10.888
	7	81.986	2.816	24.515	9.121
Bevel angle *17*	8	83.095	2.422	21.467	7.865
	9	83.926	2.128	19.091	6.922
	10	84.573	1.900	17.188	6.187
	11	85.093	1.717	15.630	5.595
	12	85.521	1.567	14.330	5.109
	14	86.182	1.335	12.286	4.356
	16	86.672	1.163	10.752	3.798
	18	87.049	1.031	9.559	3.368
	20	87.349	0.926	8.604	3.026
	22	87.593	0.841	7.822	2.747
	24	87.796	0.770	7.171	2.516
	26	87.967	0.710	6.619	2.321
	28	88.113	0.659	6.147	2.154
	30	88.240	0.615	5.737	2.009
	32	88.351	0.576	5.378	1.883
	34	88.448	0.542	5.062	1.772
	36	88.535	0.512	4.781	1.673

Bowl slope	Sides	MG°	V	BT°	V
72	4	72.828	6.180	42.260	18.173
	5	77.346	4.490	33.988	13.484
	6	79.884	3.568	28.394	10.811
	7	81.536	2.976	24.371	9.060
Bevel angle *18*	8	82.706	2.560	21.343	7.815
	9	83.583	2.249	18.983	6.880
	10	84.266	2.008	17.091	6.149
	11	84.815	1.815	15.542	5.562
	12	85.267	1.656	14.250	5.079
	14	85.966	1.411	12.218	4.331
	16	86.483	1.229	10.693	3.776
	18	86.881	1.090	9.506	3.349
	20	87.198	0.979	8.556	3.009
	22	87.456	0.889	7.779	2.732
	24	87.670	0.814	7.131	2.502
	26	87.851	0.750	6.583	2.308
	28	88.006	0.696	6.113	2.142
	30	88.140	0.650	5.705	1.998
	32	88.257	0.609	5.349	1.873
	34	88.360	0.573	5.034	1.762
	36	88.451	0.541	4.755	1.664

Bowl slope	Sides	MG°	V	BT°	V
71	4	71.966	6.511	41.958	17.981
	5	76.692	4.731	33.763	13.370
	6	79.355	3.759	28.214	10.730
	7	81.089	3.136	24.220	8.997
Bevel angle *19*	8	82.320	2.697	21.213	7.763
	9	83.242	2.370	18.868	6.835
	10	83.962	2.116	16.989	6.110
	11	84.539	1.912	15.449	5.527
	12	85.014	1.745	14.165	5.048
	14	85.750	1.486	12.146	4.304
	16	86.295	1.295	10.630	3.754
	18	86.714	1.148	9.450	3.329
	20	87.048	1.031	8.506	2.991
	22	87.320	0.936	7.733	2.716
	24	87.546	0.857	7.089	2.487
	26	87.736	0.791	6.544	2.294
	28	87.899	0.734	6.077	2.129
	30	88.040	0.684	5.672	1.986
	32	88.163	0.641	5.318	1.862
	34	88.272	0.603	5.005	1.752
	36	88.368	0.570	4.727	1.654

Bowl slope	Sides	MG°	V	BT°	V
70	4	71.118	6.840	41.641	17.783
	5	76.045	4.970	33.528	13.252
	6	78.830	3.949	28.024	10.645
	7	80.647	3.294	24.062	8.930
Bevel angle *20*	8	81.937	2.833	21.076	7.708
	9	82.904	2.490	18.747	6.788
	10	83.659	2.223	16.881	6.069
	11	84.265	2.009	15.352	5.491
	12	84.764	1.833	14.076	5.015
	14	85.536	1.561	12.070	4.277
	16	86.108	1.361	10.563	3.730
	18	86.549	1.206	9.391	3.308
	20	86.899	1.083	8.453	2.972
	22	87.185	0.984	7.685	2.699
	24	87.422	0.901	7.045	2.472
	26	87.622	0.831	6.504	2.280
	28	87.793	0.771	6.039	2.116
	30	87.941	0.719	5.637	1.974
	32	88.071	0.674	5.285	1.850
	34	88.185	0.634	4.974	1.741
	36	88.286	0.598	4.698	1.644

Bowl slope	Sides	MG°	V	BT°	V
69	4	70.284	7.167	41.311	17.577
	5	75.406	5.207	33.281	13.128
	6	78.310	4.138	27.826	10.556
	7	80.208	3.452	23.895	8.861
Bevel angle *21*	8	81.557	2.969	20.932	7.650
	9	82.569	2.609	18.621	6.739
	10	83.358	2.329	16.768	6.026
	11	83.993	2.105	15.249	5.452
	12	84.515	1.920	13.983	4.980
	14	85.324	1.636	11.990	4.247
	16	85.923	1.426	10.494	3.705
	18	86.384	1.264	9.330	3.286
	20	86.751	1.135	8.398	2.953
	22	87.050	1.031	7.635	2.681
	24	87.299	0.944	6.999	2.455
	26	87.508	0.870	6.461	2.265
	28	87.688	0.808	6.000	2.102
	30	87.843	0.753	5.600	1.961
	32	87.979	0.706	5.250	1.838
	34	88.098	0.664	4.942	1.729
	36	88.204	0.627	4.667	1.633

Bowl slope	Sides	MG°	V	BT°	V
68	4	69.464	7.492	40.967	17.365
	5	74.775	5.443	33.024	13.000
	6	77.796	4.326	27.619	10.464
	7	79.774	3.608	23.721	8.788
Bevel angle *22*	8	81.180	3.103	20.782	7.590
	9	82.236	2.727	18.489	6.687
	10	83.060	2.434	16.649	5.981
	11	83.723	2.200	15.142	5.412
	12	84.268	2.008	13.885	4.944
	14	85.113	1.710	11.907	4.217
	16	85.739	1.490	10.421	3.678
	18	86.221	1.321	9.265	3.263
	20	86.605	1.187	8.340	2.932
	22	86.917	1.077	7.582	2.662
	24	87.177	0.986	6.951	2.438
	26	87.396	0.910	6.417	2.249
	28	87.583	0.844	5.959	2.088
	30	87.745	0.787	5.562	1.948
	32	87.887	0.738	5.214	1.825
	34	88.012	0.694	4.908	1.717
	36	88.123	0.655	4.635	1.621

Bowl slope	Sides	MG°	V	BT°	V
67	4	68.658	7.815	40.609	17.148
	5	74.152	5.678	32.756	12.867
	6	77.288	4.512	27.403	10.369
	7	79.343	3.763	23.540	8.713
Bevel angle *23*	8	80.807	3.237	20.626	7.528
	9	81.906	2.844	18.351	6.634
	10	82.765	2.539	16.526	5.934
	11	83.455	2.295	15.031	5.370
	12	84.023	2.094	13.783	4.906
	14	84.904	1.784	11.820	4.185
	16	85.556	1.554	10.345	3.651
	18	86.059	1.378	9.198	3.239
	20	86.459	1.238	8.279	2.910
	22	86.785	1.124	7.527	2.643
	24	87.055	1.029	6.901	2.421
	26	88.083	0.669	6.370	2.233
	28	87.479	0.880	5.916	2.072
	30	87.648	0.821	5.521	1.933
	32	87.796	0.770	5.177	1.812
	34	87.926	0.724	4.872	1.705
	36	88.042	0.684	4.602	1.610

Bowl slope	Sides	MG°	V	BT°	V
66	4	67.867	8.135	40.239	16.925
	5	73.537	5.910	32.478	12.730
	6	76.785	4.697	27.179	10.269
	7	78.918	3.917	23.352	8.635
Bevel angle *24*	8	80.437	3.370	20.463	7.463
	9	81.579	2.961	18.207	6.578
	10	82.472	2.643	16.398	5.885
	11	83.189	2.389	14.914	5.327
	12	83.780	2.180	13.677	4.867
	14	84.696	1.857	11.729	4.152
	16	85.375	1.618	10.266	3.622
	18	85.898	1.434	9.128	3.213
	20	86.314	1.288	8.216	2.888
	22	86.653	1.170	7.470	2.622
	24	86.935	1.071	6.848	2.402
	26	87.173	0.988	6.322	2.216
	28	87.376	0.917	5.871	2.056
	30	87.552	0.855	5.480	1.919
	32	87.706	0.801	5.137	1.798
	34	87.842	0.754	4.835	1.692
	36	87.962	0.712	4.567	1.597

Bowl slope	Sides	MG°	V	BT°	V
65	4	67.090	8.452	39.856	16.696
	5	72.931	6.141	32.189	12.589
	6	76.288	4.880	26.946	10.167
	7	78.496	4.070	23.156	8.554
Bevel angle *25*	8	80.071	3.501	20.293	7.396
	9	81.255	3.076	18.058	6.521
	10	82.181	2.746	16.264	5.835
	11	82.926	2.482	14.794	5.282
	12	83.539	2.265	13.566	4.826
	14	84.490	1.929	11.635	4.118
	16	85.195	1.681	10.184	3.593
	18	85.738	1.490	9.055	3.187
	20	86.171	1.339	8.151	2.864
	22	86.523	1.215	7.411	2.601
	24	86.815	1.113	6.794	2.383
	26	87.062	1.026	6.272	2.198
	28	87.274	0.952	5.824	2.040
	30	87.457	0.888	5.086	1.780
	32	87.616	0.832	5.097	1.784
	34	87.757	0.783	4.797	1.678
	36	87.882	0.739	4.531	1.585

Bowl slope	Sides	MG°	V	BT°	V
64	4	66.329	8.767	39.460	16.463
	5	72.334	6.370	31.891	12.444
	6	75.797	5.062	26.705	10.061
	7	78.079	4.222	22.953	8.470
Bevel angle *26*	8	79.708	3.632	20.118	7.326
	9	80.935	3.191	17.903	6.461
	10	81.894	2.849	16.126	5.782
	11	82.665	2.574	14.668	5.235
	12	83.301	2.349	13.452	4.784
	14	84.286	2.001	11.537	4.082
	16	85.017	1.744	10.099	3.562
	18	85.580	1.546	8.979	3.160
	20	86.028	1.389	8.083	2.840
	22	86.394	1.261	7.349	2.579
	24	86.697	1.154	6.737	2.363
	26	86.953	1.065	6.219	2.180
	28	87.172	0.988	5.776	2.023
	30	87.362	0.921	5.391	1.887
	32	87.528	0.864	5.054	1.769
	34	87.674	0.812	4.757	1.664
	36	87.804	0.767	4.493	1.572

Bowl slope	Sides	MG°	V	BT°	V
63	4	65.582	9.080	39.053	16.226
	5	71.745	6.597	31.582	12.295
	6	75.313	5.242	26.456	9.952
	7	77.667	4.373	22.743	8.384
Bevel angle *27*	8	79.350	3.761	19.936	7.254
	9	80.617	3.305	17.743	6.399
	10	81.609	2.950	15.982	5.728
	11	82.407	2.666	14.538	5.187
	12	83.064	2.433	13.333	4.740
	14	84.084	2.072	11.436	4.046
	16	84.840	1.806	10.010	3.530
	18	85.423	1.601	8.901	3.132
	20	85.887	1.438	8.012	2.815
	22	86.265	1.305	7.285	2.557
	24	86.580	1.195	6.679	2.342
	26	86.845	1.102	6.165	2.160
	28	87.072	1.023	5.725	2.005
	30	87.268	0.954	5.344	1.871
	32	87.440	0.894	5.010	1.753
	34	87.591	0.841	4.716	1.650
	36	87.725	0.794	4.454	1.558

Bowl slope	Sides	MG°	V	BT°	V
62	4	64.851	9.389	38.634	15.985
	5	71.166	6.822	31.264	12.143
	6	74.834	5.421	26.198	9.840
	7	77.260	4.522	22.526	8.295
Bevel angle *28*	8	78.996	3.889	19.748	7.180
	9	80.303	3.417	17.577	6.336
	10	81.327	3.051	15.834	5.672
	11	82.151	2.757	14.404	5.137
	12	82.830	2.516	13.210	4.695
	14	83.884	2.143	11.331	4.008
	16	84.665	1.868	9.919	3.497
	18	85.268	1.656	8.820	3.103
	20	85.747	1.487	7.939	2.789
	22	86.138	1.350	7.219	2.533
	24	86.463	1.236	6.618	2.320
	26	86.737	1.140	6.109	2.141
	28	86.972	1.058	5.673	1.987
	30	87.175	0.987	5.296	1.854
	32	87.353	0.925	4.965	1.737
	34	87.509	0.870	4.673	1.635
	36	87.648	0.821	4.414	1.544

Bowl slope	Sides	MG°	V	BT°	V
61	4	64.135	9.696	38.203	15.740
	5	70.596	7.045	30.937	11.987
	6	74.363	5.598	25.932	9.725
	7	76.858	4.669	22.302	8.203
Bevel angle *29*	8	78.645	4.016	19.554	7.104
	9	79.993	3.529	17.406	6.270
	10	81.048	3.150	15.680	5.614
	11	81.898	2.847	14.265	5.085
	12	82.598	2.598	13.083	4.648
	14	83.686	2.213	11.223	3.968
	16	84.492	1.929	9.824	3.463
	18	85.114	1.710	8.736	3.073
	20	85.609	1.536	7.864	2.762
	22	86.013	1.394	7.150	2.509
	24	86.348	1.277	6.555	2.298
	26	86.631	1.177	6.052	2.120
	28	86.873	1.092	5.620	1.968
	30	87.083	1.019	5.245	1.836
	32	87.266	0.955	4.918	1.721
	34	87.428	0.898	4.629	1.619
	36	87.571	0.848	4.372	1.529

Table C (continued)

Bowl slope **60°** — Bevel angle *30°*

Sides	MG°	V	BT°	V
4	63.435	10.000	37.761	15.492
5	70.035	7.265	30.600	11.828
6	73.898	5.774	25.659	9.608
7	76.462	4.816	22.071	8.109
8	78.299	4.142	19.355	7.025
9	79.686	3.640	17.229	6.202
10	80.772	3.249	15.522	5.555
11	81.648	2.936	14.122	5.032
12	82.369	2.679	12.953	4.600
14	83.489	2.282	11.111	3.928
16	84.320	1.989	9.727	3.428
18	84.962	1.763	8.649	3.042
20	85.472	1.584	7.786	2.735
22	85.888	1.438	7.080	2.484
24	86.234	1.317	6.491	2.275
26	86.526	1.214	5.992	2.099
28	86.776	1.127	5.564	1.948
30	86.992	1.051	5.194	1.818
32	87.181	0.985	4.869	1.704
34	87.347	0.927	4.583	1.603
36	87.495	0.875	4.329	1.514

Bowl slope **59** — Bevel angle *31*

Sides	MG°	V	BT°	V
4	62.750	10.301	37.309	15.241
5	69.484	7.484	30.254	11.665
6	73.440	5.947	25.378	9.487
7	76.070	4.961	21.834	8.013
8	77.957	4.267	19.149	6.945
9	79.383	3.749	17.048	6.133
10	80.500	3.347	15.360	5.494
11	81.400	3.025	13.975	4.977
12	82.143	2.760	12.818	4.550
14	83.295	2.351	10.996	3.886
16	84.151	2.049	9.627	3.392
18	84.811	1.816	8.560	3.010
20	85.336	1.631	7.706	2.706
22	85.765	1.481	7.007	2.458
24	86.121	1.356	6.424	2.252
26	86.422	1.251	5.930	2.078
28	86.679	1.161	5.507	1.928
30	86.901	1.083	5.141	1.799
32	87.096	1.015	4.820	1.686
34	87.268	0.955	4.536	1.587
36	87.420	0.901	4.284	1.498

Bowl slope **58** — Bevel angle *32*

Sides	MG°	V	BT°	V
4	62.080	10.598	36.846	14.987
5	68.943	7.700	29.899	11.500
6	72.989	6.119	25.089	9.364
7	75.684	5.104	21.590	7.914
8	77.620	4.390	18.937	6.862
9	79.083	3.857	16.861	6.062
10	80.231	3.444	15.192	5.431
11	81.156	3.112	13.823	4.921
12	81.919	2.840	12.679	4.500
14	83.104	2.419	10.877	3.843
16	83.983	2.108	9.523	3.355
18	84.662	1.869	8.468	2.978
20	85.202	1.679	7.624	2.677
22	85.643	1.524	6.932	2.432
24	86.009	1.395	6.355	2.228
26	86.318	1.287	5.867	2.055
28	86.583	1.194	5.449	1.908
30	86.812	1.114	5.086	1.780
32	87.012	1.044	4.768	1.668
34	87.189	0.982	4.488	1.570
36	87.346	0.927	4.239	1.482

Bowl slope **57** — Bevel angle *33*

Sides	MG°	V	BT°	V
4	61.426	10.893	36.372	14.730
5	68.411	7.914	29.535	11.332
6	72.544	6.289	24.793	9.238
7	75.303	5.246	21.339	7.813
8	77.287	4.512	18.720	6.777
9	78.787	3.965	16.669	5.988
10	79.965	3.539	15.020	5.367
11	80.914	3.198	13.667	4.863
12	81.697	2.919	12.537	4.447
14	82.914	2.486	10.756	3.799
16	83.817	2.167	9.417	3.317
18	84.514	1.921	8.374	2.944
20	85.070	1.725	7.539	2.647
22	85.522	1.566	6.855	2.404
24	85.899	1.434	6.285	2.203
26	86.216	1.323	5.802	2.032
28	86.488	1.227	5.388	1.886
30	86.724	1.145	5.029	1.760
32	86.929	1.073	4.715	1.650
34	87.111	1.009	4.438	1.552
36	87.272	0.953	4.192	1.466

Bowl slope **56** — Bevel angle *34*

Sides	MG°	V	BT°	V
4	60.786	11.184	35.889	14.472
5	67.889	8.126	29.163	11.161
6	72.107	6.457	24.489	9.110
7	74.928	5.386	21.082	7.710
8	76.959	4.633	18.497	6.691
9	78.496	4.071	16.472	5.914
10	79.702	3.634	14.844	5.301
11	80.676	3.284	13.507	4.804
12	81.478	2.997	12.390	4.394
14	82.727	2.553	10.631	3.754
16	83.653	2.225	9.308	3.278
18	84.369	1.972	8.277	2.910
20	84.939	1.771	7.452	2.616
22	85.403	1.608	6.776	2.376
24	85.790	1.472	6.212	2.177
26	86.116	1.358	5.735	2.009
28	86.395	1.260	5.326	1.865
30	86.636	1.175	4.971	1.740
32	86.848	1.102	4.661	1.631
34	87.034	1.036	4.387	1.534
36	87.199	0.978	4.144	1.449

Bowl slope **55** — Bevel angle *35*

Sides	MG°	V	BT°	V
4	60.162	11.472	35.396	14.211
5	67.377	8.335	28.782	10.987
6	71.677	6.623	24.178	8.979
7	74.559	5.524	20.819	7.605
8	76.635	4.752	18.269	6.602
9	78.208	4.175	16.270	5.837
10	79.443	3.727	14.663	5.233
11	80.440	3.368	13.343	4.744
12	81.263	3.074	12.240	4.339
14	82.542	2.618	10.503	3.708
16	83.491	2.282	9.196	3.238
18	84.225	2.023	8.178	2.874
20	84.809	1.817	7.362	2.584
22	85.286	1.649	6.695	2.348
24	85.682	1.510	6.138	2.151
26	86.016	1.393	5.666	1.984
28	86.302	1.293	5.262	1.842
30	86.550	1.206	4.912	1.719
32	86.767	1.130	4.605	1.611
34	86.958	1.063	4.335	1.516
36	87.127	1.004	4.094	1.432

Bowl slope **54** — Bevel angle *36*

Sides	MG°	V	BT°	V
4	59.554	11.756	34.894	13.949
5	66.875	8.541	28.394	10.811
6	71.255	6.787	23.860	8.846
7	74.195	5.661	20.550	7.497
8	76.317	4.869	18.035	6.512
9	77.924	4.279	16.063	5.759
10	79.188	3.820	14.478	5.164
11	80.208	3.452	13.175	4.682
12	81.050	3.150	12.087	4.283
14	82.359	2.683	10.371	3.660
16	83.331	2.338	9.081	3.197
18	84.083	2.073	8.076	2.838
20	84.681	1.862	7.271	2.552
22	85.169	1.690	6.611	2.318
24	85.575	1.548	6.062	2.124
26	85.918	1.427	5.596	1.960
28	86.211	1.325	5.197	1.819
30	86.465	1.236	4.851	1.697
32	86.687	1.158	4.548	1.591
34	86.882	1.089	4.281	1.497
36	87.056	1.028	4.043	1.414

Bowl slope **53** — Bevel angle *37*

Sides	MG°	V	BT°	V
4	58.960	12.036	34.383	13.686
5	66.383	8.745	27.997	10.633
6	70.840	6.949	23.536	8.711
7	73.837	5.796	20.274	7.388
8	76.003	4.986	17.796	6.420
9	77.645	4.381	15.852	5.679
10	78.936	3.911	14.288	5.093
11	79.979	3.534	13.003	4.618
12	80.840	3.225	11.929	4.225
14	82.179	2.747	10.237	3.612
16	83.174	2.394	8.964	3.155
18	83.943	2.122	7.972	2.801
20	84.555	1.906	7.177	2.518
22	85.055	1.731	6.526	2.288
24	85.470	1.585	5.984	2.096
26	85.821	1.461	5.524	1.934
28	86.121	1.356	5.130	1.796
30	86.381	1.265	4.789	1.675
32	86.608	1.185	4.490	1.570
34	86.808	1.115	4.226	1.478
36	86.986	1.053	3.991	1.395

Bowl slope **52** — Bevel angle *38*

Sides	MG°	V	BT°	V
4	58.381	12.313	33.863	13.421
5	65.901	8.946	27.593	10.452
6	70.432	7.109	23.204	8.574
7	73.486	5.930	19.993	7.277
8	75.694	5.100	17.551	6.326
9	77.370	4.482	15.635	5.597
10	78.688	4.001	14.094	5.021
11	79.753	3.615	12.827	4.554
12	80.633	3.299	11.768	4.167
14	82.001	2.810	10.099	3.562
16	83.018	2.449	8.843	3.112
18	83.804	2.171	7.865	2.763
20	84.431	1.950	7.081	2.484
22	84.941	1.770	6.439	2.257
24	85.366	1.621	5.904	2.068
26	85.725	1.495	5.450	1.908
28	86.032	1.387	5.062	1.771
30	86.298	1.294	4.725	1.653
32	86.530	1.213	4.430	1.549
34	86.735	1.141	4.170	1.458
36	86.917	1.077	3.938	1.377

Bowl slope **51** — Bevel angle *39*

Sides	MG°	V	BT°	V
4	57.817	12.586	33.334	13.155
5	65.429	9.145	27.180	10.270
6	70.032	7.267	22.866	8.434
7	73.140	6.061	19.706	7.163
8	75.390	5.213	17.302	6.230
9	77.099	4.581	15.414	5.514
10	78.444	4.090	13.895	4.948
11	79.531	3.696	12.647	4.488
12	80.428	3.373	11.604	4.107
14	81.826	2.873	9.958	3.512
16	82.865	2.504	8.720	3.068
18	83.668	2.219	7.756	2.724
20	84.308	1.993	6.983	2.450
22	84.830	1.810	6.350	2.226
24	85.264	1.657	5.822	2.039
26	85.630	1.528	5.375	1.882
28	85.944	1.418	4.992	1.747
30	86.216	1.323	4.659	1.630
32	86.453	1.240	4.369	1.528
34	86.663	1.166	4.112	1.438
36	86.849	1.101	3.884	1.358

Bowl slope **50** — Bevel angle *40*

Sides	MG°	V	BT°	V
4	57.268	12.856	32.798	12.888
5	64.967	9.340	26.761	10.086
6	69.639	7.422	22.521	8.293
7	72.800	6.191	19.413	7.048
8	75.091	5.325	17.047	6.132
9	76.832	4.679	15.189	5.430
10	78.203	4.177	13.693	4.873
11	79.312	3.775	12.464	4.421
12	80.228	3.445	11.436	4.046
14	81.654	2.934	9.815	3.460
16	82.714	2.557	8.595	3.023
18	83.534	2.267	7.644	2.684
20	84.187	2.036	6.883	2.414
22	84.720	1.848	6.259	2.193
24	85.163	1.692	5.739	2.010
26	85.537	1.561	5.298	1.855
28	85.858	1.448	4.920	1.722
30	86.135	1.351	4.593	1.607
32	86.377	1.266	4.306	1.506
34	86.591	1.191	4.053	1.417
36	86.781	1.125	3.828	1.338

Bowl slope **49** — Bevel angle *41*

Sides	MG°	V	BT°	V
4	56.733	13.121	32.253	12.621
5	64.515	9.533	26.334	9.900
6	69.255	7.576	22.170	8.150
7	72.467	6.319	19.114	6.931
8	74.797	5.435	16.787	6.033
9	76.570	4.776	14.959	5.344
10	77.967	4.263	13.487	4.797
11	79.096	3.853	12.276	4.352
12	80.030	3.516	11.264	3.983
14	81.484	2.995	9.668	3.407
16	82.565	2.610	8.467	2.977
18	83.401	2.314	7.530	2.644
20	84.068	2.078	6.780	2.378
22	84.611	1.887	6.166	2.161
24	85.064	1.727	5.653	1.980
26	85.445	1.593	5.219	1.827
28	85.772	1.478	4.847	1.696
30	86.055	1.379	4.525	1.583
32	86.303	1.292	4.242	1.484
34	86.521	1.216	3.993	1.396
36	86.715	1.148	3.771	1.318

Bowl slope **48** — Bevel angle *42*

Sides	MG°	V	BT°	V
4	56.212	13.383	31.701	12.353
5	64.073	9.723	25.900	9.712
6	68.877	7.726	21.813	8.005
7	72.139	6.445	18.810	6.813
8	74.509	5.543	16.522	5.933
9	76.312	4.871	14.724	5.256
10	77.734	4.348	13.276	4.719
11	78.884	3.929	12.085	4.282
12	79.835	3.586	11.089	3.920
14	81.317	3.054	9.518	3.353
16	82.419	2.662	8.336	2.931
18	83.271	2.360	7.414	2.603
20	83.950	2.120	6.676	2.341
22	84.505	1.924	6.071	2.127
24	84.966	1.762	5.566	1.949
26	85.355	1.625	5.139	1.799
28	85.688	1.508	4.773	1.670
30	85.977	1.407	4.455	1.558
32	86.229	1.318	4.177	1.461
34	86.452	1.240	3.932	1.375
36	86.650	1.171	3.714	1.298

Bowl slope **47** — Bevel angle *43*

Sides	MG°	V	BT°	V
4	55.706	13.640	31.141	12.084
5	63.642	9.910	25.460	9.522
6	68.508	7.875	21.449	7.858
7	71.818	6.569	18.501	6.692
8	74.225	5.650	16.253	5.831
9	76.059	4.965	14.486	5.167
10	77.505	4.432	13.062	4.640
11	78.676	4.005	11.891	4.211
12	79.644	3.655	10.911	3.855
14	81.152	3.113	9.366	3.299
16	82.275	2.713	8.203	2.883
18	83.143	2.405	7.296	2.561
20	83.835	2.160	6.570	2.303
22	84.400	1.961	5.974	2.093
24	84.869	1.796	5.478	1.918
26	85.266	1.656	5.057	1.770
28	85.606	1.537	4.697	1.643
30	85.900	1.434	4.384	1.533
32	86.157	1.343	4.111	1.437
34	86.384	1.264	3.869	1.353
36	86.585	1.193	3.655	1.277

Bowl slope **46** — Bevel angle *44*

Sides	MG°	V	BT°	V
4	55.214	13.893	30.574	11.816
5	63.220	10.094	25.013	9.332
6	68.146	8.021	21.080	7.709
7	71.503	6.691	18.186	6.570
8	73.948	5.755	15.979	5.727
9	75.811	5.057	14.243	5.077
10	77.281	4.514	12.843	4.560
11	78.472	4.079	11.693	4.139
12	79.456	3.723	10.730	3.790
14	80.991	3.171	9.211	3.243
16	82.133	2.764	8.067	2.835
18	83.017	2.450	7.176	2.518
20	83.721	2.200	6.461	2.265
22	84.296	1.998	5.876	2.058
24	84.775	1.829	5.388	1.886
26	85.179	1.687	4.974	1.741
28	85.525	1.565	4.620	1.616
30	85.824	1.460	4.312	1.508
32	86.086	1.368	4.043	1.414
34	86.317	1.287	3.806	1.330
36	86.522	1.215	3.594	1.256

Bowl slope / Bevel angle	Sides	MG°	V	BT°	V
Bowl slope **45°**	4	54.736	14.142	30.000	11.547
	5	62.808	10.275	24.559	9.139
	6	67.792	8.165	20.705	7.559
	7	71.195	6.810	17.867	6.447
Bevel angle *45°*	8	73.675	5.858	15.700	5.622
	9	75.567	5.147	13.995	4.985
	10	77.061	4.595	12.621	4.478
	11	78.271	4.153	11.491	4.066
	12	79.271	3.789	10.545	3.723
	14	80.832	3.228	9.053	3.187
	16	81.994	2.813	7.929	2.786
	18	82.893	2.494	7.053	2.474
	20	83.610	2.240	6.351	2.226
	22	84.195	2.033	5.776	2.023
	24	84.682	1.862	5.296	1.854
	26	85.093	1.717	4.889	1.711
	28	85.445	1.593	4.541	1.588
	30	85.750	1.486	4.239	1.482
	32	86.016	1.393	3.974	1.390
	34	86.251	1.310	3.741	1.308
	36	86.460	1.237	3.533	1.235

Bowl slope / Bevel angle	Sides	MG°	V	BT°	V
Bowl slope **44**	4	54.271	14.387	29.419	11.278
	5	62.407	10.453	24.099	8.946
	6	67.446	8.306	20.324	7.408
	7	70.893	6.928	17.542	6.322
Bevel angle *46*	8	73.408	5.959	15.417	5.515
	9	75.328	5.236	13.744	4.892
	10	76.845	4.675	12.396	4.396
	11	78.073	4.224	11.286	3.991
	12	79.090	3.855	10.358	3.655
	14	80.676	3.284	8.892	3.129
	16	81.857	2.862	7.789	2.736
	18	82.771	2.537	6.928	2.430
	20	83.500	2.279	6.239	2.186
	22	84.095	2.069	5.674	1.987
	24	84.590	1.894	5.202	1.821
	26	85.008	1.747	4.803	1.681
	28	85.366	1.621	4.461	1.560
	30	85.676	1.512	4.164	1.456
	32	85.947	1.417	3.904	1.365
	34	86.186	1.333	3.675	1.285
	36	86.399	1.259	3.471	1.213

Bowl slope / Bevel angle	Sides	MG°	V	BT°	V
Bowl slope **43**	4	53.820	14.627	28.832	11.010
	5	62.016	10.627	23.632	8.751
	6	67.108	8.445	19.938	7.255
	7	70.598	7.044	17.212	6.196
Bevel angle *47*	8	73.147	6.059	15.129	5.407
	9	75.094	5.324	13.489	4.797
	10	76.633	4.753	12.166	4.312
	11	77.880	4.295	11.078	3.916
	12	78.913	3.919	10.167	3.587
	14	80.523	3.339	8.729	3.071
	16	81.723	2.910	7.646	2.685
	18	82.652	2.579	6.801	2.385
	20	83.393	2.317	6.124	2.146
	22	83.997	2.103	5.570	1.950
	24	84.500	1.926	5.107	1.787
	26	84.925	1.776	4.715	1.650
	28	85.289	1.648	4.379	1.532
	30	85.604	1.537	4.088	1.429
	32	85.880	1.441	3.833	1.340
	34	86.123	1.355	3.608	1.261
	36	86.339	1.280	3.408	1.191

Bowl slope / Bevel angle	Sides	MG°	V	BT°	V
Bowl slope **42**	4	53.382	14.863	28.239	10.741
	5	61.634	10.799	23.160	8.556
	6	66.778	8.581	19.546	7.100
	7	70.309	7.158	16.877	6.068
Bevel angle *48*	8	72.891	6.156	14.837	5.298
	9	74.865	5.410	13.230	4.702
	10	76.425	4.829	11.933	4.227
	11	77.691	4.364	10.866	3.839
	12	78.738	3.983	9.973	3.517
	14	80.373	3.392	8.563	3.011
	16	81.591	2.956	7.501	2.633
	18	82.535	2.621	6.672	2.340
	20	83.287	2.354	6.008	2.105
	22	83.901	2.137	5.464	1.913
	24	84.412	1.957	5.011	1.753
	26	84.844	1.805	4.626	1.618
	28	85.214	1.675	4.297	1.503
	30	85.814	1.464	4.011	1.402
	32	86.061	1.377	3.761	1.315
	34	86.280	1.300	3.540	1.237
	36	81.591	2.956	3.343	1.168

Bowl slope / Bevel angle	Sides	MG°	V	BT°	V
Bowl slope **41**	4	52.958	15.094	27.639	10.473
	5	61.263	10.967	22.682	8.359
	6	66.456	8.715	19.149	6.945
	7	70.026	7.269	16.538	5.939
Bevel angle *49*	8	72.640	6.252	14.540	5.187
	9	74.640	5.494	12.967	4.605
	10	76.222	4.904	11.697	4.141
	11	77.505	4.432	10.651	3.761
	12	78.568	4.044	9.776	3.446
	14	80.226	3.445	8.394	2.951
	16	81.462	3.002	7.354	2.581
	18	82.420	2.662	6.542	2.293
	20	83.184	2.391	5.891	2.064
	22	83.807	2.170	5.357	1.876
	24	84.326	1.987	4.912	1.719
	26	84.764	1.833	4.536	1.587
	28	85.140	1.701	4.212	1.473
	30	85.465	1.586	3.932	1.375
	32	85.749	1.487	3.687	1.289
	34	86.000	1.399	3.470	1.213
	36	86.222	1.321	3.278	1.145

Bowl slope / Bevel angle	Sides	MG°	V	BT°	V
Bowl slope **40**	4	52.546	15.321	27.034	10.205
	5	60.901	11.131	22.199	8.161
	6	66.141	8.846	18.747	6.788
	7	69.751	7.378	16.194	5.808
Bevel angle *50*	8	72.395	6.346	14.240	5.076
	9	74.421	5.576	12.700	4.507
	10	76.023	4.978	11.457	4.053
	11	77.323	4.499	10.434	3.683
	12	78.401	4.105	9.577	3.374
	14	80.082	3.497	8.223	2.890
	16	81.336	3.048	7.204	2.528
	18	82.307	2.701	6.409	2.246
	20	83.082	2.427	5.771	2.021
	22	83.715	2.203	5.249	1.837
	24	84.241	2.017	4.813	1.684
	26	84.686	1.860	4.444	1.554
	28	85.067	1.726	4.127	1.443
	30	85.397	1.610	3.853	1.347
	32	85.685	1.509	3.612	1.263
	34	85.940	1.420	3.400	1.188
	36	86.166	1.340	3.212	1.122

Bowl slope / Bevel angle	Sides	MG°	V	BT°	V
Bowl slope **39**	4	52.148	15.543	26.423	9.938
	5	60.550	11.293	21.710	7.963
	6	65.835	8.974	18.340	6.630
	7	69.481	7.485	15.846	5.677
Bevel angle *51*	8	72.156	6.438	13.936	4.963
	9	74.206	5.657	12.430	4.408
	10	75.828	5.050	11.214	3.965
	11	77.146	4.564	10.213	3.603
	12	78.237	4.165	9.374	3.302
	14	79.942	3.548	8.050	2.829
	16	81.213	3.092	7.052	2.474
	18	82.197	2.741	6.274	2.199
	20	82.983	2.462	5.650	1.979
	22	83.624	2.235	5.138	1.798
	24	84.158	2.046	4.712	1.648
	26	84.609	1.887	4.350	1.522
	28	84.996	1.751	4.040	1.413
	30	85.330	1.634	3.772	1.318
	32	85.623	1.531	3.536	1.236
	34	85.881	1.440	3.329	1.163
	36	86.110	1.360	3.144	1.099

Bowl slope / Bevel angle	Sides	MG°	V	BT°	V
Bowl slope **38**	4	51.762	15.760	25.807	9.671
	5	60.208	11.450	17.929	6.471
	6	65.536	9.099	15.493	5.544
	7	69.219	7.590	13.627	4.849
Bevel angle *52*	8	71.923	6.528	12.156	4.308
	9	73.996	5.736	10.967	3.876
	10	75.639	5.121	9.989	3.522
	11	76.972	4.628	9.169	3.228
	12	78.077	4.223	7.874	2.766
	14	79.804	3.597	6.898	2.420
	16	81.092	3.135	6.137	2.150
	18	82.090	2.779	5.527	1.935
	20	82.886	2.496	5.027	1.759
	22	83.536	2.266	4.609	1.612
	24	84.077	2.075	4.256	1.488
	26	84.534	1.914	3.953	1.382
	28	84.926	1.776	3.690	1.290
	30	85.265	1.656	3.460	1.209
	32	85.562	1.552	3.257	1.138
	34	85.824	1.460	3.076	1.075
	36	86.056	1.379	6.898	2.420

Bowl slope / Bevel angle	Sides	MG°	V	BT°	V
Bowl slope **37**	4	51.388	15.973	25.185	9.405
	5	59.876	11.605	17.512	6.311
	6	65.246	9.222	15.136	5.410
	7	68.963	7.692	13.315	4.733
Bevel angle *53*	8	71.695	6.616	11.878	4.207
	9	73.792	5.814	10.718	3.785
	10	75.453	5.190	9.762	3.441
	11	76.803	4.690	8.961	3.154
	12	77.921	4.280	7.696	2.703
	14	79.669	3.646	6.743	2.365
	16	80.974	3.177	5.999	2.102
	18	81.984	2.816	5.402	1.891
	20	82.791	2.530	4.913	1.719
	22	83.450	2.297	4.505	1.576
	24	83.998	2.103	4.160	1.455
	26	84.461	1.939	3.864	1.351
	28	84.858	1.800	3.607	1.261
	30	85.202	1.679	3.382	1.182
	32	85.502	1.573	3.183	1.112
	34	85.768	1.480	3.007	1.050
	36	86.003	1.397	6.743	2.365

Bowl slope / Bevel angle	Sides	MG°	V	BT°	V
Bowl slope **36**	4	51.027	16.180	24.559	9.139
	5	59.554	11.756	20.212	7.363
	6	64.963	9.342	17.091	6.149
	7	68.714	7.792	14.775	5.275
Bevel angle *54*	8	71.474	6.702	12.999	4.617
	9	73.593	5.889	12.999	4.617
	10	75.272	5.257	10.465	3.694
	11	76.637	4.751	9.532	3.358
	12	77.769	4.336	8.750	3.078
	14	79.538	3.693	7.516	2.639
	16	80.858	3.218	6.585	2.309
	18	81.881	2.853	5.858	2.052
	20	82.698	2.563	5.276	1.847
	22	83.365	2.326	4.798	1.679
	24	83.920	2.130	4.400	1.539
	26	84.390	1.965	4.063	1.421
	28	84.792	1.823	3.773	1.319
	30	85.140	1.701	3.522	1.231
	32	85.444	1.594	3.303	1.154
	34	85.713	1.499	3.109	1.086
	36	85.951	1.416	2.936	1.026

Bowl slope / Bevel angle	Sides	MG°	V	BT°	V
Bowl slope **35**	4	50.677	16.383	23.927	8.874
	5	59.241	11.903	19.703	7.162
	6	64.689	9.459	16.666	5.987
	7	68.472	7.890	14.410	5.139
Bevel angle *55*	8	71.258	6.786	12.680	4.500
	9	73.398	5.963	12.680	4.500
	10	75.096	5.323	10.209	3.602
	11	76.476	4.810	9.299	3.275
	12	77.620	4.390	8.537	3.002
	14	79.410	3.739	7.333	2.574
	16	80.746	3.259	6.425	2.252
	18	81.781	2.889	5.716	2.002
	20	82.608	2.595	5.148	1.802
	22	83.283	2.356	4.682	1.638
	24	83.845	2.157	4.294	1.502
	26	84.320	1.989	3.964	1.386
	28	84.727	1.846	3.682	1.287
	30	85.079	1.722	3.437	1.201
	32	85.387	1.614	3.223	1.126
	34	85.659	1.518	3.034	1.060
	36	85.901	1.433	2.865	1.001

Bowl slope / Bevel angle	Sides	MG°	V	BT°	V
Bowl slope **34**	4	50.340	16.581	23.291	8.610
	5	58.938	12.047	19.189	6.960
	6	64.422	9.573	16.236	5.824
	7	68.236	7.985	14.042	5.002
Bevel angle *56*	8	71.048	6.868	12.357	4.381
	9	73.209	6.035	11.026	3.897
	10	74.924	5.387	9.951	3.509
	11	76.319	4.869	9.064	3.191
	12	77.476	4.443	8.322	2.925
	14	79.285	3.784	7.148	2.508
	16	80.636	3.298	6.263	2.195
	18	81.683	2.924	5.572	1.951
	20	82.519	2.626	5.018	1.756
	22	83.203	2.384	4.565	1.597
	24	83.771	2.183	4.186	1.464
	26	84.252	2.013	3.865	1.351
	28	84.663	1.868	3.590	1.255
	30	85.020	1.743	3.351	1.171
	32	85.332	1.633	3.142	1.098
	34	85.607	1.536	2.958	1.033
	36	85.852	1.451	2.794	0.976

Bowl slope / Bevel angle	Sides	MG°	V	BT°	V
Bowl slope **33**	4	48.557	17.659	22.209	8.165
	5	57.320	12.830	18.421	6.661
	6	62.989	10.195	15.650	5.603
	7	66.965	8.504	13.570	4.827
Bevel angle *57*	8	69.911	7.315	11.962	4.237
	9	72.184	6.427	10.688	3.775
	10	73.992	5.738	9.654	3.402
	11	75.466	5.185	8.800	3.096
	12	76.689	4.732	8.083	2.840
	14	78.606	4.031	6.948	2.437
	16	80.039	3.513	6.091	2.134
	18	81.151	3.114	5.421	1.898
	20	82.039	2.797	4.883	1.709
	22	82.765	2.539	4.442	1.554
	24	83.370	2.325	4.074	1.424
	26	83.881	2.144	3.762	1.315
	28	84.319	1.990	3.494	1.221
	30	84.698	1.856	3.262	1.140
	32	85.030	1.739	3.059	1.069
	34	85.323	1.636	2.880	1.006
	36	85.583	1.545	2.720	0.950

Bowl slope / Bevel angle	Sides	MG°	V	BT°	V
Bowl slope **32**	4	49.700	16.961	22.006	8.083
	5	58.361	12.323	18.148	6.556
	6	63.913	9.792	15.365	5.496
	7	67.785	8.168	13.293	4.725
Bevel angle *58*	8	70.645	7.025	11.700	4.142
	9	72.846	6.173	10.442	3.686
	10	74.595	5.511	9.425	3.320
	11	76.017	4.980	8.586	3.020
	12	77.198	4.545	7.883	2.769
	14	79.045	3.871	6.772	2.375
	16	80.425	3.374	5.934	2.079
	18	81.495	2.991	5.280	1.848
	20	82.350	2.686	4.755	1.664
	22	83.048	2.439	4.325	1.513
	24	83.629	2.233	3.966	1.387
	26	84.121	2.059	3.662	1.280
	28	84.542	1.911	3.401	1.189
	30	84.906	1.783	3.175	1.110
	32	85.225	1.671	2.977	1.040
	34	85.507	1.572	2.803	0.979
	36	85.757	1.484	2.647	0.925

Bowl slope / Bevel angle	Sides	MG°	V	BT°	V
Bowl slope **31**	4	49.398	17.143	21.358	7.821
	5	58.087	12.455	17.622	6.353
	6	63.670	9.898	14.923	5.330
	7	67.570	8.256	12.913	4.585
Bevel angle *59*	8	70.453	7.101	11.367	4.021
	9	72.673	6.240	10.146	3.579
	10	74.437	5.570	9.158	3.224
	11	75.873	5.034	8.343	2.933
	12	77.065	4.594	7.660	2.690
	14	78.930	3.913	6.581	2.307
	16	80.324	3.410	5.767	2.020
	18	81.405	3.023	5.131	1.796
	20	82.269	2.715	4.621	1.617
	22	82.974	2.465	4.203	1.470
	24	83.562	2.257	3.855	1.348
	26	84.058	2.082	3.559	1.244
	28	84.484	1.932	3.306	1.155
	30	84.852	1.802	3.086	1.078
	32	85.174	1.688	2.894	1.011
	34	85.459	1.589	2.724	0.952
	36	85.711	1.500	2.573	0.899

Table C (continued)

Bowl slope	Sides	MG°	V	BT°	V
30°	4	49.107	17.321	20.705	7.559
	5	57.822	12.584	17.091	6.149
	6	63.435	10.000	14.478	5.164
	7	67.361	8.341	12.529	4.445
Bevel angle	8	70.266	7.174	11.031	3.899
60°	9	72.505	6.304	9.847	3.471
	10	74.284	5.628	8.888	3.128
	11	75.733	5.086	8.098	2.846
	12	76.936	4.641	7.435	2.610
	14	78.819	3.953	6.388	2.239
	16	80.226	3.445	5.598	1.960
	18	81.318	3.054	4.981	1.743
	20	82.190	2.743	4.486	1.569
	22	82.902	2.490	4.080	1.427
	24	83.496	2.280	3.742	1.308
	26	83.997	2.103	3.455	1.208
	28	84.427	1.952	3.209	1.121
	30	84.799	1.820	2.996	1.047
	32	85.125	1.706	2.809	0.981
	34	85.412	1.605	2.644	0.924
	36	85.667	1.515	2.498	0.872

Bowl slope	Sides	MG°	V	BT°	V
29	4	48.826	17.492	20.048	7.299
	5	57.566	12.709	16.557	5.946
	6	63.208	10.099	14.029	4.997
	7	67.159	8.424	12.143	4.303
Bevel angle	8	70.086	7.246	10.692	3.776
61	9	72.342	6.367	9.545	3.363
	10	74.136	5.684	8.616	3.030
	11	75.597	5.136	7.850	2.758
	12	76.811	4.687	7.208	2.530
	14	78.711	3.993	6.193	2.170
	16	80.131	3.479	5.427	1.900
	18	81.233	3.084	4.829	1.690
	20	82.113	2.771	4.350	1.521
	22	82.833	2.515	3.956	1.383
	24	83.432	2.303	3.628	1.268
	26	83.938	2.124	3.350	1.171
	28	84.372	1.971	3.112	1.087
	30	84.748	1.839	2.905	1.015
	32	85.077	1.723	2.724	0.951
	34	85.367	1.621	2.564	0.896
	36	85.624	1.530	2.422	0.846

Bowl slope	Sides	MG°	V	BT°	V
28	4	48.557	17.659	19.388	7.038
	5	57.320	12.830	16.019	5.742
	6	62.989	10.195	13.576	4.830
	7	66.965	8.504	11.753	4.161
Bevel angle	8	69.911	7.315	10.350	3.653
62	9	72.184	6.427	9.240	3.254
	10	73.992	5.738	8.342	2.933
	11	75.466	5.185	7.601	2.669
	12	76.689	4.732	6.979	2.448
	14	78.606	4.031	5.996	2.101
	16	80.039	3.513	5.255	1.840
	18	81.151	3.114	4.676	1.636
	20	82.039	2.797	4.212	1.473
	22	82.765	2.539	3.831	1.339
	24	83.370	2.325	3.513	1.228
	26	83.881	2.144	3.244	1.134
	28	84.319	1.990	3.013	1.053
	30	84.698	1.856	2.813	0.983
	32	85.030	1.739	2.637	0.921
	34	85.323	1.636	2.483	0.867
	36	85.583	1.545	2.345	0.819

Bowl slope	Sides	MG°	V	BT°	V
27	4	48.299	17.820	18.725	6.779
	5	57.083	12.947	15.477	5.538
	6	62.778	10.288	13.120	4.662
	7	66.777	8.582	11.360	4.018
Bevel angle	8	69.743	7.381	10.005	3.528
63	9	72.032	6.486	8.933	3.144
	10	73.854	5.790	8.065	2.834
	11	75.339	5.232	7.348	2.579
	12	76.572	4.775	6.748	2.366
	14	78.505	4.067	5.798	2.031
	16	79.950	3.545	5.081	1.778
	18	81.071	3.142	4.522	1.582
	20	81.967	2.822	4.073	1.424
	22	82.700	2.562	3.704	1.295
	24	83.310	2.346	3.397	1.187
	26	83.825	2.164	3.137	1.096
	28	84.267	2.008	2.914	1.018
	30	84.650	1.873	2.720	0.950
	32	84.985	1.755	2.550	0.891
	34	85.280	1.651	2.401	0.839
	36	85.543	1.559	2.268	0.792

Bowl slope	Sides	MG°	V	BT°	V
26	4	48.051	17.976	18.058	6.521
	5	56.855	13.060	14.932	5.333
	6	62.574	10.378	12.661	4.493
	7	66.595	8.657	10.965	3.875
Bevel angle	8	69.580	7.446	9.657	3.403
64	9	71.885	6.543	8.623	3.033
	10	73.720	5.841	7.785	2.734
	11	75.216	5.278	7.094	2.489
	12	76.459	4.817	6.515	2.284
	14	78.407	4.103	5.598	1.960
	16	79.864	3.576	4.906	1.717
	18	80.995	3.170	4.366	1.527
	20	81.898	2.847	3.932	1.375
	22	82.637	2.585	3.577	1.250
	24	83.252	2.367	3.280	1.146
	26	83.772	2.183	3.029	1.058
	28	84.217	2.025	2.813	0.983
	30	84.603	1.889	2.626	0.917
	32	84.941	1.770	2.463	0.860
	34	85.239	1.666	2.318	0.810
	36	85.504	1.573	2.190	0.765

Bowl slope	Sides	MG°	V	BT°	V
25	4	47.814	18.126	17.388	6.263
	5	56.636	13.169	14.383	5.129
	6	62.379	10.465	12.199	4.324
	7	66.421	8.729	10.566	3.731
Bevel angle	8	69.424	7.508	9.307	3.278
65	9	71.744	6.597	8.311	2.922
	10	73.591	5.890	7.504	2.634
	11	75.098	5.322	6.838	2.398
	12	76.350	4.857	6.280	2.201
	14	78.313	4.137	5.396	1.889
	16	79.781	3.606	4.729	1.655
	18	80.921	3.196	4.209	1.472
	20	81.831	2.871	3.791	1.325
	22	82.576	2.606	3.448	1.205
	24	83.196	2.386	3.162	1.105
	26	83.720	2.201	2.920	1.020
	28	84.169	2.042	2.712	0.947
	30	84.559	1.905	2.532	0.884
	32	84.899	1.785	2.374	0.829
	34	85.199	1.680	2.235	0.780
	36	85.466	1.586	2.111	0.737

Bowl slope	Sides	MG°	V	BT°	V
24	4	47.587	18.271	16.715	6.006
	5	56.427	13.275	13.832	4.924
	6	62.191	10.549	11.734	4.154
	7	66.253	8.799	10.165	3.586
Bevel angle	8	69.273	7.568	8.955	3.151
66	9	71.608	6.650	7.996	2.810
	10	73.468	5.937	7.221	2.534
	11	74.984	5.365	6.580	2.307
	12	76.245	4.896	6.043	2.117
	14	78.222	4.170	5.193	1.818
	16	79.701	3.634	4.551	1.592
	18	80.849	3.222	4.050	1.416
	20	81.767	2.894	3.648	1.275
	22	82.517	2.627	3.318	1.160
	24	83.142	2.405	3.043	1.063
	26	83.670	2.218	2.810	0.982
	28	84.123	2.059	2.610	0.912
	30	84.515	1.920	2.437	0.851
	32	84.859	1.800	2.285	0.798
	34	85.161	1.693	2.151	0.751
	36	85.430	1.598	2.032	0.709

Bowl slope	Sides	MG°	V	BT°	V
23	4	47.370	18.410	16.039	5.750
	5	56.226	13.376	13.277	4.719
	6	62.011	10.629	11.266	3.984
	7	66.093	8.866	9.761	3.440
Bevel angle	8	69.129	7.626	8.599	3.025
67	9	71.477	6.701	7.680	2.697
	10	73.349	5.982	6.935	2.433
	11	74.875	5.406	6.320	2.215
	12	76.145	4.933	5.804	2.033
	14	78.135	4.202	4.988	1.746
	16	79.624	3.662	4.372	1.529
	18	80.781	3.246	3.890	1.360
	20	81.705	2.916	3.504	1.225
	22	82.461	2.647	3.188	1.114
	24	83.090	2.424	2.923	1.021
	26	83.623	2.235	2.699	0.943
	28	84.079	2.074	2.507	0.876
	30	84.474	1.935	2.341	0.818
	32	84.820	1.813	2.195	0.767
	34	85.125	1.706	2.066	0.722
	36	85.396	1.611	1.952	0.681

Bowl slope	Sides	MG°	V	BT°	V
22	4	47.164	18.544	15.360	5.494
	5	56.034	13.473	12.720	4.515
	6	61.839	10.706	10.795	3.814
	7	65.939	8.930	9.354	3.295
Bevel angle	8	68.991	7.681	8.242	2.897
68	9	71.352	6.749	7.361	2.584
	10	73.235	6.025	6.647	2.331
	11	74.771	5.445	6.058	2.123
	12	76.048	4.969	5.564	1.948
	14	78.051	4.232	4.782	1.673
	16	79.550	3.689	4.191	1.466
	18	80.715	3.270	3.730	1.304
	20	81.646	2.937	3.360	1.174
	22	82.407	2.666	3.056	1.068
	24	83.041	2.441	2.803	0.979
	26	83.577	2.252	2.588	0.904
	28	84.036	2.089	2.404	0.840
	30	84.434	1.949	2.244	0.784
	32	84.782	1.826	2.104	0.735
	34	85.089	1.718	1.981	0.692
	36	85.362	1.622	1.871	0.653

Bowl slope	Sides	MG°	V	BT°	V
21	4	46.967	18.672	14.679	5.239
	5	55.852	13.566	12.160	4.310
	6	61.675	10.780	10.322	3.643
	7	65.792	8.992	8.945	3.148
Bevel angle	8	68.858	7.734	7.882	2.769
69	9	71.232	6.796	7.040	2.470
	10	73.125	6.067	6.358	2.229
	11	74.670	5.482	5.795	2.030
	12	75.956	5.003	5.322	1.863
	14	77.971	4.262	4.574	1.600
	16	79.480	3.714	4.009	1.402
	18	80.652	3.292	3.568	1.247
	20	81.589	2.957	3.214	1.123
	22	82.355	2.685	2.923	1.021
	24	82.993	2.458	2.681	0.937
	26	83.533	2.267	2.476	0.865
	28	83.995	2.104	2.300	0.803
	30	84.396	1.962	2.147	0.750
	32	84.746	1.839	2.013	0.703
	34	85.056	1.730	1.895	0.662
	36	85.331	1.634	1.790	0.625

Bowl slope	Sides	MG°	V	BT°	V
20	4	46.781	18.794	13.995	4.985
	5	55.678	13.655	11.597	4.104
	6	61.519	10.851	9.847	3.471
	7	65.652	9.051	8.534	3.001
Bevel angle	8	68.732	7.785	7.521	2.640
70	9	71.118	6.840	6.718	2.356
	10	73.021	6.106	6.067	2.126
	11	74.575	5.518	5.529	1.936
	12	75.867	5.036	5.079	1.777
	14	77.895	4.290	4.365	1.527
	16	79.413	3.738	3.826	1.337
	18	80.592	3.314	3.405	1.190
	20	81.535	2.977	3.067	1.072
	22	82.306	2.702	2.790	0.975
	24	82.948	2.474	2.559	0.894
	26	83.491	2.282	2.363	0.825
	28	83.956	2.118	2.195	0.766
	30	84.359	1.975	2.049	0.715
	32	84.712	1.851	1.921	0.671
	34	85.024	1.742	1.808	0.631
	36	85.300	1.644	1.708	0.596

Bowl slope	Sides	MG°	V	BT°	V
19	4	46.727	18.829	13.335	4.741
	5	55.627	13.680	11.047	3.905
	6	61.473	10.871	9.378	3.303
	7	65.611	9.068	8.127	2.856
Bevel angle	8	68.696	7.799	7.161	2.513
71	9	71.085	6.853	6.396	2.242
	10	72.991	6.118	5.776	2.023
	11	74.547	5.529	5.264	1.843
	12	75.842	5.045	4.835	1.692
	14	77.872	4.298	4.155	1.453
	16	79.393	3.745	3.642	1.273
	18	80.574	3.320	3.241	1.133
	20	81.519	2.982	2.920	1.020
	22	82.291	2.707	2.656	0.928
	24	82.934	2.479	2.436	0.851
	26	83.479	2.286	2.249	0.786
	28	83.945	2.122	2.089	0.730
	30	84.349	1.979	1.950	0.681
	32	84.702	1.855	1.829	0.639
	34	85.014	1.745	1.721	0.601
	36	85.291	1.647	1.626	0.568

Bowl slope	Sides	MG°	V	BT°	V
18	4	46.437	19.021	12.621	4.478
	5	55.356	13.820	10.465	3.694
	6	61.229	10.982	8.888	3.128
	7	65.392	9.160	7.705	2.706
Bevel angle	8	68.499	7.879	6.791	2.382
72	9	70.906	6.923	6.067	2.126
	10	72.828	6.180	5.480	1.919
	11	74.397	5.585	4.995	1.748
	12	75.703	5.097	4.587	1.605
	14	77.753	4.341	3.943	1.379
	16	79.288	3.784	3.456	1.208
	18	80.480	3.354	3.076	1.075
	20	81.434	3.013	2.771	0.968
	22	82.214	2.735	2.521	0.880
	24	82.863	2.504	2.312	0.807
	26	83.413	2.310	2.135	0.745
	28	83.884	2.143	1.983	0.692
	30	84.292	1.999	1.851	0.646
	32	84.649	1.873	1.736	0.606
	34	84.964	1.763	1.634	0.570
	36	85.244	1.664	1.543	0.539

Bowl slope	Sides	MG°	V	BT°	V
17	4	46.280	19.126	11.931	4.226
	5	55.209	13.896	9.896	3.489
	6	61.096	11.042	8.406	2.955
	7	65.272	9.211	7.288	2.558
Bevel angle	8	68.391	7.922	6.424	2.252
73	9	70.809	6.961	5.739	2.010
	10	72.739	6.214	5.184	1.814
	11	74.315	5.616	4.725	1.653
	12	75.628	5.125	4.340	1.518
	14	77.687	4.365	3.730	1.304
	16	79.230	3.804	3.270	1.143
	18	80.429	3.372	2.910	1.017
	20	81.387	3.029	2.621	0.916
	22	82.171	2.750	2.385	0.833
	24	82.824	2.518	2.187	0.764
	26	83.377	2.322	2.020	0.705
	28	83.850	2.155	1.876	0.655
	30	84.260	2.010	1.751	0.612
	32	84.619	1.884	1.642	0.573
	34	84.936	1.772	1.546	0.540
	36	85.217	1.673	1.460	0.510

Bowl slope	Sides	MG°	V	BT°	V
16	4	46.132	19.225	11.239	3.974
	5	55.070	13.968	9.324	3.284
	6	60.970	11.100	7.922	2.783
	7	65.160	9.258	6.869	2.409
Bevel angle	8	68.289	7.963	6.055	2.121
74	9	70.717	6.997	5.410	1.894
	10	72.655	6.247	4.886	1.710
	11	74.238	5.645	4.454	1.558
	12	75.556	5.151	4.091	1.430
	14	77.625	4.388	3.516	1.229
	16	79.175	3.824	3.083	1.077
	18	80.380	3.390	2.743	0.958
	20	81.343	3.045	2.471	0.863
	22	82.131	2.764	2.248	0.785
	24	82.787	2.531	2.062	0.720
	26	83.343	2.334	1.904	0.665
	28	83.818	2.166	1.769	0.618
	30	84.231	2.021	1.651	0.576
	32	84.592	1.894	1.548	0.541
	34	84.910	1.781	1.457	0.509
	36	85.193	1.682	1.377	0.481

Bowl slope 15° — Bevel angle 75°

Sides	MG°	V	BT°	V
4	45.993	19.319	10.545	3.723
5	54.939	14.036	8.750	3.078
6	60.853	11.154	7.435	2.610
7	65.054	9.303	6.448	2.260
8	68.194	8.002	5.684	1.991
9	70.630	7.031	5.079	1.777
10	72.576	6.277	4.587	1.605
11	74.166	5.672	4.182	1.462
12	75.489	5.176	3.841	1.343
14	77.567	4.409	3.302	1.154
16	79.124	3.843	2.894	1.011
18	80.334	3.406	2.576	0.900
20	81.302	3.060	2.320	0.810
22	82.093	2.778	2.111	0.737
24	82.753	2.543	1.936	0.676
26	83.311	2.346	1.788	0.624
28	83.789	2.177	1.661	0.580
30	84.203	2.030	1.550	0.541
32	84.565	1.903	1.454	0.508
34	84.885	1.790	1.368	0.478
36	85.170	1.690	1.293	0.451

Bowl slope 14 — Bevel angle 76

Sides	MG°	V	BT°	V
4	45.864	19.406	9.850	3.472
5	54.818	14.099	8.175	2.873
6	60.742	11.204	6.948	2.437
7	64.955	9.345	6.025	2.111
8	68.104	8.038	5.312	1.860
9	70.549	7.063	4.746	1.661
10	72.502	6.305	4.287	1.499
11	74.098	5.698	3.908	1.366
12	75.426	5.200	3.590	1.255
14	77.513	4.429	3.086	1.078
16	79.076	3.860	2.705	0.945
18	80.291	3.422	2.408	0.841
20	81.263	3.074	2.169	0.757
22	82.058	2.790	1.973	0.689
24	82.720	2.555	1.810	0.632
26	83.281	2.356	1.671	0.583
28	83.761	2.187	1.552	0.542
30	84.177	2.040	1.449	0.506
32	84.541	1.911	1.359	0.474
34	84.862	1.798	1.279	0.447
36	85.148	1.698	1.208	0.422

Bowl slope 13 — Bevel angle 77

Sides	MG°	V	BT°	V
4	45.744	19.487	9.153	3.222
5	54.705	14.158	7.598	2.668
6	60.640	11.251	6.458	2.264
7	64.863	9.385	5.601	1.961
8	68.021	8.072	4.938	1.728
9	70.473	7.093	4.413	1.543
10	72.433	6.332	3.986	1.394
11	74.034	5.722	3.634	1.270
12	75.368	5.222	3.338	1.166
14	77.462	4.448	2.869	1.002
16	79.031	3.876	2.515	0.879
18	80.251	3.436	2.239	0.782
20	81.227	3.087	2.017	0.704
22	82.025	2.802	1.835	0.641
24	82.690	2.566	1.683	0.587
26	83.253	2.366	1.554	0.542
28	83.735	2.196	1.443	0.504
30	84.153	2.048	1.347	0.470
32	84.518	1.919	1.263	0.441
34	84.841	1.806	1.189	0.415
36	85.128	1.705	1.123	0.392

Bowl slope 12 — Bevel angle 78

Sides	MG°	V	BT°	V
4	45.633	19.563	8.454	2.973
5	54.600	14.213	7.020	2.463
6	60.545	11.295	5.967	2.090
7	64.777	9.421	5.176	1.812
8	67.944	8.103	4.564	1.596
9	70.403	7.120	4.078	1.426
10	72.369	6.356	3.684	1.288
11	73.975	5.744	3.358	1.174
12	75.313	5.242	3.085	1.078
14	77.415	4.465	2.652	0.926
16	78.990	3.891	2.325	0.812
18	80.214	3.449	2.069	0.723
20	81.194	3.098	1.864	0.651
22	81.995	2.813	1.696	0.592
24	82.662	2.576	1.555	0.543
26	83.227	2.375	1.436	0.501
28	83.711	2.204	1.334	0.466
30	84.130	2.056	1.245	0.435
32	84.497	1.927	1.168	0.408
34	84.821	1.813	1.099	0.384
36	85.109	1.712	1.038	0.362

Bowl slope 11 — Bevel angle 79

Sides	MG°	V	BT°	V
4	45.531	19.633	7.754	2.723
5	54.504	14.264	6.440	2.257
6	60.458	11.335	5.475	1.917
7	64.699	9.455	4.749	1.661
8	67.873	8.132	4.187	1.464
9	70.339	7.146	3.742	1.308
10	72.310	6.379	3.380	1.181
11	73.921	5.765	3.082	1.077
12	75.263	5.261	2.831	0.989
14	77.371	4.481	2.433	0.850
16	78.952	3.905	2.133	0.745
18	80.180	3.462	1.899	0.663
20	81.163	3.109	1.710	0.597
22	81.967	2.823	1.556	0.543
24	82.636	2.585	1.427	0.498
26	83.203	2.384	1.318	0.460
28	83.689	2.212	1.224	0.427
30	84.109	2.063	1.143	0.399
32	84.478	1.934	1.072	0.374
34	84.803	1.819	1.009	0.352
36	85.091	1.718	0.953	0.333

Bowl slope 10 — Bevel angle 80

Sides	MG°	V	BT°	V
4	45.439	19.696	7.053	2.474
5	54.416	14.310	5.858	2.052
6	60.378	11.372	4.981	1.743
7	64.627	9.485	4.321	1.511
8	67.808	8.158	3.810	1.332
9	70.280	7.169	3.405	1.190
10	72.256	6.400	3.076	1.075
11	73.872	5.783	2.804	0.980
12	75.218	5.278	2.576	0.900
14	77.332	4.496	2.214	0.773
16	78.917	3.918	1.941	0.678
18	80.149	3.473	1.728	0.603
20	81.135	3.120	1.557	0.543
22	81.941	2.832	1.416	0.494
24	82.613	2.593	1.299	0.453
26	83.181	2.392	1.199	0.419
28	83.668	2.219	1.114	0.389
30	84.091	2.070	1.040	0.363
32	84.460	1.940	0.975	0.340
34	84.786	1.825	0.918	0.320
36	85.076	1.723	0.867	0.303

Bowl slope 9 — Bevel angle 81

Sides	MG°	V	BT°	V
4	45.280	19.805	6.351	2.226
5	54.266	14.389	5.276	1.847
6	60.242	11.435	4.486	1.569
7	64.504	9.538	3.892	1.361
8	67.697	8.204	3.432	1.199
9	70.179	7.209	3.067	1.072
10	72.164	6.435	2.771	0.968
11	73.787	5.815	2.526	0.882
12	75.139	5.307	2.320	0.810
14	77.264	4.520	1.995	0.697
16	78.857	3.940	1.749	0.611
18	80.095	3.492	1.557	0.543
20	81.086	3.137	1.402	0.490
22	81.897	2.848	1.276	0.445
24	82.572	2.607	1.170	0.408
26	83.144	2.405	1.080	0.377
28	83.633	2.232	1.004	0.350
30	84.058	2.082	0.937	0.327
32	84.429	1.951	0.879	0.307
34	84.757	1.835	0.827	0.289
36	85.048	1.733	0.781	0.273

Bowl slope 8 — Bevel angle 82

Sides	MG°	V	BT°	V
4	45.280	19.805	5.648	1.978
5	54.266	14.389	4.692	1.642
6	60.242	11.435	3.990	1.395
7	64.504	9.538	3.462	1.210
8	67.697	8.204	3.053	1.067
9	70.179	7.209	2.728	0.953
10	72.164	6.435	2.465	0.861
11	73.787	5.815	2.247	0.785
12	75.139	5.307	2.064	0.721
14	77.264	4.520	1.775	0.620
16	78.857	3.940	1.556	0.543
18	80.095	3.492	1.385	0.483
20	81.086	3.137	1.248	0.436
22	81.897	2.848	1.135	0.396
24	82.572	2.607	1.041	0.363
26	83.144	2.405	0.961	0.336
28	83.633	2.232	0.893	0.312
30	84.058	2.082	0.834	0.291
32	84.429	1.951	0.782	0.273
34	84.757	1.835	0.736	0.257
36	85.048	1.733	0.695	0.243

Bowl slope 7 — Bevel angle 83

Sides	MG°	V	BT°	V
4	45.214	19.851	4.944	1.730
5	54.204	14.423	4.108	1.436
6	60.185	11.461	3.493	1.221
7	98.000	-2.811	3.031	1.059
8	67.651	8.223	2.673	0.934
9	70.137	7.225	2.389	0.834
10	51.000	16.196	60.000	34.641
11	73.752	5.829	1.968	0.687
12	75.107	5.319	1.808	0.631
14	77.236	4.531	1.554	0.543
16	78.832	3.949	1.362	0.476
18	80.073	3.500	1.213	0.423
20	81.066	3.144	1.092	0.381
22	81.878	2.854	0.994	0.347
24	82.555	2.613	0.911	0.318
26	83.128	2.410	0.842	0.294
28	83.619	2.237	0.782	0.273
30	84.044	2.086	0.730	0.255
32	84.417	1.955	0.684	0.239
34	84.745	1.839	0.644	0.225
36	85.037	1.737	0.609	0.212

Bowl slope 6 — Bevel angle 84

Sides	MG°	V	BT°	V
4	45.157	19.890	4.239	1.482
5	54.150	14.451	3.522	1.231
6	60.136	11.484	2.996	1.047
7	64.409	9.579	2.599	0.908
8	67.611	8.239	2.293	0.801
9	70.101	7.240	2.049	0.715
10	72.092	6.463	1.851	0.646
11	73.721	5.840	1.688	0.589
12	75.078	5.330	1.550	0.541
14	77.211	4.540	1.333	0.465
16	78.810	3.956	1.168	0.408
18	80.054	3.507	1.040	0.363
20	81.049	3.150	0.937	0.327
22	81.862	2.860	0.852	0.298
24	82.541	2.619	0.782	0.273
26	83.114	2.415	0.722	0.252
28	83.606	2.241	0.671	0.234
30	84.033	2.091	0.626	0.219
32	84.406	1.959	0.587	0.205
34	84.735	1.843	0.553	0.193
36	85.027	1.740	0.000	0.000

Bowl slope 5 — Bevel angle 0

Sides	MG°	V	BT°	V
4	45.109	19.924	3.533	1.235
5	54.037	14.511	2.936	1.026
6	60.094	11.503	2.498	0.872
7	64.371	9.595	2.167	0.757
8	67.577	8.253	52.000	25.599
9	70.070	7.252	1.708	0.596
10	72.064	6.474	1.543	0.539
11	73.695	5.850	1.407	0.491
12	75.055	5.339	1.293	0.451
14	77.190	4.547	1.111	0.388
16	78.792	3.963	0.974	0.340
18	80.037	3.513	72.064	61.789
20	81.034	3.156	0.781	0.273
22	81.849	2.865	0.711	0.248
24	82.528	2.623	0.652	0.228
26	83.103	2.419	0.602	0.210
28	83.596	2.245	0.559	0.195
30	84.023	2.094	0.522	0.182
32	84.396	1.962	0.489	0.171
34	84.726	1.846	0.461	0.161
36	85.019	1.743	0.435	0.152

Bowl slope 4 — Bevel angle 86

Sides	MG°	V	BT°	V
4	45.070	19.951	2.827	0.988
5	54.066	14.495	2.350	0.821
6	60.060	11.519	1.999	0.698
7	64.340	9.608	1.734	0.606
8	67.549	8.264	1.530	0.534
9	70.045	7.262	1.367	0.477
10	72.041	6.483	1.235	0.431
11	73.674	5.858	1.126	0.393
12	75.035	5.346	1.034	0.361
14	77.173	4.554	0.889	0.310
16	78.777	3.969	0.780	0.272
18	80.024	3.518	0.694	0.242
20	81.022	3.160	0.625	0.218
22	81.838	2.869	0.569	0.199
24	82.518	2.627	0.522	0.182
26	83.094	2.423	0.482	0.168
28	83.587	2.248	0.447	0.156
30	84.015	2.097	0.418	0.146
32	84.389	1.965	0.392	0.137
34	84.719	1.849	0.369	0.129
36	85.012	1.746	0.348	0.122

Bowl slope 3 — Bevel angle 87

Sides	MG°	V	BT°	V
4	45.039	19.973	2.121	0.741
5	54.037	14.511	1.763	0.616
6	60.034	11.531	1.499	0.524
7	64.316	9.618	1.301	0.454
8	67.528	8.273	1.148	0.401
9	70.025	7.269	1.026	0.358
10	72.023	6.489	0.927	0.323
11	73.658	5.864	0.845	0.295
12	75.020	5.352	0.776	0.271
14	77.160	4.559	0.667	0.233
16	78.765	3.973	0.585	0.204
18	80.013	3.522	0.521	0.182
20	81.012	3.163	0.469	0.164
22	81.829	2.872	0.427	0.149
24	82.510	2.629	0.391	0.137
26	83.086	2.425	0.361	0.126
28	83.580	2.250	0.336	0.117
30	84.008	2.099	0.313	0.109
32	84.383	1.967	0.294	0.103
34	84.713	1.851	0.277	0.097
36	85.007	1.747	0.261	0.091

Bowl slope 2 — Bevel angle 88

Sides	MG°	V	BT°	V
4	45.017	19.988	1.414	0.494
5	54.017	14.522	1.175	0.410
6	60.015	11.540	1.000	0.349
7	64.299	9.626	0.868	0.303
8	67.512	8.279	0.765	0.267
9	70.011	7.275	0.684	0.239
10	72.010	6.494	0.618	0.216
11	73.646	5.869	0.563	0.197
12	75.009	5.356	0.518	0.181
14	77.150	4.562	0.445	0.155
16	78.757	3.976	0.390	0.136
18	80.006	3.524	0.347	0.121
20	81.005	3.166	0.313	0.109
22	81.823	2.874	0.285	0.099
24	82.505	2.631	0.261	0.091
26	83.081	2.427	0.241	0.084
28	83.575	2.252	0.224	0.078
30	84.004	2.101	0.209	0.073
32	84.378	1.969	0.196	0.068
34	84.709	1.852	0.184	0.064
36	85.003	1.749	0.174	0.061

Bowl slope 1 — Bevel angle 89

Sides	MG°	V	BT°	V
4	45.004	19.997	0.707	0.247
5	54.004	14.529	0.588	0.205
6	60.004	11.545	0.500	0.175
7	64.289	9.630	0.434	0.151
8	67.503	8.283	0.383	0.134
9	70.003	7.278	0.342	0.119
10	72.003	6.497	0.309	0.108
11	73.639	5.872	0.282	0.098
12	75.002	5.358	0.259	0.090
14	77.145	4.564	0.223	0.078
16	78.752	3.978	0.195	0.068
18	80.001	3.526	0.174	0.061
20	81.001	3.167	0.156	0.055
22	81.819	2.875	0.142	0.050
24	82.501	2.633	0.131	0.046
26	83.078	2.428	0.121	0.042
28	83.572	2.253	0.112	0.039
30	84.001	2.102	0.105	0.036
32	84.376	1.970	0.098	0.034
34	84.707	1.853	0.092	0.032
36	85.001	1.750	0.087	0.030

Bowl slope 0 — Bevel angle 90

Sides	MG°	V	BT°	V
4	45.000	20.000	0.000	0.000
5	54.000	14.531	0.000	0.000
6	60.000	11.547	0.000	0.000
7	64.286	9.631	0.000	0.000
8	67.500	8.284	0.000	0.000
9	70.000	7.279	0.000	0.000
10	72.000	6.498	0.000	0.000
11	73.636	5.873	0.000	0.000
12	75.000	5.359	0.000	0.000
14	77.143	4.565	0.000	0.000
16	78.750	3.978	0.000	0.000
18	80.000	3.527	0.000	0.000
20	81.000	3.168	0.000	0.000
22	81.818	2.876	0.000	0.000
24	82.500	2.633	0.000	0.000
26	83.077	2.428	0.000	0.000
28	83.571	2.253	0.000	0.000
30	84.000	2.102	0.000	0.000
32	84.375	1.970	0.000	0.000
34	84.706	1.853	0.000	0.000
36	85.000	1.750	0.000	0.000

Inches to millimetres

in	mm	in	mm	in	mm	in	mm	in	mm
1/64	0.3969	25/64	9.9219	49/64	19.4469	2 1/8	53.9751	13	330.201
1/32	0.7937	13/32	10.3187	25/32	19.8437	2 1/4	57.1501	14	355.601
3/64	1.1906	27/64	10.7156	51/64	20.2406	2 3/8	60.3251	15	381.001
1/16	1.5875	7/16	11.1125	13/16	20.6375	2 1/2	63.5001	16	406.401
5/64	1.9844	29/64	11.5094	53/64	21.0344	2 5/8	66.6751	17	431.801
3/32	2.3812	15/32	11.9062	27/32	21.4312	2 3/4	69.8501	18	457.201
7/64	2.7781	31/64	12.3031	55/64	21.8281	2 7/8	73.0251	19	482.601
1/8	3.1750	1/2	12.7000	7/8	22.2250	3	76.2002	20	508.001
								21	533.401
9/64	3.5719	33/64	13.0969	57/64	22.6219	3 1/8	79.3752	22	558.801
5/32	3.9687	17/32	13.4937	29/32	23.0187	3 1/4	82.5502	23	584.201
11/64	4.3656	35/64	13.8906	59/64	23.4156	3 3/8	85.7252	24	609.601
3/16	4.7625	9/16	14.2875	15/16	23.8125	3 1/2	88.9002		
13/64	5.1594	37/64	14.6844	61/64	24.2094	3 5/8	92.0752	25	635.001
7/32	5.5562	19/32	15.0812	31/32	24.6062	3 3/4	95.2502	26	660.401
15/64	5.9531	39/64	15.4781	63/64	25.0031	3 7/8	98.4252	27	685.801
1/4	6.3500	5/8	15.8750	1	25.4001	4	101.500	28	711.201
								29	736.601
17/64	6.7469	41/64	16.2719	1 1/8	28.5751	5	127.000	30	762.002
9/32	7.1437	21/32	16.6687	1 1/4	31.7501	6	152.400	31	787.402
19/64	7.5406	43/64	17.0656	1 3/8	34.9251	7	177.800	32	812.802
5/16	7.9375	11/16	17.4625	1 1/2	38.1001	8	203.200	33	838.202
21/64	8.3344	45/64	17.8594	1 5/8	41.2751	9	228.600	34	863.602
11/32	8.7312	23/32	18.2562	1 3/4	44.4501	10	254.001	35	889.002
23/64	9.1281	47/64	18.6531	1 7/8	47.6251	11	279.401	36	914.402
3/8	9.5250	3/4	19.0500	2	50.8001	12	304.801		

Millimetres to inches

mm	in	mm	in	mm	in	mm	in	mm	in
1	0.03937	21	0.82677	41	1.61417	160	6.29922	360	14.1732
2	0.07874	22	0.86614	42	1.65354	170	6.69292	370	14.5669
3	0.11811	23	0.90551	43	1.69291	180	7.08662	380	14.9606
4	0.15748	24	0.94488	44	1.73228	190	7.48032	390	15.3543
5	0.19685	25	0.98425	45	1.77165	200	7.87402	400	15.7480
6	0.23622	26	1.02362	46	1.81103				
7	0.27559	27	1.06299	47	1.85040	210	8.26772	410	16.1417
8	0.31496	28	1.10236	48	1.88977	220	8.66142	420	16.5354
9	0.35433	29	1.14173	49	1.92914	230	9.05513	430	16.9291
10	0.39370	30	1.18110	50	1.96851	240	9.44883	440	17.3228
						250	9.84252	450	17.7165
				60	2.36221	260	10.2362	460	18.1103
11	0.43307	31	1.22047	70	2.75591	270	10.6299	470	18.5040
12	0.47244	32	1.25984	80	3.14961	280	11.0236	480	18.8977
13	0.51181	33	1.29921	90	3.54331	290	11.4173	490	19.2914
14	0.55118	34	1.33858	100	3.93701	300	11.8110	500	19.6851
15	0.59055	35	1.37795						
16	0.62992	36	1.41732	110	4.33071	310	12.2047	600	23.6221
17	0.66929	37	1.45669	120	4.72441	320	12.5984	700	27.5591
18	0.70866	38	1.49606	130	5.11811	330	12.9921	800	31.4961
19	0.74803	39	1.53543	140	5.51181	340	13.3858	900	35.4331
20	0.78740	40	1.57480	150	5.90552	350	13.7795	1000	39.3701

ABOUT THE AUTHOR

Ron Hampton has been turning since 1993. He is a dentist by profession but enjoys writing about turning and teaching turning as a hobby.

He likes to learn new techniques and then write articles about them. His goal is to make difficult techniques easy. He has published more than 70 articles in journals such as *Woodturning*, *More Woodturning*, *American Woodturner*, *The Woodturner*, *Woodworker's Journal*, and *The Woodworker*. This is Ron's third woodturning book, following *Mini-Lathe Magic: Big Projects From a Small Lathe*, and *A Turner's Guide to Veneer Inlays*, both published by Schiffer Publishing Ltd. He has also been a demonstrator at the AAW national symposia in 1998 and 2000. He has demonstrated for the last four years at the 'Texas Turn or Two', which is the second- or third-largest woodturning event in the United States.

For some years Ron has been trying to create 'the world's best woodturning website' at Woodturning Plus (http://www.woodturningplus.com). This is a site where turners can come for information or inspiration. Many of the world's best turners are represented here.

A founding member of Ark-La-Tex Woodturners, Ron stays busy as its president and programme director. It is very common for new members to visit his shop during the week for individual instruction or to get help in making their own tools.

He lives with his wife Barbara in Texarkana, Texas.

Index